MOUNT ATHOS

MOUNT ATHOS
RENEWAL IN PARADISE

by
Graham Speake

Yale University Press
New Haven and London

for Tony

Copyright © by Yale University Press 2002

Designed by Beatrix McIntyre
Set in Ehrhardt Mt
Printed in Singapore

Cover illustration: The monastery of Simonopetra seen from the west © Graham Speake. Endpapers: (front) The monastery of Xenophontos; (back) The monastery of Koutloumousiou. Both were drawn by the Russian pilgrim Vasily Barsky in 1744 on his second visit to the Mountain.

ISBN   0 300 093535

Library of Congress Control Number: 2002112133

CONTENTS

The Mother of God as ephor ('overseer') of Athos, a modern icon hugely popular on the Mountain today (Bourazeri).

PREFACE

For many years I resisted the temptation to write a book such as this, just as I resisted the temptation to become Orthodox. In the end I found myself compelled to do both. I became Orthodox largely as a consequence of the numerous visits that I had made to Mount Athos. My spiritual journey into Orthodoxy was initially facilitated by the fathers of the monastery of Vatopedi who are now my brothers. Since my reception it has been steered by my spiritual father, Bishop Kallistos of Diokleia. Bishop Kallistos is the closest approximation I know to an Athonite elder outside Athos and I feel deeply honoured to be numbered among his many spiritual children. My debt to him and to the Vatopedi fathers is incalculable. I wrote this book because it seemed to me that there was a need for it. It is in no sense, I hasten to add, a 'convert's confession': that will be a very different book, if indeed I ever write it.

In writing this book, I have received generous assistance from the same quarters. Bishop Kallistos has read the whole text and provided me with numerous suggestions for its improvement. The fathers of Vatopedi, probably without realizing it, have contributed to it at every stage, and have provided the answers to many of my questions over the years. I am particularly grateful for their assistance with Chapter 7, which I should not have been able to write unaided. It goes without saying that any remaining imperfections are mine alone.

I have written this book for my friend Anthony Hazledine, who has accompanied me on many memorable journeys to Athos. It is for him, and others like him, who may not necessarily be academic or religious, but who have spiritually inquiring minds and who share a desire to know something more about the mysterious mountain of the monks, both its past and its present. Athos remains one of the most fascinating places on earth. The renewal that is currently taking place there makes it also one of the most challenging and dynamic. If in this book I succeed in conveying something of that fascination and that challenge, then it will have been worth writing.

Graham Speake
Pentecost 2001

ACKNOWLEDGEMENTS

For permission to quote from E. Amand de Mendieta's *Mount Athos: The Garden of the Panaghia* I am grateful to Akademie Verlag GmbH, Berlin; for permission to quote from the works of the late Philip Sherrard I am grateful to his widow, Denise Harvey.

For assistance of various kinds in procuring illustrations I am indebted to the Holy Community of Mount Athos, the Abbot and Fathers of Vatopedi, Fr Ioustinos of Simonopetra, Bishop Kallistos of Diokleia and Mr John Leatham of Athens.

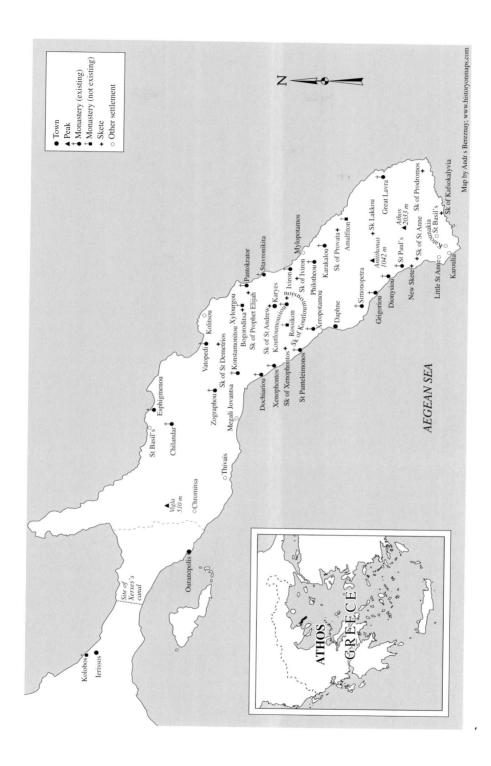

Town ●
Peak ▲
Monastery (existing) †■
Monastery (not existing) ■
Skete +
Other settlement ○

N

Map by Andrś Bereznay: www.historyonmaps.com

St Basil's ○
Esphigmenou +
Chilandar ●
Zographou +
Megali Jovantsa ●
Thivaïs ○
Chromitsa ○
Vigla *510 m* ▲
Ouranopolis ●
Kolobos ■
Ierissos ●
Site of Xerxes's canal

Vatopedi ●
Sk of St Demetrios †
Konstamonitou †
Bogoroditsa †■
Sk of Prophet Elijah +
Koliтsou ○
Xylourgou
Pantokrator †■
Stavronikita +
Docheiariou +
Xenophontos ●
Sk of Xenophontos +
St Panteleimonos +
Sk of St Andrew +
Koutloumousiou +
Karyes ●
Rossikon +
Sk of Koutloumousiou +
Iviron ●
Sk of Iviron ○
Mylopotamos +
Philotheou +
Xeropotamou +
Daphne ●
Simonopetra ●
Karakalou ●
Sk of Provata +
Amalfiton +
Grigoriou +
Dionysiou ●
New Skete ○
Antithonus 1042 m ▲
St Paul's ●
Sk of St Anne +
Little St Anne ○
Kausokalyvia ○
Karoulia ○
St Basil's ○
Sk of Kafsokalyvia ○
Sk of St Lakkou +
Great Lavra ●
Athos 2033 m ▲
Sk of Prodromos ○

AEGEAN SEA

ATHOS
GREECE

IX

N

Ouranopolis

Chilandar

St Panteleimonos

Dionysiou

Esphigmenou

Zographou

Konstamonitou

Vatopedi

Dochiariou

Pantokrator

Xenophontos

Karyes

Stavronikita

St Panteleimonos

Koutloumousiou

Xeropotamou

Iviron

Daphne

Simonopetra

Philotheou

Karakalou

Grigoriou

Dionysiou

St Paul's

AEGEAN SEA

Great Lavra

† Monastery
● Town

Monastic landholdings on Mount Athos today.

INTRODUCTION

When Robert Byron stood on the peak of Athos at sunset one September evening in 1926, he claimed that to the east he could see not only Lemnos but also the coast of Asia Minor beyond: 'the plains of Troy, whence Tozer saw this platform of ours "towering up from the horizon, like a vast spirit of the waters, when the rest of the peninsula is concealed below"'. To the north he looked down on the coastline of Thrace stretching away to the Dardanelles, 'with Turkey's remnant hovering in soft eternity'; to the west, he saw the two other fingers of Chalkidiki and beyond them Mount Olympus; to the south, the islands of Euboea and Skiathos (literally, the shadow of Athos). But even he was forced to admit that 'the flat dome of St Sophia rose only in the mind'.[1] There is a tension between physical and spiritual topography that sometimes stretches the limits of credulity.

If geography shapes the pattern of events, it dominates the history of Greece. Consider the following natural configurations and the images they bring to mind: the pass of Thermopylae, the island of Salamis, the island of Sphakteria, the bay of Navarino, the volcanic peaks of the Meteora, the mountains of Souli. It is largely thanks to geography that the flames of the holy beacon that is Mount Athos have continued to burn so brightly to this day. Our first definition of Athos must therefore be a geographical one.

Athos is a peninsula. The French word *presqu'île* is so much more graphic—almost an island. Indeed Xerxes turned it into an island in 482 BC when he cut a canal across the isthmus to save his ships from the rocks at the southernmost point. The canal has long since silted up; but many people still think of Athos as an island, perhaps because the only (legitimate) way to get there is by sea. It has many of the characteristics of an island but it is in fact part of the mainland of northern Greece, being the most easterly of the three prehensile claws that Chalkidiki extends into the Aegean Sea.

From the isthmus in the north-west to Cape Akrathos in the south-east the distance, as the eagle flies, is about 56 kilometres; that from the west coast over the ridge to the Aegean Sea on the east is rarely more than eight kilometres. The border between Athos and Greece is marked by a wall which runs from coast to coast roughly eight kilometres south of the isthmus, at the point where the land begins to climb. It continues to rise, steeply at first, to densely wooded peaks of 500 and 600 metres. Then it levels off and remains at approximately that height until a point no more than ten kilometres short of the tip, when suddenly it rises dramatically to a majestic marble peak of 2030 metres before making its final plunge into the waves immediately below. Few peaks of such relatively modest dimensions can have been endowed with so spectacular a setting.

From physical geography we move to the anthropology of Athos, which is the prime reason for embarking on its history. Athos is the spiritual capital of the Orthodox Christian world. Such awesome surroundings inevitably result in divine associations and even in antiquity Athos was a holy mountain, sacred to Zeus. For the last thousand years or so it has been dedicated to the glorification of the Virgin Mary, the Theotokos or Mother of God as she is known to the Orthodox. Among Greeks, indeed among all Orthodox Christians, Mount Athos is known simply as *the* Holy Mountain. Road signs direct motorists to 'Agion Oros', even though there is no road to the Mountain, and letters to the inhabitants must be so addressed.

Athos is a self-governing monastic enclave. All its permanent inhabitants are monks, each of whom owes allegiance to one of the twenty ruling monasteries scattered over the peninsula. Not all the monks live in monasteries, but only the monasteries may own land and property; and though there are many smaller settlements and hermitages, all of them are dependencies of one or another of the monasteries. The monasteries are called 'ruling' because between them they govern the Mountain by means of a democratically elected parliament (known as the Holy Community) to which each monastery sends an elected representative. The Holy Community meets in Karyes, the capital of Athos, a small town situated high up in the hills roughly in the middle of the peninsula. Karyes has a population of 300 or 400. Most of them are monks, dressed uniformly in black from head to toe.

Athos is a male preserve. No woman may reside on the Mountain or even set foot on its soil. All domestic animals must be male: only the birds and wild animals (and evidently cats) are exempt from this ruling. The dedication to the Mother of God means that she alone is held to represent her sex, and the monks believe that she herself issued the decree. They are not all misogynists, but they regard the presence of women as a distraction from their vocation. The exclusion of female animals apparently owes more to a desire to avoid the inevitable interruptions that milking would cause to the monastic routine than to any offence that might be given by their breeding, although the official line given to monks has always been 'because you have absolutely renounced all female beings'.[2]

Athos is in Greece, but it is not Greek, it is Orthodox; more than that, it is pan-Orthodox. The Greek government appoints a civil governor who with the support of the Greek police is responsible for maintaining law and order. But for all other purposes the monks govern themselves. A majority of the monasteries—seventeen of the surviving twenty—are Greek-speaking and mostly peopled by Greeks. But there is one monastery for Russians, one for Serbs, and one for Bulgarians; and there are two sketes (dependent houses) reserved for Romanian monks. In addition to these monks from the traditional Orthodox heartlands, there are today monks from all over the world in most monasteries—from Western Europe, the United States, Australia, even Peru. Throughout its history Athos has been a supranational centre and at more than one stage Greeks have formed a minority of the population. Unlike the Greek Church, which is autocephalous (i.e. with its own archbishop as head), Athos falls directly under the spiritual jurisdiction of the Ecumenical Patriarch of Constantinople.

Athos celebrated its millennium in 1963. It was then a thousand years since the foundation of the first monastery, the Great Lavra, though there had been communities of monks on the Mountain for some time before that. The celebrations included high-level visits, impressive publications, even the construction of a road—the first on Athos—from the port of Daphne up to the town of Karyes. But despite the junketing there was no hiding the fact that the monasteries gave every appearance of being in terminal decline. Monks were becoming noticeably older and fewer, buildings were falling into disrepair through lack of use, standards of spirituality were not all that they might be, and there was serious talk of at least one monastery having to close.

The response to this disturbing situation was predictable, if—with hindsight—alarmist. As long ago as 1935 Michael Choukas concluded his perceptive sociological study of the Holy Mountain with these words:

> [The Mountain's] secularization looms imminent. And the next generation of monks may be predestined by human providence to put the final stamp of failure upon the material remnants of this greatest of all human experiments of our millennium—to close up shop and return to their homes and their worldly occupations. To predict that this will happen within the next generation is hazardous—not because it may not happen; but because it may occur sooner.[3]

All the monasteries of Athos were originally founded as *coenobia*, that is communities of monks living and working together and contributing any wealth that they either brought with them or that they earned to the common purse. In the late Byzantine period the so-called idiorrhythmic system was introduced, allowing monks to retain their personal wealth and the profits from any work that they might do. This made nonsense of the monastic vow of poverty, though it served its purpose by attracting wealthy aristocrats to the monasteries at a time when the future of the empire, and that of the Mountain, hung in the balance and, in theory at least, it allowed for a greater measure of austerity than was available in the *coenobia*. Later, however, the system began to be abused and Choukas feared that the idiorrhythmic system would sweep through the whole Mountain, driving before it any remnants of true, cenobitic monasticism. Happily his prediction was not fulfilled.

A more equivocal note was sounded by Philip Sherrard, an English convert to Orthodoxy who knew and loved the Mountain as well as anyone from outside. In 1960 he estimated that the total number of monks was no more than 3000 (in fact the total was then well below 2000):

This number continues to dwindle. New recruits to the monasteries each year are few, firstly because in Greece itself a spirit hostile to the demands and purposes of the monastic life continues largely to dominate both publicly and privately; and secondly because the Greek state, for reasons not unconnected with that tendency to destroy Athos as an Orthodox centre and to turn it into a purely Greek concern, either directly prohibits or makes extremely difficult the admission of probationers of non-Greek nationality, as, for instance, the Roumanians. Whether this policy will have the effect it seems designed to promote, and Athos be reduced to a kind of glorified Byzantine museum and a valuable tourist attraction—one eminent Greek politician has proposed that the monasteries be converted into casinos—remains to be seen.[4]

Most depressing of all were the comments of another English visitor, John Julius Norwich, who wrote in 1966:

Athos is dying—and dying fast. In nearly every monastery the writing looms, all too plainly, on the wall. We have suggested why this should be; we have even discussed what may happen when, probably within the lifetime of most readers, the thousand-year history of the Holy Mountain comes to an end. What we have not done is to make any proposals as to how the disaster may be averted. There are none to make. The disease is incurable. There is no hope.[5]

With hindsight we may commend the remarks of Constantine Cavarnos, a Greek-American academic who visited the Mountain several times during the 1950s. In the first of two books based on his visits, he wrote in 1959:

How to stop this unfortunate trend towards a decrease of the monastic population of Athos, and to increase the number of monks there, is the biggest and most vital problem that now concerns many Athonite monks. There are today about two thousand monks living in the twenty Athonite monasteries and their dependencies, whereas at the beginning of the century there were nearly seven and a half thousand. The problem, as the monks themselves see it, is not merely to increase their number, but especially to increase the number of *younger* monks . . . Although serious, the problem is not one without parallel in the past, and it does not cause the monks to think that the Mountain will soon cease to be a living reality and become a mere library or museum . . . they believe that this unique Pan-Orthodox democracy of monks will continue to exist until the end of time.[6]

Professor Cavarnos went on to report some practical ways of solving the problem that were being put forward by the monks:

As to the measures that should be taken in order to reverse the present trend, they [the monks] specify the following. First, steps should be taken to strengthen the piety of men...Secondly, the economic problem must be solved. The Greek government must furnish regularly adequate financial compensation to the monasteries for the estates it has expropriated…Thirdly, bishops in Greece must stop taking monks from Athos and employing them as deacons, priests, and preachers of their dioceses…Finally, Athonite monks, as well as friends of Athos, should strive to provide a better understanding and appreciation of the ideals of Athonite monasticism.[7]

The fact that so many of these 'measures' have subsequently been realized lends weight to the prophetic traditions of Athonite divines. In his later book, written after another visit in 1965 and published in 1973, Cavarnos returned to the same theme:

During the last four decades, there has been much speculation and concern about the survival of monasticism on the Holy Mountain, prompted by (a) the reduction of the number of monks, (b) the anti-monastic spirit of our age, and (c) the invasion of Athos by tourism . . . Of the three dangers which I have discussed, the first—the reduction in the number of monks—is regarded by the Athonites as the most fearful. But these pious and determined men believe that they will confront this danger, as well as the others, successfully.[8]

What is especially commendable in Cavarnos's account is his description of the then very recent changes at the monastery of Stavronikita.[9] He reports that in 1968 the monastery had been forced to close 'because there were no more monks there'. Later in the same year it reopened under new management. Archimandrite Vasileios Gontikakis, a theology graduate of the University of Athens, was appointed abbot; a number of other devout monks joined him and the monastery changed from the idiorrhythmic to the cenobitic system. 'Thus the temporary closing down of the Monastery of Stavronikita turned out to be not a disaster, but an opportunity for inaugurating there a stricter mode of monasticism.' Cavarnos cannot have known that the changes at Stavronikita were the first manifestation of a revival that was to overtake the monasteries of Athos in the course of the following quarter-century. The seeds of revival had been sown many years earlier in the cells and hermitages in the most remote parts of the Mountain, although the fruits were not to become apparent for some years to come. Describing this revival is my first and principal motive for writing this book.

A second motive is that, although much has been written about various aspects of the Holy Mountain, few authors to my knowledge have attempted a complete history from earliest times to the present. The task has been made more laborious and more rewarding as well as more necessary by the monasteries' ongoing publication of their archives. These archives represent a uniquely valuable resource and include countless charters, chrysobulls and other documents covering the entire period of Athonite monasticism from the ninth century onwards. The information they provide extends way beyond purely monastic or even ecclesiastical concerns and touches on political, economic, legal, social and cultural matters. Their publication, in a systematic and scholarly series initiated in Paris in 1937 by Gabriel Millet and continued by Paul Lemerle, is an undertaking of immense historical importance which, when complete, will add immeasurably to our understanding of the Orthodox world throughout the Byzantine and Ottoman periods.

Neither of these motives would be sufficient justification for the book if Athos were not itself important. Athos matters to different people for different reasons. I shall select four areas of concern, all equally important.

The first concern must be the spiritual tradition. For more than a thousand years Athos has functioned as the principal centre of Orthodox monasticism and spirituality. At one time it is said to have sheltered 40,000 monks. The Great Lavra alone has been the nursery of 26 patriarchs and more than 144 bishops. The monastery of Vatopedi has produced more than 44 recognized saints. In the twentieth century there was a decline in numbers of monks, but spiritual traditions were maintained, saints continued to emerge and, as Archimandrite Gabriel (1886–1983), Abbot of Dionysiou for fifty years, has written,

> The splendour and grandeur of the Holy Mountain is not to be judged by the small or large number of monks who dwell on it. This fluctuation has occurred many times during its thousand-year period of monastic life . . . We Hagiorites steadfastly believe that our holy abodes on Mount Athos will soon be filled with monks . . . We believe that the Mountain, by the Grace of God, will continue in existence till the end of time. The piety of Orthodox people will always envelop Athos, and souls beloved by God will never cease coming to it, because its spirituality will always have the power of attracting those who are heavy laden with sin, and its holiness those who are pure in heart.[10]

Fr Gabriel was just one of the most recent in an unbroken tradition of holy men, scholars, teachers and ascetics that stretches back to the ninth century. They are the men who have provided the Mountain with its life-blood and its means of self-perpetuation. For Athonites are biologically incapable of reproducing themselves: they cannot survive without an intake from the world, and that intake will only present itself if there are enough men like Fr Gabriel to draw them. That is why the current revival is so important. It is in no sense a reform. It is simply yet another manifestation of the Mountain regenerating itself in the way that it has always done—from within—and attracting new blood that will enable it not just to survive but to shine with the mystical radiance of an authentic icon.

Secondly, Athos is important for historical reasons. From the moment of its inauguration by the emperor Constantine the Great in 330, the Byzantine empire was a uniquely God-centred institution. However reduced his circumstances might become, the emperor remained God's viceroy on earth, supreme among all other Christian princes, anointed by God, acknowledged by all Orthodox patriarchs, bishops and peoples. Although his territories might be threatened and even occupied by the enemy, God's authority would soon be restored over the full extent of the ancient Roman empire. This remained the confident belief of all Byzantines, one of the most devoutly religious people of all times. The patriarch and other members of the hierarchy enjoyed enormous prestige and great wealth, but oddly enough it was individual monks and holy men who were far more influential in Byzantine society in general, and if there was a conflict between the monks and the bishops it was the monks who commanded the support of the people. This was one reason why emperors were so generous with their monastic endowments, and it accounted for the great wealth and power the monasteries acquired.

As the principal monastic survivor of the turmoil created by the Fourth Crusade and the Latin empire of 1204–61, Athos emerged in a position of great strength. The monks were able to influence political affairs, dominate religious debate, and play an unprecedented part in the administration of the Church. This was perhaps their most glorious period in terms of worldly power. After the fall of the empire in 1453 they acquired a new role: they became the guardians of Hellenism. During the long centuries of Ottoman rule, it was largely the monasteries that kept alive the spirit of the Greeks as a people, reminding them of their heritage, preserving the traditions of Orthodoxy, and in due course fostering the idea of nationalism. Orthodoxy and Hellenism had long been inextricably intertwined and it is impossible to separate the secular aspect from the religious in this development. But it is perhaps true to say that after the Greek War of Independence in 1821–32 and the eventual disintegration of the Ottoman empire in 1922 the monasteries were temporarily bereft of part of their *raison d'être*. It was as if they suddenly had to cast around for a new role and the search for that role may be part of the explanation for the decline in the number of monks in the half-century following the liberation of northern Greece in 1912.

The third area in which Athos is of supreme importance is its cultural heritage—the buildings themselves and what they contain. Architecturally the monasteries are an amalgam. They represent an accumulation of structures of all periods from the tenth century to the present day, when once again they are being forced to expand in order to accommodate the new influx of monks. Among the earliest surviving structures are the principal churches of some of the first monasteries such as the Great Lavra, Vatopedi and Iviron and the church of the Protaton in Karyes, the only basilica on the Mountain, all of which date (at least in part) from the tenth century. Apart from some early fortifications and towers, not much else survives from the Byzantine period. But the cells and other monastic buildings scattered over the peninsula represent by far the best witness we have to domestic architecture in Greece during the Ottoman period, with an interesting admixture of Russian, Serbian, Bulgarian, Romanian and Georgian styles thrown in.

All Orthodox churches are decorated in an attempt to make them worthy symbols of heaven on earth, and the decoration of Athonite churches is eminently suited to the earthly paradise which the monks are proud to inhabit. Some of the best Byzantine artists and craftsmen were attracted to Athos, and glorious examples of their work may still be admired in many of the monasteries. In addition to the frescos which colour the walls, roofs and domes of many a church and refectory, there are priceless collections of icons, many of them believed to possess miracle-working properties. Icon-painting is a tradition still practised by monks today and more than one skete houses a school of painting. As well as icons, all monasteries have collections of relics—mostly bones of the saints, fragments of the 'True Cross', and other items associated with the early Church. Many of these are preserved in elaborate reliquaries and put on display for pilgrims to venerate. Most monasteries also have rich and important collections of medieval and later manuscripts. The majority of these are liturgical, biblical or patristic texts, some of them resplendent with fine illuminations, but an important minority are of ancient pagan literature. Libraries and treasuries often house other valuable items such as jewelled book-covers, vessels of silver and gold, embroidered vestments, mosaic icons, and countless gifts from benefactors which together comprise the celebrated wealth of the Athonite houses.

Finally, as a fourth area of special importance, there is the natural environment. Due to its varied topography, geology and climate, the peninsula is home to a wide range of flora, including a number of endemic species on the peak itself. As a result of the exclusion of female domestic animals and the consequent absence of flocks, the slopes of the Mountain have been very little grazed and therefore retain much of their natural vegetation. Most impressive to the visitor is the forest cover which, despite numerous fires, extends over more than 90 per cent of the Mountain. In the north the commonest tree is the Aleppo pine, but in the uplands of the central region there is an extensive zone of deciduous broadleaved forest in which the Spanish chestnut predominates. In springtime the visitor will also be struck by the profusion of wild flowers which seem to carpet every available slope and meadow. If he is lucky, he may be awakened by the sound of jackals howling at night, and though the last wolves are said to have died out there have been reports of their reintroduction.

In short, the environment of Athos in the twenty-first century is practically unchanged since the first monks arrived in the ninth. It is perhaps the nearest thing to a natural landscape anywhere in southern Europe. It goes without saying that it is almost indescribably beautiful and naturally conducive to religious activity. Conservationists have toured the peninsula and have made the monks aware of the value and the fragility of their natural surroundings. The survival of this unique environment depends upon preserving the seclusion of the Holy Mountain, which remains inviolate after more than a thousand years of monkish activity. This is perhaps the most important of all the areas of concern, since should it ever be lost the rest will surely perish with it. And such an eventuality is unthinkable.

I

ATHOS BC

Athos is an extraordinary place. Its unusual physiognomy is conducive to religious activity, and it is largely in that context that we think of it today. But its pre-Christian past helps to explain something of the numinous quality that the place already possessed before the arrival of the monks. In fact, for its size and its relative remoteness from the centres of contemporary cultural activity Athos has a pagan past of quite exceptional importance. Three particular episodes merit narration, each connected with a momentous event in Greek history, each the direct result of the peninsula's geography.

THE TROJAN WAR

Robert Byron may have been blessed with exceptional eyesight, or perhaps with a creative imagination, when he described what he could see from the peak of Athos on that evening in 1926 (see above, p. 1), but it is significant that the first two places he mentioned were Lemnos and the plains of Troy. The site of Troy had been positively identified by Heinrich Schliemann some fifty years earlier, and there was no more celebrated episode in the annals of prehistory than the capture of Troy by the Greeks after a ten-year siege. News of the victory was relayed almost instantly to Argos, where Clytaemnestra, Agamemnon's faithless queen, was waiting to proclaim the joyful tidings to her people. How did she know so quickly, what messenger could come so fast? Aeschylus explains it thus:

> Hephaestus, launching a fine flame from Ida,
> Beacon forwarding beacon, despatch-riders of fire,
> Ida relayed to Hermes' cliff in Lemnos
> And the great glow from the island was taken over third
> By the height of Athos that belongs to Zeus,
> And towering then to straddle over the sea . . .
> Blazing and bounding till it reached at length
> The Arachnaean steep, our neighbouring heights;
> And leaps in the latter end on the roof of the sons of Atreus
> Issue and image of the fire on Ida . . .
> Such is the proof I offer you, the sign
> My husband sent me out of Troy.[1]

Scholars argue over the precise location of some of the beacons, but the principle is perfectly sound. Beacons were lit on hilltops all over England in 1988 to commemorate the manner in which news of the defeat of the Spanish Armada had been signalled 400 years earlier. Athos was one of the best-known eminences in the Aegean and a landmark familiar to all sailors. Even the Argonauts, the most dauntless of all mythology's mariners, were gratified to catch sight of it as they struck out across the open sea towards the Hellespont, and the poet comments on the famous shadow which at sunset the mountain casts as far as the island of Lemnos, a distance of some fifty miles.[2] Athos was therefore well placed to join the chain of beacons between Troy and Argos that night.

THE PERSIAN WARS

The next time that the Greeks became involved in a major foreign war occurred early in the fifth century BC when they were twice invaded by the Persians. On each occasion Athos played a prominent role.

By the end of the sixth century the Persians were by far the strongest power in the eastern Mediterranean and had established their rule from the north Aegean as far as Egypt and India. In 492 BC a fleet under the command of Mardonius, son-in-law of King Darius, was dispatched to re-establish Persian authority over Thrace and Macedonia, which had supported a recent rebellion. While a land army crossed the Hellespont and began its march through Thrace, the fleet overran the island of Thasos and then turned its attention to the mainland. Herodotus tells the story:

> From Thasos the fleet stood across to the mainland and proceeded along the coast to Acanthus, and from there attempted to double Athos; but before they were round this promontory, they were caught by a violent northerly gale, which proved too much for the ships to cope with. A great many of them were driven ashore on Athos and smashed up—indeed, report says that something like three hundred were wrecked, and over twenty thousand men lost their lives. The sea in the neighbourhood of Athos is full of man-eating monsters, so that those of the ships' companies who were not dashed to pieces on the rocks, were seized and devoured. Others, unable to swim, were drowned; others, again, died of cold.[3]

The rocks are still there off the southern tip of the peninsula for all to see. As for the man-eating monsters, Athos has seen stranger things in its time. Undeterred, the Persians continued with their invasion, only to be driven back into the sea by the Athenians when they landed at Marathon in 490 BC.

Ten years later they were ready to try again. As before, the invasion was planned by both land and sea, but this time Xerxes, who had succeeded to

1 The isthmus of Athos from the south-west. Xerxes' canal ran close to the line of the modern road.

the throne of his father Darius, decided to cut a canal through the isthmus of Athos rather than risk his fleet on the rocks at the southern point. This immense operation took three years to complete, with labour provided by the inhabitants of Athos as well as by the soldiers of the Persian army based in the Thracian Chersonese. Herodotus breaks off at this point to give an engaging description of the peninsula. 'Everyone knows Mount Athos', he writes,

> that lofty promontory running far out into the sea. People live on it, and where the high land ends on the landward side it forms a sort of isthmus with a neck about a mile and a half wide, all of which is level, except for a few low hills, right across from the coast by Acanthus to the other side near Torone. On this isthmus to the north of the high ground stands the Greek town of Sane, and south of it, on Athos itself, are Dium, Olophyxus, Acrothoon, Thyssus, and Cleonae—the inhabitants of which Xerxes now proposed to turn into islanders.[4]

Herodotus gives a detailed description of how the canal was dug and concludes that the enterprise was primarily intended as propaganda to demonstrate the extent of Persian power. Whatever the motive for building the canal, the fleet escaped the rocks of Athos this time and the Persians went on to sack the Athenian Acropolis. But their triumph was short-lived. Their ships came to grief in the narrows off Salamis, and their army was routed at Plataea in 479 BC. The Persian threat had been decisively beaten off and Greece was free to enjoy a cultural golden age.

Xerxes' enterprise aroused the curiosity of a number of eighteenth- and nineteenth-century travellers and surveyors. The Comte de Choiseul-Gouffier, subsequently French ambassador to the Sublime Porte and Elgin's rival for possession of the Parthenon marbles, was on the scene in 1776 and published a description of the canal together with a map.[5] Then the military surveyor William Martin Leake examined the site after his tour of the Athos peninsula in October–November 1806. Leake had a professional concern with the canal's military potential and after a detailed description concluded that 'it might . . ., without much labour, be renewed; and there can be no doubt that it would be useful to the navigation of the Aegean'.[6] In 1838 another British officer, Lieutenant T. Spratt R.N. of H.M.S. *Beacon* was detailed to survey it and published his results, again with a map, in 1847.[7] And in 1901 yet another survey was conducted and published, together with another map, by A. Struck.[8]

Perhaps surprisingly, it was to be ninety years before modern archaeological techniques were applied to the canal. In 1991–2 a topographical survey and various geophysical investigations were carried out under the auspices of the British School at Athens and the somewhat inconclusive results were published in 1994–6.[9] More positive results were claimed by a team of Greek scientists who used seismic resistivity techniques to establish the existence of a substantial channel which they have calculated to be 65 feet wide at its base, 114 feet broad at the top, and up to 47 feet deep. The depth of the water was probably between seven and ten feet, which would have allowed two unladen triremes to pass through the canal abreast.[10] It begins to look as if there may indeed be detectable traces of what the British excavator B.S.J. Isserlin has called 'not only the most impressive surviving monument of Persia's short-lived imperial presence in Europe, but also one of the most important pieces of ancient marine communication engineering anywhere'.[11]

And the evidence of local tradition, which is often more graphic and more colourful than that of the spade or the sledge-hammer, should not be ignored. Joice Loch, an Australian who lived in the Byzantine tower at Prosphori (now Ouranopolis) from 1928 until her death in 1982, records in her autobiography that in the 1920s caiques were still being hauled across the narrowest part of the isthmus on wooden rollers by teams of bullocks, as had been the custom, she says, from before the time of Xerxes.[12] If there was indeed a canal there, those bullocks would surely be following its route.

THE CONQUESTS OF ALEXANDER THE GREAT

It was ostensibly to avenge the sack of Athens 150 years earlier that in 334 BC Alexander III of Macedon set out to conquer the Persian empire. He succeeded in his ambition and went on to become master of the known world, taking Greek culture as far as Upper Egypt and Central Asia. Megalomaniac he may have been, but no Greek has equalled his achievement before or since. Pandering to the general's vanity and confident in his own ideas and skill, the young architect Dinocrates came up with an equally astonishing scheme to commemorate the conquests and reflect Alexander's scarcely concealed pretensions to divinity. What Dinocrates proposed was nothing less than the transformation of the whole of Mount Athos into a monumental sculpture of the king. With his left hand he would embrace the walls of a very extensive city, with his right a bowl overflowing with water channelled from all the rivers that spring from that mountain.

The reaction of Alexander, as reported by the Roman architect Vitruvius writing more than 300 years later, was entirely pragmatic. The scheme was a bold one; but could the mountain grow enough corn to feed the population of such a city? Dinocrates was forced to admit that the terrain was too mountainous for the plough and that supplies of corn would have to be imported. The king then congratulated the young architect on his originality but quietly dismissed the idea on practical grounds:

> I perceive that if anyone leads a colony to that place, his judgment will be blamed. For just as a child when born, if it lacks the nurse's milk cannot be fed, nor led up the staircase of growing life, so a city without cornfields and their produce abounding within its ramparts, cannot grow, nor become populous without abundance of food, nor maintain its people without a supply. Therefore, just as I think your *planning* worthy of approval, so, in my judgement, the *site* is worthy of disapproval.[13]

However the young architect was not laughed out of court and his services were retained for other projects that were even dearer to the heart of the king—first (according to Vitruvius), the design of the new city of Alexandria in Egypt and later (according to Plutarch), the fantastically grandiose tomb of Alexander's adored friend Hephaestion in Babylon.[14] As for Athos, 'let the mountain stand as it is', Alexander is said to have declared; 'it is sufficient that another king perpetuated his arrogance by having a canal cut through it.'[15]

Thus Mount Athos, which would ultimately have a very different commemorative role, was spared this proposed assault on its craggy features. The hubristic fantasy of Dinocrates was also condemned by the Renaissance architect Leon Battista Alberti in his influential study of Vitruvius, written in

1452. In fact he criticizes it twice, the first time for purely practical reasons:

> In choosing the region it will be proper to have it such, that the inhabitants may find it convenient in all respects, both as to its natural properties, and as to the neighbourhood and its correspondence with the rest of mankind . . . For this reason, more than any other, Alexander was perfectly in the right in not building a city upon Mount Athos (though the invention and design of the architect Policrates [sic] must needs have been wonderful) because the inhabitants could never have been well supplied with conveniences.[16]

Later in the same work Alberti attacks the plan again—for lacking a sense of proportion, for contravening nature, and for being plain unnecessary:

> What the hand or wit of man can add to the region, either of beauty or dignity, is hardly discoverable; unless we would give in to those miraculous and superstitious accounts which we read of some works. Nor are the undertakers of such works blamed by prudent men, if their designs answer any great conveniency; but if they take pains to do what there was no necessity for, they are justly denied the praise they hunt after. For who would be so daring as to undertake, like Stasicrates (according to Plutarch) or Dinocrates (according to Vitruvius) to make Mount Athos into a statue of Alexander, and in one of the hands to build a city big enough to contain ten thousand men? . . . But let us leave it to mighty kings to be delighted with such undertakings: let them join sea to sea by cutting the land between them: let them level hills: let them make new islands, or join old ones to the continent: let them put it out of the power of any others to imitate them, and so make their names memorable to posterity: still all their vast works will be commended not so much in proportion to their greatness as their use.[17]

Alberti's strictures however did nothing to discourage later artists from depicting a realization of the scheme in order to appeal to the vanity of their patrons or demonstrate their own antiquarian learning. Thus Pietro da Cortona in about 1655 portrayed himself kneeling before Pope Alexander VII together with Dinocrates, who directs attention to the anthropomorphic mountain as if to commend the new pope's propitious choice of name and his ambition to be remembered as Rome's greatest builder. In his *Sketch of Historical Architecture* (1721), the Baroque architect Johann Bernard Fischer von Erlach included a dramatic representation of the Athonite colossus with fine detailing of the imagined city and the flowing streams. And in 1796 a blatantly political statement by the French artist Pierre-Henri de Valenciennes shows a tranquil Arcadian pastoral scene in the foreground under the watchful eye of the monumental Alexander, who represents the benign but immutable authority of the republican state in the background. The irony is that Alexander, epitome of the ruthlessly autocratic monarch, had now become an icon of republican virtues for the delectation of supporters of the French Revolution.[18]

No such *volte-face* took place in the staunchly royalist waters of the

2 *Mount Athos Carved as a Monument to Alexander the Great* by Pierre-Henri de Valenciennes (1796), a recreation of the scheme of Dinocrates made during the Revolutionary period in France.

north Aegean, infested as they are thought to be by man-eating Gorgons (can they be the same monsters that are referred to by Herodotus?). According to the folklorists, these creatures usually surface on Saturday nights in particularly stormy seas and, grasping the stern of a caique in distress, ask the captain, 'Is King Alexander living?' To this question he must reply, 'He lives and reigns and keeps the world at peace.' Provided the correct response is given, the Gorgon will disappear and the storm will subside. But if the captain is so foolish as to reply that the king is dead, the ship will invariably be lost with all hands. No hero from antiquity is more celebrated in modern Greek folklore than Alexander the Great.[19]

THE END OF ANTIQUITY

We have observed Mount Athos implicated in or associated with three of the most heroic episodes in ancient history—the Trojan War, the defeat of Persia, and the conquests of Alexander the Great. Such associations are the life-blood of legend, though none of these associations would have come about were it not for the mountain's remarkable geography. It is also worth remarking at this point that by the first centuries AD the inhabitants of Athos had acquired a reputation for longevity, the reason for which may or may not be related to the mountain's geography.[20] However it came about, the reputation is well deserved, as is borne out by the experience of many of its latter-day residents.

Given its history, and the fact that we know of the existence of at least five cities on the shores of the peninsula in antiquity, it is perhaps surprising that so little of its pre-Christian past survives. The site of none of them is known for certain.[21] And apart from a very few fragments of ancient masonry or sculpture reused in the walls or preserved in the treasuries of one or two of the monasteries, nothing of any substance has come to light. But then archaeology is officially forbidden on Athos; monks, if they are not positively prejudiced against it, take very little interest in the pagan past of their present surroundings; and if any casual find is ever made, the chances of its becoming widely known are remote.

Nor is the fate of those ancient cities recorded. It must be assumed, however, that by late antiquity they had become depopulated. Their citizens may have sailed away in search of more fertile land elsewhere, or they may have succumbed to some deadly plague, or they may simply have faded away like old soldiers. The one thing that seems certain is that they were not driven away by enemy action or by any occupying force. There is nothing to suggest that when the first monks arrived they had to win the land by conquest or displace an existing population. It seems that they found a deserted peninsula, suitable in every respect for the purpose they had in mind. The President of the Immortals had ended his sport with the mountain and graciously surrendered his seat to the Holy Mother of God.

The Garden of the Mother of God

A visit to Mount Athos requires careful preparation. The pilgrim—and every visitor is by definition a pilgrim—must prepare himself not only materially and physically but also intellectually and spiritually. For the journey he is about to make is no ordinary pilgrimage, no mere passage through time and space, but a journey to another world. He must prepare himself to leave this world and to enter a world where every stone breathes prayers, a world where he will experience a foretaste of paradise, a world known to its inhabitants as the Garden of the Mother of God. It will be helpful if the reader too makes these preparations, for they will help him or her (and readers, unlike pilgrims, may be of either sex) to acquire the intellectual agility required to enter into the Athonite *mentalité*. On Athos things are not always what they seem to be, and people do not always think or behave in the way you expect them to. A different set of assumptions needs to be applied. Facts that appear to be black and white in the world suddenly acquire many different hues on the Mountain. Conversely, notions and beliefs that are subjected to endless scrutiny or uncertainty in the world may be accepted as gospel by Athonites. It does not mean that they are demented or brain-washed or naïve: they simply do things differently there.

The Visit of the Virgin Mary to Athos

According to Athonite tradition, after the Ascension of our Lord the Virgin Mary accepted an invitation to visit Lazarus, the brother of Mary and Martha, who was ministering to the Church in Cyprus as the bishop of Kition. In the course of the voyage her ship was blown off course, and when it finally came to land, it was on the east coast of Mount Athos, near where the monastery of Iviron stands today. There was then a pagan temple there, and an oracle of Apollo. She went ashore, and immediately all the idols cried out and called on the people living roundabout to go and meet the Holy Mother of God. The people abandoned their pagan practices and were converted to Christianity. The Virgin for her part was so enchanted with what she found that she fell on her knees and besought her Son to grant her the land on which she knelt as her personal domain. Her prayer was granted and before she departed she announced that the Mountain was hers and blessed Athos and all its residents.

The conversion of the inhabitants reminds us that in antiquity Athos was not a deserted land. Another tradition relates that the pagan cities were in time depopulated, by divine providence and through the intercession of the Mother of God, to make way for the arrival of the monks. This process became a reality in the fourth century when, according to tradition, the Christian emperor Constantine the Great founded three great churches on the Mountain, on sites that are now occupied by the monasteries of Iviron and Vatopedi and the church of the Protaton in Karyes.[1] Constantine was indeed a great church builder, but sadly no traces have come to light on Athos to confirm his activity there.

Ever since the arrival of the first monks the Virgin is believed to have continued to visit the Mountain and reveal herself as its patron and protector. Her words to St Peter the Athonite, one of the first hermits known by name to be living on Athos in the ninth century, are recorded by St Gregory Palamas:

> In Europe there is a mountain, very high and very beautiful, which extends towards the south and very deeply into the sea. This is the mountain that I have chosen out of all the earth, and I have decided to make of it the country of the monastic order. I have consecrated it to be henceforth my dwelling: this is why people will call it the 'Holy Mountain'. All who shall come to live there after having decided to fight the battle against the common enemy of the human race will find me at their side throughout their lives. I will be their invincible aid, I will teach them what they must do and what they must avoid. I myself shall be their tutor, their physician, their nurse. I shall take care to give them both food and the care that their bodies require, and that which is necessary for their souls, to inspire and invigorate them, so they depart not from virtue. And all who finish their lives on this mountain in a spirit of love for God and repentance, I promise to recommend to my Son and God that He accord them complete remission of their sins.[2]

This declaration by the Mother of God provides every Athonite with his *raison d'être*. The Mountain is her garden and she is ever present in it. She is the archetype of monasticism, the paradigm of Christian holiness, the abbess of the whole Mountain, every monk's guide to the Kingdom of Heaven. Her role is symbolized in the famous nineteenth-century Russian image that portrays her dressed as an abbess, complete with purple cloak and pastoral staff, presiding on clouds of glory over Mount Athos. Every monk is deeply conscious of her presence and her protection. This is why she occupies so exclusive and privileged a place on the Holy Mountain.

The Role of the Virgin Mary in Orthodoxy

For all Orthodox Christians the Virgin Mary occupies a very special position among the saints.[3] She is revered as the most exalted of God's creatures. In the words of the *Axion estin* ('It is meet'), a hymn to the Virgin sung at the Divine Liturgy and at other services, she is 'greater in honour than the Cherubim, incomparably more glorious than the Seraphim, without corruption you gave birth to God the Word; truly the Mother of God, we magnify you.' She is revered, venerated and honoured, but in no sense is she worshipped. She was chosen as a virgin to be the Mother of God, but she herself did not become God, nor does she rank with the members of the Trinity.

Mary's name is frequently mentioned in the course of Orthodox church services and she is generally referred to by her full title: 'Our most holy, pure, most blessed and glorious Lady, Mother of God and Ever-Virgin Mary'. This title incorporates the three principal epithets with which she is endowed: *Theotokos*, meaning God-birthgiver, the Mother of God, a title awarded to her by the Council of Ephesus (AD 431); *Aeiparthenos*, Ever-Virgin, assigned by the Council of Constantinople (AD 553); and *Panagia*, All-Holy, a title which was never dogmatically defined but is nevertheless used by all Orthodox.

The title Theotokos is particularly important because it defines the reason why Mary is honoured—because she is the Mother of God. She is revered not in her own right, but because of her relationship with her Son; veneration of her in this role is to be encouraged specifically because it provides a defence for the doctrine of her Son as 'the Word made flesh'. She accepted this role of her own free will: 'Here am I, the servant of the Lord; as you have spoken, so let it be' (Luke 1:38). She is therefore the model of co-operation between God's purpose and human freedom, and a voluntary participant in the mystery of the Incarnation. Bishop Kallistos quotes the fourteenth-century theologian St Nicolas Cabasilas: 'The Incarnation was not only the work of the Father, of His Power and His Spirit . . . but it was also the work of the will and faith of the Virgin . . . Just as God became incarnate voluntarily, so He wished that His Mother should bear Him freely and with her full consent.'[4] Just as Christ is regarded as the Second Adam, who came into the world to reverse the effects of the first Adam's disobedience, so Mary is the Second Eve, who by her voluntary submission to the will of God counteracts the first Eve's disobedience in the Garden of Eden.

The virginity of Mary is important because it acts as a pointer to the uniqueness of her Son, and it does so in three distinct but closely connected ways. First, the absence of an earthly father underlines the divinity of the Son: He is truly human, but He is not only human. He is of this world, but He also transcends the world. He is at the same time both completely man and perfect God. Secondly, the virginity of Mary demonstrates the fact that the birth of Christ was the result not of sexual union between a man and a woman but of divine initiative; it was, truly, literally and uniquely, an act of God. Thirdly, it emphasizes the fact that the birth of Christ did not result in the creation of a new person but rather the incarnation of the second person of the Trinity, the already existing Son of God, who was and is before the world began. It therefore reflects the eternal presence of the Son.

The Orthodox Church regularly refers to Mary as 'All-Holy' (*Panagia*) and as 'pure' or 'spotless' (*achrantos*), but it has never proclaimed a doctrine of the Immaculate Conception such as was defined by the Roman Catholic Church in 1854. The Orthodox view is that such a doctrine is unnecessary and unhelpful, since it would divorce Mary from the saints of the Old Testament, the descendants of Adam, among whom, together with John the Baptist, she is the greatest and the last representative. Similarly, the Orthodox subscribe to the bodily Assumption of the Virgin and believe that after her death she was taken up into heaven where she dwells, both physically and spiritually, in eternal glory with her Son. For the Orthodox the Virgin is 'the joy of all creation' (Liturgy of St Basil), 'the precious treasure of the whole world' (St Cyril of Alexandria), 'the flower of the human race and gate of heaven' (*Dogmatikon* in Tone One). And the feast of the Dormition or 'Falling Asleep' of Mary on 15 August is celebrated with great joy and intensity throughout the Orthodox world. But the Assumption of Our Lady has never been affirmed as a dogma by the Church.

The twentieth-century theologian of the Eastern Church Vladimir Lossky summarizes the Orthodox view of the Virgin as follows:

> The Mother of God was never a theme of the public preaching of the Apostles; while Christ was preached on the housetops, and proclaimed for all to know in an initiatory teaching addressed to the whole world, the mystery of his Mother was revealed only to those who were within the Church . . . It is not so much an object of faith as a foundation of our hope, a fruit of faith, ripened in Tradition. Let us therefore keep silence, and let us not try to dogmatize about the supreme glory of the Mother of God.[5]

As Bishop Kallistos has written, 'The doctrines of the Trinity and the Incarnation have been proclaimed as dogmas, for they belong to the public preaching of the Church; but the glorification of Our Lady belongs to the Church's inner Tradition.'[6] Her role in the world, as the supreme offering made by the human race to God, is perhaps best summed up in the words of a hymn sung during the Great Vespers of Christmas:

> What shall we offer thee, O Christ,
> Who for our sakes hast appeared on earth as man?

Every creature made by thee offers thee thanks.
The angels offer thee a hymn; the heavens, a star;
The magi, gifts; the shepherds, their wonder;
The earth, its cave; the wilderness, a manger;
And we offer thee—a Virgin Mother.

THE ROLE OF THE VIRGIN MARY ON ATHOS

On Athos the role of the Mother of God is no different from what it is in the world, except that it is more sharply focused. If she is the Second Eve, Athos is the Second Garden, her Garden, and she is everywhere present in it, not only in spirit but in body too. *Axion estin* is not only the name of a hymn sung at the Divine Liturgy. It is also the name of the most celebrated icon on the Holy Mountain which is preserved in the sanctuary of the church of the Protaton in Karyes. It is of course an icon of the Mother of God, credited with miracle-working properties, and by tradition it dates from the tenth century. *Axion estin* is also the name of one of the ferries operating between Ouranopolis and the Athonite port of Daphne; as such, it provides the pilgrim's first contact with the Mountain and serves to remind him whose territory he is approaching.

The majority of the most important icons on Athos represent the Mother of God. One such is the so-called Portaïtissa, or Our Lady of the Gate, at the monastery of Iviron. It is said to have travelled to Athos of its own accord during the reign of the iconoclast emperor Theophilos (829–42) and to have arrived off Iviron in a pillar of fire. The monks, or rather the hermit monk Gabriel whom the icon asked for by name, took it from the sea and placed it in the *katholikon* (that is, the main church) of the monastery, only to find next day that it had removed itself to a spot over the old entrance gate of the monastery. They took it back to the church, and again it repositioned itself over the gate. This happened three times, after which the Virgin appeared in a vision to Fr Gabriel and told him that a special chapel should be built for the icon next to the gate, 'for I have not come here for you to guard me, but for me to guard you'. The chapel was duly built and to this day it houses the icon, which is therefore known as Our Lady of the Gate.

Another icon of the Mother of God said to date from the period of icon-oclasm is the so-called Tricherousa, or Our Lady with Three Hands, at the monastery of Chilandar which is dedicated to the Presentation of the Virgin. This icon apparently belonged to the eighth-century theologian St John of Damascus, whose hand was cut off by the Caliph when he mistak-enly thought John was plotting against him. The mistake was discovered and the hand restored, in gratitude for which John had a silver hand

3 The *Axion estin* icon of the Mother of God, the holiest icon on Athos (Protaton, Karyes).

attached to the icon. In the twelfth century the Tricherousa was given to St Savvas, archbishop of Serbia and co-founder (with his father Stefan Nemanya) of the monastery of Chilandar, though the icon itself did not reach Athos until 1371. As at Iviron, the monks placed it in the chancel of the katholikon, where it remained until a dispute occurred over the election of a new abbot. Then one morning the monks noticed that the icon had repositioned itself over the abbot's throne. They put it back in the chancel, and again it removed itself to the throne. This happened three times, after which a hermit told the monks that the Mother of God had appeared to him in a vision and told him that this was her way of settling the dispute. From now on she would take the role of abbot and the monks should elect only a deputy abbot. And to this day the abbot's throne is occupied by the Tricherousa.

The most cherished sacred treasure at the monastery of Vatopedi is the so-called Holy Zone, the girdle of the Mother of God, which is the only surviving relic of her earthly life. Now in three pieces, it is made of camel's hair, supposedly fashioned by the Virgin herself. At her Assumption she gave it to St Thomas and it remained in Jerusalem until the fourth century, when the emperor Arcadius removed it to Constantinople. Always prized as

4 The Virgin Hodegetria ('she who shows the way'), a twelfth–century mosaic icon from Chilandar, traditionally associated with the foundation of the monastery in 1198.

5 This fine reliquary contains the holy girdle of the Mother of God. Its feast day, 13 September, is the occasion for a major celebration at Vatopedi.

an agent of healing, it cured the empress Zoë, wife of Leo VI, and in gratitude she embroidered it with the gold thread that still adorns it today. After further adventures in Bulgaria and Serbia the girdle was presented to Vatopedi by the Serbian prince Lazarus I (1372–89) and since then has resided in the sanctuary of the katholikon of the monastery. Over the years it has performed many miracles, particularly in the case of barren women, and it is still occasionally taken out into the world to heal the faithful.

Vatopedi alone has no fewer than eight other miracle-working icons, all of them representations of the Virgin (Vimatarissa, Paramythia, Esphagmeni, Antiphonitria, Eleousa, Elaiovrytissa, Pyrovolitheisa, and Pantanassa). Each one has a miraculous legend attached to it dating from some point in the monastery's 1000-year history, and many of them continue to work miracles of healing to this day. The collection at Vatopedi is especially large, but nearly every monastery has at least one or two such icons: the Koukouzelissa at the Great Lavra, the Phoveraprostasia at Koutloumousiou, the Gerontissa at Pantokrator, the Glykophilousa and another Gerontissa at Philotheou, the Gorgoypekoös at Dochiariou, the Myrovlitissa at Dionysiou, and many others.

Several monasteries are dedicated to the Virgin: Vatopedi and Philotheou to the Annunciation; St Paul's to the Purification; Chilandar to the Presentation of the Virgin; and Iviron to her Dormition. All these feasts are celebrated with enthusiasm throughout Athos, none more so than that of the Dormition (15 August). The church of the Protaton shares this dedication with the monastery of Iviron, and since it is a public holiday in Greece, many pilgrims converge on the Holy Mountain to celebrate the *panegyri* there.

THE EXCLUSION OF WOMEN ON ATHOS

In those days, we are told, Athos was visited by the Virgin. It became her personal domain and the whole Mountain is dedicated to her glorification. It is linked directly with the events and characters of the New Testament. It is holy ground. But why then is it closed to all other women? Can it really be that the Pantanassa is so possessive a queen that she denies access to her garden to all others of her sex? Many monks offer some such explanation.[7] Indeed the icon of Our Lady Antiphonitria (which means 'she who answers back') at Vatopedi is so called because when the empress Galla Placidia, daughter of Theodosius the Great, is said to have visited the monastery her family was building and prepared to enter the church, she heard a voice from the icon saying: 'Stop! Come no closer; for another queen than you reigns here.'

But the exclusion of women on Athos is in fact based on the time-honoured principle of *abaton* (literally a 'no-go' area) which is common to all monasteries, whether for men or for women, and which enables them, in so far as they wish to enforce it, to close their doors to members of the opposite sex. The *abaton* is by no means peculiar to Athos. Women were at first excluded from Patmos by imperial chrysobull (a document bearing the emperor's gold seal) when the monastery there was being built, but the ban had to be rescinded when it proved impossible to recruit celibate construction workers. Meteora banned women from entering the monastic area in the fourteenth century and other holy mountains facilitated the exclusion of women from men's monasteries by allowing them to establish a house of their own. In the case of Athos the principle is extended to cover the whole Mountain, as if it were one huge monastery. Furthermore, it is an unwritten law. Legislation exists to prohibit eunuchs and beardless youths and even female animals, but there is no ancient monastic rule or Byzantine law that specifically excludes women from Athos. Such an exclusion order is implied in certain legal documents, such as the *typikon* (charter) for the Great Lavra of about 970 which states: 'You will not own any animal of the female sex, for the purpose of doing any work which you require, because you have absolutely renounced all female beings.'[8] The *typikon* for Athos of

6 Mount Athos, its monasteries, their founders and saints, surveyed by the Mother of God and groups of archangels and apostles: a Romanian icon dated 1859 from the skete of Prodromos (St John the Baptist).

1045[9] begins with the exclusion of eunuchs and beardless youths, presumably because this rule had been flouted; and in another *typikon* of 1406 the reason for it is given: 'a woman wearing masculine dress and pretending to be a eunuch or beardless youth might dare to enter the monastery'.[10] The document of 1045 also remarks on the presence on the Mountain of domestic animals—sheep, goats, even cows—despite earlier legislation banning them. The reason for this too is given in the later source: so that the monks may be pure in all respects and 'may not defile their eyes with the sight of anything female'.[11] Here again the exclusion of women is implied, but it is never specifically stated. Presumably it was considered unnecessary to do so. The principle of *abaton* was so well established, so widely understood and so deeply respected that there was no need to spell it out. No one ever questioned it; and so it has (almost) always been.[12]

TALES OF EARLY FOUNDATIONS

There is no documentary evidence for any monastery prior to the foundation of the first monastery, the Great Lavra, in AD 963, but, as usual on Athos, legends abound. We have already noted the tradition of Constantine the Great's activities at Iviron and Vatopedi and at the Protaton and the story of Galla Placidia's visit to Vatopedi in the early fifth century. What are we to make of these tales? Let us look at the traditions at Vatopedi.

According to the monks, the monastery was first built by the emperor Constantine the Great (324–37), was subsequently destroyed by Julian the Apostate (360–3), and refounded by Theodosius the Great (379–95) as a thank-offering for the miraculous rescue of his infant son Arcadius. The story is told that Arcadius was shipwrecked off Athos, saved from drowning by the Mother of God and found by the sailors in a bramble bush on the shore. In gratitude for his son's delivery the emperor founded the monastery on the spot where the child was found. The story also accounts for the monastery's name, *vatos* meaning a bramble bush and *paidi* a child. To this day the monks prefer the spelling Vatopaidi out of respect for the tradition (as opposed to Vatopedi, from *pedion* which means a plain) and they revere a holy well near the *arsanas* (landing stage) where they say the miracle occurred. The water for this well is said to spring from another well which is now in the sanctuary of the katholikon.

The same tradition goes on to relate that this monastery was in turn destroyed by Syrian pirates in the early tenth century. In the course of the raid the sacristan (*vimataris*), whose name was Savvas, concealed the so-called cross of Constantine together with an icon of the Virgin and a candle beside it inside a well. Savvas himself was taken prisoner and carried off to Crete. After the liberation of Crete in 961 he regained his freedom and, now an old man, returned to the monastery after an absence of seventy years. Remembering the well, he instructed the younger monks to open it, and inside they found the cross with the icon standing upright on the water and the candle still burning beside it. The well is the one now under the sanctuary of the katholikon. The cross to this day stands on the high altar. And the icon, the miraculous Virgin of the Sacristan (Vimatarissa), with its inextinguishable light beside it, keeps a constant watch over the holiest part of the monastery. Because these events took place at the time of the historical foundation of the monastery (or refoundation, as the monks would have it) around the year 972, the icon is also known as the Ktitorissa (from *ktitor* meaning founder). The events are commemorated every Tuesday, when the Divine Liturgy is celebrated in the katholikon (weekday liturgies are normally celebrated in one of the many smaller chapels scattered around the monastery).

What are we to make of stories like these? Similar tales are told by the monks at many of the monasteries: that Karakalou was founded by the pagan emperor Caracalla in the third century; Xeropotamou by the empress Pulcheria and Esphigmenou by the emperor Theodosius II in the fifth century; Xenophontos by a sixth-century St Xenophon, and so on. Furthermore, as if to add credence to the myth, a portrait of the 'founder', labelled *ktitor* for the avoidance of doubt, is generally included among the saints represented on the walls of the monastery concerned. Earlier writers like F.W. Hasluck have generally written off such stories as 'pious patriotism':

> Athos, where miracles and wonders were (and doubtless are) seen almost daily by fasting anchorites, is not a place where we should expect a critical spirit, and, now that the beginnings of monastic life on the Mountain have been investigated, there is less reason than ever to give credence to legends of foundations earlier than the tenth century…These and other such legends obviously spring partly from pious credulity, partly from a desire to give one monastery or another exalted status.[13]

Hasluck's judgement is perhaps a little harsh. In most instances he may be right, but tradition does not usually manufacture itself out of thin air. It is often created in order to provide an explanation for something that happened that could not otherwise be explained. In the case of Vatopedi, it is quite likely that the monastery stands on the site of one of the ancient cities of Athos. Some fragments of ancient sculpture are built into the exterior walls of the katholikon and others are preserved in various parts of the monastery. Recent investigations of the shape and layout of the courtyard have led architectural historians to draw some highly tentative but potentially very interesting conclusions:

> The general layout of this enclosure [the lower part of the courtyard of Vatopedi] clearly echoes that of late Roman and early Byzantine fortifications, as we learn from the numerous *Kastra* and *Kastella* of the Roman Frontiers. It is fascinating to speculate on the existence, beneath the present-day monastery, of such an earlier foundation; this would support the monastic tradition which attributes the origins of Vatopedi to Theodosius the Great.[14]

Perhaps it is wise to conclude with the monks themselves: 'Tradition and history are interlaced, giving us the beauty of today's reality, which has been handed down by the elders to the younger members continuously for more than a thousand years.'[15]

THE NATURAL HISTORY OF THE GARDEN

Because of its history and the unusual circumstances of its dedication to the Mother of God for more than a thousand years, Athos embodies a unique cultural landscape. This landscape cannot be described as entirely natural, since even monks make some impact on their environment, but it is probably closer to being a natural landscape than any other area of comparable size in the eastern Mediterranean. As such, it is of inestimable value to the ecologist, before the results of any human activity are taken into account. A number of factors have combined to create it.[16]

The Mountain enjoys wide variety in both its relief and its geology. From sea level south of the isthmus Megali Vigla rises sharply to a peak of 510 metres within 1.5 kilometres of the frontier, creating a natural barrier against the outside world. This is followed by undulating hills that run down the spine of the peninsula, gradually increasing in altitude until they become a mountain range with heights of between 450 and 900 metres. At the southern tip the range shoots up to a rocky eminence of 2033 metres before plunging headlong into the sea. The relief is so dramatic that it is perhaps a matter for some surprise that only 20 per cent of the area of the peninsula is above 500 metres.

Geologically Athos, unlike its peninsular neighbours, is a continuation of the Rhodope Mountains of western Bulgaria and contains both igneous and metamorphic rocks. Much of the peninsula consists of granite, and there are also bands of schist and gneiss in the central area, but the peak itself is made of pale marble, stands of which are strikingly visible from the sea. These are all highly durable rocks which are resistant to erosion and weathering and provide an environment hospitable to dense vegetation. Despite the durability of the rocks, however, the land has risen rapidly (by some 14 metres in the last 2500 years). This means that caves that were once hollowed out by marine action now stand well clear of the water line and are available for human occupation. It also means that the whole peninsula is an area of maximum earthquake intensity.[17]

Athos also develops its own micro-climates which give considerable variation according to the altitude. In the lower regions the climate is mild and typically Mediterranean. As the height increases, so does the rainfall and even the snow, which on the peak lies for some months into the summer. The whole peninsula is subject to strong winds from the north or north-east which frequently result in stormy seas, and the climate on the higher slopes is distinctly harsh.

This combination of relief, geology and climate, together with the general inaccessibility of the region and the absence of destructive flocks of sheep and goats, is conducive to the development of forest and woodland

7 The east coast of Athos from Stavronikita. The last rays of the setting sun illuminate the peak, which for once is free of its customary cap of cloud.

and enables the Mountain to enjoy a dense and varied vegetation cover. As a result, the forest cover, which includes maquis, extends to more than 90 per cent of the peninsula, and the landscape is astonishingly varied. Bare hillsides, however, which characterize so much of the Greek landscape elsewhere, are not a feature of the Holy Mountain.

As the land rises, so the vegetation changes and passes through a number of zones. Above the coastal strip, there is first a zone of broadleaved maquis consisting mainly of evergreen shrubs and small trees. These include the strawberry tree or *Arbutus*, which in autumn is hung with great clusters of cream-coloured flowers; the laurel or bay, which flourishes particularly beside streams, where also oriental plane, alder, and white willow are found; the kermes oak (*Quercus coccifera*) and holm oak or *Quercus ilex*, and the wild olive. The cultivated olive and vine are common in the immediate vicinity of monasteries; elsewhere their appearance on crumbling terraces often indicates an abandoned grove or orchard, dating from a time when there were more mouths to feed, now gently reverting to the wild. Other flowering trees at this level include the Judas tree with its unmistakable splash of purple in early spring and the flowering ash, which produces sprays of creamy-white flowers in May.

The Aleppo pine (*Pinus halepensis*) accounts for more than a quarter of

8 Mixed woodland on the slopes of the mountain itself near the skete of Lakkou.

the total forest cover. It is especially widespread in the north of the penin-sula, perhaps because that area has suffered more from forest fires, and there it more or less takes the place of the broadleaved maquis found further south. Above the broadleaved maquis is a zone of deciduous broadleaved for-est in which the sweet chestnut is dominant. Mixed forests, with deciduous oaks and other species and an endemic fir, perhaps of hybrid origin, are less common than they used to be as a result of long-term coppicing, but in some parts these species survive, as does beech on some north–west-facing slopes. Other trees found at this level include the lime, aspen, hop hornbeam and sev-eral acers. Higher up, there are stands of black pine and juniper.

The export of timber has long provided the monks with a source of income; but while disciplined forestry is entirely beneficial for the environ-ment, overexploitation of the reserves is not. 'Do not pick the flowers', warns a notice to pilgrims; 'this is the Virgin's garden.' But the trees are just as much a part of the garden as the flowers. Bishop Kallistos is fond of quot-ing the words of the late Fr Amphilochios of Patmos (*d*.1970): 'whoever does not love the trees, does not love Christ.'

Finally, above 1500 metres, is the alpine zone of the peak itself. Here, above the tree line, there are a number of endemic species. According to K. Ganiatsas, who has studied the vegetation and flora of the Mountain,[18] there

9 Left: Vegetable gardens and cypress trees near the monastery of Zographou in the northern part of the peninsula where gradients are less steep.

10 Above: Bees and olive trees make important contributions to the monks' economy.

11 The west coast from near Simonopetra. In April the Mountain blossoms but the higher slopes are still streaked with snow.

are 35 plants that are endemic to Athos, most of them found on the peak. This compares with only 82 for the whole of the north Aegean (which of course includes Athos) and 206 for Crete. The botanical names for the varieties peculiar to Athos are often quite charming: *Crocus athous* and *Viola athois* are named after the Mountain itself; others recall the names of monasteries or sketes such as *Campanula lavrensis* and a pink called *Centaurea sanctae-annae*; *Astragalus monachorum* is called after the monks; and *Campanula rotundifolia* subsp. *sancta*, a harebell, and *Armeria sancta*, a thrift, are reminders of the sanctity of the garden.

Wildflowers are one of the most arresting and memorable features of the Athonite landscape at every level and in every season. Botanists tell us that the flora is not as rich as in other parts of Greece, and in terms of the sheer number of species this is no doubt true, though elsewhere the depredations of flocks and herbicides, not to mention human intervention, often create a contrary impression. On Athos, especially in springtime, the profusion and richness of the flowers can only support the belief that horticulture there is in good hands. Bulbs, corms and tubers are among the most attractive plants, notably crocus, anemone, cyclamen and fritillary, and as many as thirty different orchids have been identified. Monks also seem to cultivate flowers and flowering shrubs with a greater enthusiasm than most people in Greece, either because they are more in tune with nature or because they simply have more leisure.

One might expect that so secluded an environment would provide the ideal habitat for a wide variety of wild animals, but it seems that the fauna of the Mountain is less interesting than the flora. It is unclear whether there are still wolves. Certainly there were until recently; then came reports that they were extinct, perhaps exterminated, then that they had been reintroduced. The same goes for red deer. Hunting is officially prohibited on Athos, but that does not mean that it does not take place and both species would represent an attractive bag. Other mammals roaming the Mountain include jackal, wild boar, roe deer, fox, hare, red squirrel, badger, hedgehog and wild cat. Lizards are ubiquitous; snakes are said to abound, but are less often seen; most commonly heard is the edible frog which frequents the environs of many a monastery. The monk seal, however, is an endangered species and is rarely seen. The bird population includes eagles, hoopoes and some hawks, but around monasteries these are uncommon. Swifts, swallows and martins arrive with the spring, when the monastic vicinity is also well nightingaled. The butterflies are out of this world.

ANOTHER WORLD

Despite a climate that is at times harsh, vegetation that is often impenetrable and rock formations that challenge the most experienced of climbers, Athos presents a landscape that is unmatched in Europe and, to most observers, incomparably beautiful. Perhaps the two most striking attributes are its seclusion and its variety. This variety is well described by Professor Dimitrios Kotoulas of the University of Thessaloniki in an evocative description of the Holy Mountain's natural environment:

> The steep slopes, the deep gorges, the tall cliffs and the outcrops of rock, the shades of green of the vegetation, changing in autumn to variations of yellow and russet, the bare boughs of the trees in winter, the deep or light azure of the sea— these all ease the eye; the roaring of the gales, the lapping of the waves, and the cries of birds delight the ear, and the sweetness of the natural aromas and the fresh air make glad the visitor's sense of smell. All together, these features make up the incomparable natural harmony of Mt Athos, to which the lissom cypresses around the monasteries and along the stream beds add a note of austere gravity, sanctity and peaceful melancholy. The grandeur of the physical environment is the natural background in which the monks of Mt Athos, guardians of the ancient institutions of Orthodoxy and the Greek race, root their mystic life and spiritual presence.[19]

As for the seclusion, the quality of the silence that is to be found on Athos, there is no more moving account than that of Gerald Palmer, an Englishman who visited the Mountain nearly every year from 1948 until his death in 1984:

This stillness, this silence, is everywhere, pervades all, is the very essence of the Holy Mountain. The distant sound of a motorboat serves only to punctuate the intensity of the quiet; the lizard's sudden rustling among the dry leaves, a frog plopping into a fountain, are loud and startling sounds, but merely emphasize the immense stillness. Often as one walks over the great stretches of wild country which form much of this sacred ground, following paths where every stone breathes prayers, it is impossible to hear a sound of any kind. Even in the monastery churches, where the silence is, as it were, made more profound by the darkness, by the beauty and by the sacred quality of the place, it seems that the reading and chanting of priests and monks in the endless rhythm of their daily and nightly ritual is no more than a thin fringe of a limitless ocean of silence.

But this stillness, this silence, is far more than a mere absence of sound. It has a positive quality, a quality of fullness, of plenitude, of the eternal Peace which is there reflected in the Veil of the Mother of God, enshrouding and protecting her Holy Mountain, offering inner silence, peace of heart, to those who dwell there and to those who come with openness of heart to seek this blessing.[20]

The creative response that the Mountain inspires in its visitors and residents has taken many forms. Poetry, painting, music of one form or another can all be cited. But probably the commonest response, and certainly the one that unites all its inhabitants, is prayer. The monks do not regard themselves as living in the same world as the rest of mankind. They often refer to themselves as the living dead. In order to be a monk on Mount Athos, it is said, a man has to die and be born again. He must cast himself off from this world, and through a process of purification he must achieve union with the divine and must himself become God-like, a process known as *theosis* (deification). Each day the monk undergoes a new martyrdom; each day he grows closer to Christ; Christ is his bridegroom, his cell his bridal chamber. Thus it is that the Garden of the Mother of God is also known as the gate of heaven. It is a foretaste of Paradise, truly another world. It is time to examine how and when the first monks arrived there.

3
BYZANTINE ATHOS

Nearly everything about Athos, even today, is Byzantine, but of course there have been changes. There is nothing Byzantine about the computers that many monks now operate, or about the Unimog four-by-four vehicles they drive, or the hot water, central heating and telephone systems that most monasteries have recently installed. But these are merely ephemeral conveniences that enable monks to manage their lives and communicate with each other and with the world in a suitably pragmatic fashion. The fundamentals of Athonite life, the things that matter most—the monastic way of life, the forces that drive monks to Athos, the inspired teaching of charismatic elders, the austere humility of the hermit in the desert, the commanding presence of the abbot in his ruling monastery—these things have not changed at all. These are the things that make Athos important and unique; they are the reasons why it is there and why it has survived. And everyone knows that if they were to change, Athos would cease to survive; there would be no reason for its existence and it would die. There have been moments when Athos seemed moribund and prophets of doom have sounded the death knell. But Athos has an inner resilience that is at times latent; it has reserves of strength that are not always apparent to the casual observer, and, most importantly to the monks, it lies under the ever-loving protection of the Mother of God. So the prophets have been confounded; monastery gardens have blossomed again, and Athos is as much alive today as it was when God's chosen representative reigned in Constantinople—a paradigm of Byzantine monasticism but not a museum. Far from being stuck in a fourteenth-century time-warp, Athos looks forward to the third millennium and the opportunities it will provide to perpetuate eternal principles that were initially put into practice in the first.

In this chapter we shall trace the evolution of Athos from its first beginnings as a monastic centre until the end of the Latin empire in 1261. To avoid the tedium of a chronicle, I shall try to concentrate on the activities of a number of individuals or groups of individuals who have illuminated and characterized the passage of time.

THE FIRST HERMITS

Icons and Orthodoxy are inseparable, but it was not ever thus. There was a movement, known as iconoclasm, that sought to deny the sacred value of icons and to forbid their veneration.[1] This movement had much earlier origins but it gained ground rapidly in the early eighth century, when the empire had suffered a number of humiliating reverses, and it became official imperial policy when in 730 the emperor Leo III ordered the destruction of all icons of the saints and in 754 Constantine V decreed that the veneration of icons and relics was idolatrous. The policy was enforced until the 780s, most rigorously in the capital, and was revived, with somewhat less enthusiasm, in the early ninth century; those who resisted it were persecuted. Monks were (and still are) among the most enthusiastic iconophiles, and many fled to escape the persecution. It is in this context that some historians have suggested that the first monks came to Athos, by then an uninhabited peninsula sufficiently far from Constantinople to be undisturbed by iconoclastic emperors. It is an attractive notion, but sadly there is no evidence for it, and it has been demonstrated that most monastic centres have their origins in the immediate vicinity where their founders lived.[2] We can say no more than that it is possible that among the first monks to settle on the Holy Mountain there may have been some refugees from iconoclasm.

Iconoclasm came to an end in the year 843, when the empress Theodora and Patriarch Methodios I led a procession through the streets of Constantinople to the great church of Hagia Sophia (formerly an iconoclast stronghold) and celebrated a liturgy to mark what has since been known as the Triumph of Orthodoxy. Eager participants in the procession were monks from a number of holy mountains, among them Athos, according to the chronicler Genesios. Genesios is an unreliable source writing a century after the event, but there is no reason to doubt him here and we can assume that by 843 there were monks on Athos in sufficient numbers for a contingent of them to be worth remarking upon in the celebrations to mark the end of iconoclasm.[3] The Triumph of Orthodoxy is commemorated annually by the Orthodox on the first Sunday in Lent, nowhere with greater enthusiasm than on Athos.

Some ninth-century Athonites are known to us by name, and we even know something about their lives from surviving hagiographical accounts.[4] There was, for example, one Euthymios, St Euthymios the Younger as he is now known, who had lived for many years on another holy mountain, Mount Olympus in Bithynia, before moving to Athos in about 859 'because he had heard of its tranquillity'.[5] For three years he lived alone in a cave. When he emerged, he found a number of other monks had taken up residence around him and were waiting for him to become their spiritual father. This he did, and in so doing founded the first known *lavra* or informal group of hermits on Athos. Among his disciples a few years later we hear of one John Kolobos, who was said to be 'already advanced in spirituality'. John went on to found the first known example of a monastery on Athos, in the northern part of the peninsula near Ierissos; he received a chrysobull from Emperor Basil I (before 881) giving him and his monastery jurisdiction over the Mountain and its hermits. After John's death the monks of his monastery attempted to take over the territory of the hermits, who promptly appealed to Constantinople. The hermits sent as their negotiator Fr Andreas, who held the office of 'first hesychast' (*protos hesychastes*), subsequently shortened to Protos (as the primate of Athos is still known). As a result of Andreas's appeal the emperor issued another chrysobull guaranteeing the independence of the monks. There were by now several monastic houses and, although the difficulties with the monks of the monastery of Kolobos were overcome, the need was felt for a central meeting-point or council of elders; this was established at Karyes, where it still meets today. Three times a year, at Christmas, Easter and the Dormition, they had assemblies (*synaxeis*) of representatives of all the communities, including the smallest, and matters of common concern were discussed.

Perhaps the best-known figure of ninth-century Athos is Peter, or St Peter the Athonite as he is always called. As a young man Peter vowed to become a monk but instead went as a soldier to Syria where he was captured by the Arabs, a misfortune he ascribed to his broken vow. On his release he travelled to Rome and was tonsured by the pope. He began the journey back to the eastern Mediterranean but his ship was miraculously diverted to Athos, where he saw a vision of the Mother of God. Despite favourable winds, the ship would sail no further, and Peter realized that this was a sign for him to be put ashore. Scrambling up the hillside, he found a dark cave, 'surrounded by thick vegetation, and in which there were more crawling animals than the sky has stars or the sea sand, and with them a host of demons nesting, who raised up a swarm of trials against the holy man such as no tongue could recount or ear could credit'.[6] Peter made this cave his home for the next fifty years, living, according to a contemporary source, 'like Elias on Mount Carmel'. When he died, around 890, his relics were deposited in the monastery of Clement, where Iviron stands today.

THE FIRST MONASTERIES

Thus by the end of the ninth century the eremitical tradition was well established on Athos and it was as a hermit (*eremites* in Greek) that St Athanasios first moved to Athos around the year 958. He went on to found the first of the monasteries that still survive today, the Great Lavra. We shall return to this momentous event in the history of the Mountain shortly, but for reasons that will emerge we should first consider the earliest imperial document concerned with the organization of the Mountain as a whole, the so-called *Tragos* signed by the emperor John Tzimiskes around the year

972.[7] This is one of the earliest documents to survive on Athos and one of the greatest treasures in the collection of the Protaton in Karyes. It is called *Tragos* ('goat') because it is written on a goatskin parchment. Its provisions are conveniently summarized by E. Amand de Mendieta:[8]

> The three customary gatherings of the whole Athonite community, formerly held at Karyes at Christmas, Easter, and the Assumption, are reduced to only one, on the Assumption. In future these gatherings are only to be attended by the Protos, with three followers, by Athanasios, with two, by Paul of Xeropotamou, with one, and by the other hegoumenoi [abbots], unaccompanied. This is done to avoid the disorders and disputes which have occurred very frequently at these gatherings.
>
> The Protos cannot legally do anything without the agreement of the assembly of the hegoumenoi, nor can the assembly do anything without his agreement, even if it is a matter for the common good.
>
> A novice must undergo a period of one year's probation before he can take his vows as a monk. All novices must be put in the charge of a spiritual father or the head of their monastery, and must obey him. The novice may not apply to join another monastery without his permission.
>
> Monks who have made their vows in other places and have come to the Mountain are not allowed to buy land or to settle on unoccupied land, unless they get the permission of the Protos and the assembly.
>
> Every hegoumenos may sell, give, or transfer his property, his house, and his cultivated land to his own disciples, or to some other person who has no property, but any gift of a house or land to any monastery is forbidden. Wills relating to such transfers of property are valid and effect is given to them. Any resale for the sake of profit is disgraceful and is forbidden.
>
> Only those monks who have received a training in discipline, under the supervision of a spiritual father, and have proved themselves suitable, may (under supervision) retire to hermitages as solitary ascetics or hesychasts.
>
> A monk may not return to the world after he has taken his vows.
>
> Monks may not go for visits to towns or to country places, act as sponsors, or join in associations with lay persons.
>
> Wine, made in excess of the maker's requirements, and pinewood may not be sold outside the Mountain. Such goods may be sold to monks who need them. If in need and stricken with poverty, monks may however sell them to laymen living on the Mountain.
>
> During Great Lent all manual work is forbidden except on Saturdays. All visiting and conversation is forbidden during this season which must be devoted to prayer and contemplation.
>
> Priests from outside cannot be admitted unless they bring letters of introduction.
>
> It is forbidden to bring in pack animals belonging to the monastery of Kolovou, near Ierissos, unless it is threatened with an attack by barbarians. Any question as to the admission of animals which normally enter Athos is to be decided by the elders.
>
> Eunuchs and beardless youths (even the children of masons and labourers) are forbidden to enter Athos.

The hegoumenoi are forbidden to force kelliots or hermits, living in cells or kellia, to undertake any work.

No pair of oxen may be kept on the Mountain, except for one pair allowed at Lavra. This monastery is very big and clearly needs beasts.

The existing rules regarding the election of the Protos are to be strictly enforced.

The administrator of Mese [the old name for Karyes] must render an account of his receipts and expenditure to the assembly each August. He is eligible for re-election by the Protos and hegoumenoi.

The adminstrator must prevent all scandalous talk and quarrelling in Mese. If any scandal is reported to him from some other part of the Mountain, he is to go there, accompanied by three or four hegoumenoi living in the district in which the trouble has occurred, and to take such action as is required.

This document is signed not only by the emperor and by Athanasios, hegoumenos (abbot) of the Great Lavra, but by no fewer than 46 other hegoumenoi as well. It shows how many houses were already in existence at this very early date and makes us wonder therefore to what extent the Lavra, founded in 963, was such an innovation.

FOUNDATION OF THE GREAT LAVRA (963)

Let us now retrace our steps to the arrival of St Athanasios on Mount Athos as a hermit in 958.[9] What sort of a Mountain did he find then? And what changes did he make to it?

Athanasios was born into a prosperous family in Trebizond some time between 925 and 930 and baptized with the name Avraamios. Orphaned young, he was sent to Constantinople to be educated. Here he came into contact with Michael Maleinos, hegoumenos of the lavra of Mount Kyminas in Bithynia, and with his nephews Leo and Nikephoros Phokas (the future emperor). He worked as a teacher in Constantinople for a while, and then went to Kyminas with Michael where he became a monk with the name Athanasios. Kyminas was one of several 'holy mountains' in western Asia Minor which may have been formed as a result of monks fleeing to the west in the face of the Muslim conquests of the seventh century, though the connection has yet to be proved.[10] It was also among the communities that sent monks to Constantinople to celebrate the Triumph of Orthodoxy in 843. Pending archaeological investigation, we have little idea what form these lavras took, but it is likely that they were scattered settlements of semi-solitary monks rather than full coenobia, and they may have operated and looked a bit like the idiorrhythmic sketes on Mount Athos today. After four years working as a humble and obedient copyist, Athanasios was given

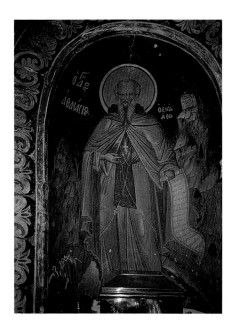

12 St Athanasios of Athos, founder of the Great Lavra, depicted in a fresco at the cell of Mylopotamos. Hymns sung on his feast day (5 July) liken him to the dawn and the morning star.

permission to become a hermit. At about the same time Nikephoros Phokas, who was then serving as a general on the eastern frontier, visited Kyminas to see his uncle and renewed his friendship with Athanasios. Shortly after this Michael announced his intention to retire and name Athanasios his successor; alarmed at the prospect and desirous of greater solitude, Athanasios fled to Athos.

For a while he retained his anonymity, living in seclusion at Zygos in the north of the peninsula, but Nikephoros got the authorities to trace him and provide him with a cell near Karyes. Here he was visited by Leo, who gave him money to extend the church at Karyes. Then he moved to the remote southern tip of the peninsula, occupying a cell at Melana. Still there was no peace. Nikephoros sought him out again: he was about to sail for Crete with a view to liberating that island from occupation by Arab pirates and he wanted Athanasios's company as his spiritual father. Athansios agreed to go. After the recovery of Crete, in March 961, the two men discussed plans to found a monastery on the strength of their Cretan spoils and Nikephoros promised to become a monk.

In 961 Athanasios returned to Athos and started to build. But what he built was not a lavra of the sort that he had lived in himself at Kyminas, a collection of cells grouped round a central church like a modern Athonite skete, but a fully fledged cenobitic monastery such as existed in Constantinople in the Stoudios monastery of St John the Baptist. No such monastery had previously existed on Athos. The other 46 signatories of the

Tragos can be assumed to have been hegoumenoi of lavras—no doubt perfectly well-run holy houses in their way, but they lacked the architectural grandeur of the Great Lavra, and they lacked its staying power too.

The katholikon was completed in 963 and the foundation of the monastery has always been associated with that date. In the same year Nikephoros, who had contributed so much thought and money to this new venture, was crowned emperor. Athanasios was distraught and went to Constantinople to protest at his friend's broken promise. Nikephoros begged his spiritual father to forgive him, undertaking to abdicate as soon as possible and become a monk, and he continued to give the monastery his full support. He presented it with a number of relics, including a fragment of the True Cross; he appointed Athanasios hegoumenos and gave the brotherhood the right to elect his successor; he fixed the number of monks at eighty and he granted the monastery an annuity of 244 gold *nomismata*.

The success of this new-style monastery, with its grand buildings, its imperial connections, its special privileges, its artificially created spiritual associations, and its fabulous wealth, was offensive to the older inhabitants of the Mountain, who practised a simpler life-style in their lavras and hermitages elsewhere on the peninsula. No doubt they were jealous of it too. They protested to Athanasios that he had brought 'the world' to Athos and they feared for their independence in the face of this huge monastery with its numerous brotherhood and its imperial backing. In December 969 the emperor Nikephoros was murdered by his nephew John Tzimiskes. The lavriots and hermits of the old Athos seized their opportunity and sent a delegation to Constantinople to plead their case with the new emperor. They were well received, but to get the full picture, the emperor summoned Athanasios too. With the help of his friend John of Georgia (later one of the founders of Iviron), Athanasios won over the emperor and gained yet more support for his monastery with a doubling of the annuity, the allotment to Lavra of a monastery in Thessaloniki, and an increase in the size of the brotherhood from eighty to 120.

Despite this further success Athanasios was persuaded that something must be done to address the hermits' grievances and to put an end to the frequent disturbances and arguments that broke out at meetings of the whole community at Karyes. With this in view the emperor instructed Euthymios, a senior monk of the Stoudios monastery in Constantinople, to visit the Mountain and settle the differences between the various parties. On arriving in Karyes, Euthymios summoned the hegoumenoi of all the lavras to a meeting in the church of the Protaton and together they drafted the first *typikon* or charter for the whole Mountain. Once it had been agreed,

13 Overleaf: Walls and towers of the Great Lavra, the largest and oldest of the surviving monasteries.

14 The katholikon of the Lavra, seen here from the east. Built by the founder in the tenth century, it was the model for all subsequent churches on Athos.

Athanasios got the emperor to sign it as well so that it acquired the force of law and became the basis for the settlement of disputes between the various communities and the hermits. The charter also confirmed the fact that the cenobitic system, as employed at the Stoudios monastery according to the rule of St Basil, was now established on Athos. That document, duly signed by the emperor John Tzimiskes and all the hegoumenoi of the time and still preserved in Karyes, is the *Tragos*, the provisions of which have been described above.

The Mountain a City

Athanasios was equally renowned for his piety, for his learning, and for his qualities as a ruler. He was abbot of the monastery from its foundation in 963 until his death nearly forty years later. During that time not only the Lavra but the whole of Athos flourished, attracting monks from all over eastern Europe and even from Armenia and Italy. By the time of Athanasios's death there were more than three thousand monks on the Mountain. Through Athanasios, as his biographer wrote, 'the whole moun-

15 Vatopedi from the north-east. The houses along the seafront are for fishermen and other workers. The grain store, beyond the quay, is kept well stocked.

tain became a city',[11] a conscious echo of the Life of St Antony of Egypt which stated that through him 'the desert became a city'.

Though himself a product of the lavra at Kyminas, Athanasios was entirely converted to the principles of cenobitic monasticism as propounded by St Basil and practised at the Stoudios monastery in Constantinople. This he believed was the best system for the vast majority of monks and he enshrined it in a charter or *typikon* he drafted for the Lavra in about 970,[12] shortly before the ratification of the *Tragos*. Taking as his model the monastic programme established by St Theodore the Stoudite (759–826), Athanasios laid stress on the links between the monastic life and martyrdom. He expected monks to struggle, 'like athletes and martyrs'. He also expected them to devote their lives to prayer and had chosen a remote site for his monastery specifically so that they should be 'undistracted and free from external activities'. Everything was to be shared under a rule of obedience to the abbot. 'Let the only things that you call your own be your body and soul, and let even these be shared in an equality of love among all your spiritual children and brethren.' Poverty was the rule, not only for individuals, but also for the house as a whole: the monastery was to own no slaves. 'Nor will you own any animals of the female sex, for the purpose of doing any work which you require, because you have absolutely renounced all

16 The interior of the katholikon at Vatopedi, a close approximation to heaven on earth. The marble floor dates from the time of the foundation in the late tenth century; the mosaics of the Annunciation, high up on the columns that support the dome, from the mid-eleventh.

female beings.' The abbot was elected for life and exercised supreme author-ity within the monastery. Yet he too was to a lead a simple life, not travelling abroad and neglecting his flock but wherever possible sharing in the life of the monks. And according to his biographer, Athanasios practised what he preached: he was both 'leader and yet servant of all . . . both humble and exalted', a 'most shepherdly' pastor to his flock.[13]

17 Vatopedi has a fine collection of icons. One of the earliest is this eleventh-century image of St George carved in green steatite.

18 Vatopedi's library is one of the richest on Athos. This illumination of St Mark is from a gospel book dated 948 which is older than the monastery itself.

In one respect, however, Athanasios departed from his Stoudite model. While proclaiming the cenobitic system as ideal for most monks, he also accepted the idea that a small minority should be allowed to live as solitaries. Their number was limited to five. They should live outside the walls of the monastery, but not too far away. Each should be allowed to have one disciple with him and the monastery should take care of their material needs, 'so that they may be free from all care concerning bodily matters and entirely undisturbed'.[14] Thus Athanasios made provision for the eremitic system to coexist with the cenobitic, as it has continued to do on Athos ever since.

The katholikon built by Athanasios remains the principal church of the monastery, though it has seen many changes and accretions. Probably in the year 1002 the finishing touches were being put to the dome and the abbot was anxious to see how the work was progressing. On 5 July, as he inspected the church, the dome collapsed without warning, killing Athanasios and four others. The saint's tomb is within the church, in the chapel of the Forty Martyrs, and is said to have the power to drive away evil-doers. His name is commemorated on 5 July in all Orthodox churches.

Athanasios's achievement was monumental and enduring. He had built a great monastery, a fully fledged coenobium on the Stoudite model, that was to be a 'city' in its own right, a fully independent and self-governing community. Since its foundation in 963 the Great Lavra has held first place in the hierarchy of Athonite monasteries; the model was copied many times—within Athanasios's lifetime some half-dozen other monasteries were founded on the Mountain—but the supremacy of the Lavra has never been challenged. At the same time Athanasios had contrived a reconciliation with the older inhabitants of the Mountain. He accepted that there was a place for the eremitic life alongside the cenobitic and that the cenobitic houses should take responsibility for the material needs of their eremitic dependants. Athanasios's *typikon* remains the model for Athonite monasticism to this day. No significant changes have been made to its principles and more than a thousand years after they were first laid down they are still in force today.

VATOPEDI AND IVIRON

Of the monasteries that were founded during Athanasios's lifetime, not all of which survive, particular mention must be made of two that do. Second in the hierarchy, though the third to be founded,[15] is the monastery of Vatopedi. According to tradition there were three founders, noblemen from Adrianople named Athanasios, Nicholas and Anthony, who visited Mount Athos while the Great Lavra was being built. With the support of Athanasios of Lavra the tradition is that they founded, or rather refounded,

19 Iviron, a tenth-century Georgian foundation, seen from the east. This has been a predominantly Greek house since the mid-fourteenth century.

the monastery of Vatopedi further north on the east coast of the peninsula. There is also a tradition that they are buried beneath the sarcophagus that stands at the south end of the *mesonyktikon* (the part of the katholikon between the nave and the narthex). This tradition has now been confirmed by archaeology: three burials were indeed placed in an underground tomb which is contemporary with the church itself, and the relics of three men were subsequently placed in the sarcophagus above it. Their names are commemorated daily at the end of Vespers, when the priest reads a Trisagion (the Thrice-Holy Hymn of the Angels) over the tomb.

The word 'founder' (*ktitor*) is often used rather loosely by Athonites to refer to any major benefactor of a monastery whose generosity or services have been on such a scale that he deserves to be ranked among the 'founders'. This may help to reconcile the apparent discrepancy between the archaeological evidence (which supports the tradition) and the archival (which superficially does not). The monastery is first mentioned in a document of 985,[16] where the name of the abbot is indeed Nicholas. Nicholas of Adrianople, no doubt the monastery's actual founder, signs last, after all the other hegoumenoi, and presumably the monastery was then very new and very small. But it flourished, the number of monks grew quickly, and

20 Iviron also has a fine collection of manuscripts. This illustrated copy of the romance of *Barlaam and Ioasaph* carries a French translation alongside the Greek text and dates from the early thirteenth century, the time of the Latin empire.

by 1010 it was reckoned as one of the great monasteries, on a par with the Lavra and Iviron. Athanasios was abbot from 1020 to 1048, and in 1045, when the emperor Constantine IX Monomachos issued his *typikon* for the Holy Mountain,[17] he signed second, immediately after the hegoumenos of Lavra. This second 'founder', Athanasios, also from Adrianople, had clearly been responsible for the monastery's ascent to the summit of the hierarchy. As abbot of Vatopedi he was granted many privileges in this new *typikon* which he exercised in common with the abbots of Lavra and Iviron, and the monastery itself gained privileges, such as the right to have a ship and keep a yoke of oxen, which set it above the majority of Athonite houses. The contribution of Anthony, the third 'founder', is uncertain, but there is a reference in 1142 to another abbot by the name of Anthony with whom he may perhaps be identified.[18]

The association of the monastery with Adrianople at this point in its history is interesting. As the capital of the Byzantine theme (province) of Macedonia, Adrianople was a major centre of the landowning aristocracy of the empire. This aristocracy became increasingly powerful in the course of the eleventh century and in 1081 the landowning family of the Komnenoi seized the throne and founded a new dynasty. Given Vatopedi's close con-

21 A mosaic icon of
St George dating
from the second half
of the twelfth century,
one of a pair of
mosaic icons (the
other being of St
Demetrios) preserved
at the monastery of
Xenophontos.

nections with Adrianople, it was inevitable that the monastery should thrive in the wake of the local landowners. Though it had no imperial endowment at first, it quickly established itself as what Nikos Oikonomides has called 'a monastery of the high aristocracy'. To some extent, it has retained that reputation ever since. Not for nothing did Osbert Lancaster term it the Christ Church of Athos.[19]

The second surviving monastery whose tenth-century foundation deserves special mention is Iviron. It identifies itself as the monastery of the Iberians (i.e. Georgians: Iberia was the Greek name for Georgia) and its foundation is due to the presence on the Mountain of a group of Georgian monks who after 963 became disciples of St Athanasios at the Lavra. They were led by John the Iberian and his son Euthymios, who were members of the distinguished Georgian family of the Tornikioi. They were joined there by the head of the family, who had also been tonsured a monk with the name John. Georgia was an independent kingdom outside the territory of the Byzantine empire but cultural contacts between the two states were close and the Georgian Church was (and still is) in communion with Constantinople. Tornikios was well connected with the court in Constantinople, but earlier requests (in 972 to John Tzimiskes and in 976 to Basil II) for a monastery on Athos to be handed over to the Georgians had been rejected. When in 976 the general Bardas Skleros staged a rebellion in the east, the emperor Basil II summoned Tornikios to his assistance. In return for his services, which contributed to the defeat of the rebels in 979, the emperor granted Tornikios a number of rewards, including agreement to his proposal for the foundation of a Georgian monastery on Mount Athos. That the grant was a personal one, to John himself rather than to the Athonites as a whole, provoked an outburst of anti-Georgian xenophobia on the Mountain which was only quelled by generous donations to the Protaton.

The monastery of Iviron was founded in 979 or 980 on the site of the earlier monastery of Clement, on the east coast of the peninsula between Vatopedi and the Lavra. The foundation was strengthened by the gift of extensive landholdings in Chalkidiki and Thessaloniki which were granted by imperial chrysobull and which had until 979 been the property of the monastery of Kolobos at Ierissos.[20] The material prosperity of Iviron, which placed it on a level with the Great Lavra, was matched by spiritual and intellectual developments within the monastery. The founders together possessed a combination of talents that underpinned its success. John the Iberian, a true ascetic who provided his flock with spiritual leadership, was appointed abbot in 980 with the full support of St Athanasios. He was succeeded in 1005 by his son Euthymios, who had received an excellent education in Greek culture and devoted himself to the translation of Greek patristic literature into Georgian. Meanwhile Tornikios had the necessary organizational skills to ensure the physical well-being of the monastery and

superintend the restoration of its buildings. In addition to the building of the katholikon they also made provision for a library and scriptorium in which liturgical texts could be copied for use by the monks. The library of Iviron is still one of the richest on Athos and includes the largest collection of Georgian manuscripts outside Georgia and the largest of Byzantine music in the world. Already in the tenth century the monastery was acting as an international cultural entrepôt disseminating Greek culture to Georgia and Georgian to Byzantium.

THE LATIN MONASTERY OF THE AMALFITANS

Before the end of the tenth century, the international standing of the Holy Mountain was further enhanced by the foundation of a Benedictine monastery which no longer survives.[21] Amalfi, on the south-west coast of Italy, was an independent state outside the territory of the Byzantine empire (though until 839 it had belonged to the Byzantine duchy of Naples). Its ships traded throughout the Mediterranean and its traders were granted a quarter of their own in Constantinople. Monks from Amalfi were first attracted to Athos by the charismatic reputation of St Athanasios, but it was John the Iberian who helped them found a monastery of their own in about 985 on the east coast of the peninsula between the Lavra and Iviron.

This was a house of substance, with estates in Macedonia and the right to keep a large ship enabling the monks to trade with their compatriots in Constantinople. It was founded by a Benedictine monk named Leo who came from Benevento with six disciples; they were no doubt joined by others from the Amalfitan colony in Constantinople, with whom they would have maintained close contact. Nor was it the only Italian monastery recorded: a monastery 'of the Sicilians' was founded in 986 and a monastery 'of the Calabrians' in 1080, though both of these were Greek houses and both were dissolved in 1108. The Amalfitan monastery was ranked in fifth place in the hierarchy in the eleventh century. The fact that it endured for more than 300 years, surviving not only the exchange of anathemas in 1054 (traditionally held to mark the 'great schism' between the Orthodox east and Latin west) but also the Latin empire of 1204–61, is a tribute to the truly ecumenical nature of Athonite monasticism at the time. The house was eventually absorbed by the Lavra in 1287, but its tall lonely tower, which still stands on a wooded eminence above the bay of Morphonou, is a forlorn reminder of this once great Latin monastery.

22 Previous page: The tower of the Amalfitan monastery of St Mary, all that survives of this tenth-century Benedictine foundation, seen from the north in winter.

THE LAVRA OF THE PROTATON AT KARYES

It is now time to examine the pan-Athonite institutions at Karyes and how they came into being. Karyes (which means 'hazel nuts') is the administrative centre of the whole Mountain, a status that is made more explicit by its earlier, more prosaic name, Mese ('centre'). As such, it was in existence by the mid-tenth century, by which time it had become the seat of a governor (*Protos*) who administered the affairs of the monks and represented them in the outside world. Before then the administration had been based at Zygos in the north of the peninsula, where assemblies of elders representing all the communities on Athos were held every year at Christmas, Easter and the Dormition of the Virgin to discuss matters of common interest under the presidency of the Protos. The increase in numbers of monks and the foundation of new monasteries compelled the Protos to move his base to a more central location and it seems that Karyes (or Mese) was first founded then as one of the new lavras.

This lavra came to be known as the Protaton (by association with the office of the Protos) and initially it owned all the buildings that sprang up in Karyes. Its wealth was therefore considerable, and it was able to build a substantial church, still known as the church of the Protaton, which is the

23 The church of the Protaton in Karyes, seen here from the south-east. The oldest church on Athos, it dates from the first half of the tenth century.

oldest church on the Mountain (dating from the first half of the tenth century) and the only one in the style of a basilica. This church, dedicated to the Dormition of the Virgin, has seen many alterations over the centuries, but it still stands as a proud reminder of the now defunct lavra of Karyes and it remains the usual focus for any form of pan-Athonite worship. If Karyes is a capital city, then the Protaton is its cathedral, or its Parthenon as some have described it.

As the administrative centre of Athos, it is natural that Karyes should be the depository for archival material relating to the Mountain as a whole, and although the lavra of the Protaton has not survived, its archives remain. They are stored today in the magnificently refurbished interior of the Protaton Tower, where they are available for the use of scholars.

The *Typikon* of Constantine IX Monomachos

In the eleventh century the Byzantine empire reached its zenith. Victories won by the emperor Basil II over the Arabs and the Bulgarians brought a period of peace and stability. There was an intellectual and artistic flowering in the city of Constantinople and emperors felt free to indulge their taste (or cultivate their image) by making lavish endowments. Monasteries flourished as never before, especially on Athos; new foundations elsewhere included the Mangana in Constantinople itself and the Nea Mone on Chios, both resulting from the munificence of Constantine IX Monomachos, who reigned from 1042 to 1055.

The increase in the numbers of monks on Athos—by 1045 there were 700 at the Lavra alone and a similar number at Vatopedi—brought new problems and, not surprisingly, the legislation of seventy years earlier was inadequate to answer all of them. The rules were being flouted in several respects: underage boys were found to be living on the Mountain; the lavra at Karyes had turned into an open market where even eunuchs were for sale; the larger monasteries were absorbing portions of the common land for their own use and some were in dispute with their neighbours; there was widespread use of illegal boats and animals, and it was alleged that the hegoumenoi were plotting against the Protos. The monks asked the emperor to intervene to restore order. This he did by sending a representative to Karyes with the task of enforcing the existing law.

After a period of consultation with all 180 hegoumenoi[22] in Karyes, a second *typikon* was drawn up in September 1045 and ratified by imperial chryso-

24 Left: The tower of the Protaton, adjoining the headquarters of the Holy Community in Karyes, acts as a depository for an important collection of archives, manuscripts, and treasures. There is a reading room on the top floor.

bull in June 1046 by Constantine IX Monomachos.[23] Once again I quote the provisions of this document as summarized by E. Amand de Mendieta.[24]

It is absolutely forbidden to receive or to tonsure any eunuch or beardless youth; it is equally forbidden to give them shelter in any monastery or cell. All such must be sent away from the Holy Mountain.

It is equally forbidden to keep large boats. By means of these many monks are engaged in illegal trade, under a variety of pretexts . . . It is agreed that monks are allowed to own small boats (up to 10 tons burden), in which they might sail to Thessaloniki and there sell their surplus produce. Any person breaking this rule is to be punished by the confiscation of his boat. An exception is made in favour of any monastery which requires a larger boat and has imperial authority for it. For example, the Latin monastery of the Amalfitans was supported by help which it received from the Amalfitan colony at Constantinople.

No monk is allowed, on any pretext, to leave Athos during Lent.

Once again, the ban on the keeping of sheep, goats and cattle is repeated. The Great Lavra is allowed to keep cows, to supply milk, cheese and butter for the aged and sick, but these animals must be kept at least 12 miles from any monastery. Lavra is also allowed three further pairs of oxen (making four in all) for making dough. These animals are not to be used for other work or for cultivation.

The monastery of Vatopedi, by reason of its size, is allowed one pair of oxen ...

No monk may move from one monastery to another; but any hegoumenos, with the approval of the brotherhood of which he is the head, may send one of its members to another monastery.

It is forbidden to refuse to fulfil contracts such as sales, gifts and exchanges of small farms or of monastic lands, if these have been made in good faith . . .

Any person may collect firewood in any place . . .

It is, for the future, forbidden to give away or to sell any part of the lands owned by the whole community of Athos.

Karyes has become a market town, where illegal trading, even in eunuchs, takes place. Therefore the old regulations must be enforced.

Some persons have ordained, as deacons, as priests, and as hegoumenoi, monks who were under twenty years of age. This practice is strictly forbidden.

The hegoumenoi of the larger monasteries have been in the habit of coming to the assemblies with many servants. This practice leads to quarrels and disorder. Therefore it is laid down that, for the future, the Protos may be accompanied by three servants only, the hegoumenos of Lavra by six, the hegoumenoi of Vatopedi and Iviron by four each, and other hegoumenoi by one only.

In future, all important matters must be decided by the Karyes General Assembly; less important matters will be dealt with by the Protos with the help of from five to ten hegoumenoi.

This document is important in a number of respects. First and foremost, it re-established the rule of law. It also established that it was the task of the Protos and the assembly to govern the affairs of the Mountain as a whole, to settle any disputes (for example, over boundaries), to enforce proper behaviour at meetings, and to apportion land to monasteries. The Protos also confirmed the election of all Athonite hegoumenoi and he came to represent the official face of the Mountain to the civil and ecclesiastical authorities of the surrounding area. We may also note the first official reference to Athos as 'the Holy Mountain', though it had borne this title unofficially since 985. When ratifying this *typikon* with his own seal, the emperor confirmed all previously granted imperial rights and privileges. Further privileges were granted by Alexios I Komnenos (1081–1118), giving the monks complete autonomy, independence from the authority of both the bishop of Ierissos and the Ecumenical Patriarch, and exemption from all taxation. The personal interest displayed by successive Byzantine emperors in the development of the Mountain was very important to its survival, to its well-being, and to its credibility: until 1312 the Protos was appointed directly by the emperor himself.

VLACH SHEPHERDS (AND SHEPHERDESSES) ON THE MOUNTAIN

The Vlachs are a transhumant people with their own (Latin) language who inhabit the mountains of northern Greece and the central Balkans. Most Byzantine references to Vlachs are unflattering, no doubt because as nomadic shepherds, and given to treachery, they were largely outside the law and thus made uncertain tax payers. That they should have infiltrated the Athonite peninsula is no great surprise; that they should have done so with the complicity of the monks was cause for great scandal.

From the start of the twelfth century as many as 300 Vlachs had strayed on to the peninsula with their flocks. Their presence was at first tolerated by the monks in return for a share of their produce. But they abused this licence by bringing in their wives and daughters, disguised as men, some of whom entered into the service of the monasteries and befriended the monks. One monk wrote, 'It would be disgraceful to tell or to hear what happened between them and some of the monks.'[25] Many of the monks were horrified by this lawless behaviour and, having failed to persuade the assembly at Karyes to evict the intruders, took their complaint to the Patriarch, Nicholas Grammatikos. He issued a severe warning to the offending monks but apparently stopped short of direct interference in the affairs of the Mountain, whereupon the leader of an opposing group, who was the hegoumenos of the Lavra, took the law into his own hands and forged an imperial command ordering the expulsion of the Vlachs. His action resulted in further protests, followed by further delegations of Athonites to Constantinople. No one seemed willing to take responsibility for the situation until eventually, in 1111, when the Patriarch was on his deathbed, a farcical scene took place in the presence of the emperor at which the dying Patriarch demonstrated from his own records that the command was not in his own hand and the abbot then arrived to confess to the forgery. Even more amazing is the later revelation that, despite all his denials, the Patriarch had indeed issued such a command.

No one emerges with credit from this sorry affair, for which there is full documentary evidence which has absorbed many generations of scholars.[26] The dispute, and others related to it, went unresolved for much of the twelfth century. As a result of it many monks left the Mountain, but many more took their places, and soon the physical and economic resources of the Mountain were insufficient to accommodate the growing population. This led to disputes over landownership, further delegations to Constantinople, and numerous recriminations affecting all those concerned. Reflecting the state of the empire, the Mountain descended into a state of unrest and faction. Rosemary Morris, whose masterly survey of monks and laymen in Byzantium terminates in the year 1118, paints a gloomy picture of the years to follow the death of Alexios I Komnenos:

> The practitioners of the monastic life became increasingly subject to criticism and rebuke, their individuality stifled in a new era of repression and conformity. Holy men there were, but their continuing popularity in many quarters was against a barrage of criticism from court-orientated intellectuals and the secular church. Where once miracle working, predictions and cures had been admired, now scepticism and fear of charlatans was evident. The monastic saints were deemed to be figures of the past; the present was a world in which the figure of the monk had, for many, lost much of its spiritual aura.[27]

THE COMING OF THE SLAVS

Ever since the days of St Athanasios the Holy Mountain had been an international centre, attracting monks from all parts of the Byzantine world. The Byzantines had been particularly successful in spreading their influence across Central Europe in the second half of the ninth century and they had responded with enthusiasm to the request of Rastislav of Moravia for Christian missionaries with a knowledge of the Slavonic language to visit his country. In 863 the emperor Michael III sent the brothers Constantine (whose monastic name was Cyril) and Methodios (who was the abbot of a monastery on Mount Olympus in Asia Minor) to preach Christianity to the Moravians in their own language. Having devised a suitable alphabet (known as the Glagolitic), the brothers translated the Liturgy of St John Chrysostom, the New Testament and various other Greek texts into Slavonic and also established a local church in Moravia. This language, now

25 The Russian skete of Bogoroditsa stands on the site of Xylourgou, the first Russian monastery on Athos.

known as Old Church Slavonic, became the ecclesiastical and literary lingua franca of all the peoples who gained entry to the Byzantine Commonwealth—Russians and Serbs, Bulgarians and Romanians—though the Moravian state, where it had been devised, soon fell to the Magyars and lost its allegiance to Byzantium. By the end of the ninth century the Glagolitic alphabet was replaced by the simpler 'Cyrillic', named after Constantine Cyril but devised by a disciple after his death, and the peoples of Eastern Europe now shared a religious bond with Byzantium, having all accepted Orthodox Christianity.

Politically, relations between Byzantium and the Slavs were often strained. After a series of wars Bulgaria was finally defeated and brought within the empire in 1018, but Serbia remained independent and there was often tension with the principalities of Kievan Rus'. Culturally, however, close contacts were maintained and relations were entirely harmonious and mutually tolerant, especially on ecclesiastical matters. There is evidence for a monastery 'tou Rhos' (i.e. of the Rus') on Athos as early as 1016; this was probably the monastery of Xylourgou, the first cenobitic Russian house, mentioned by name in documents from 1030 on. In the

26 The courtyard of Chilandar, the Serbian monastery founded in 1198. In the foreground stands the
phiale ('canopied basin') in which water for use in the church is blessed at the start of each month.

mid-eleventh century ascetics from Kiev visited Athos and spent some
time attached to the monastery of Esphigmenou, eventually returning to
Kiev where they founded the so-called Lavra of the Caves, 'with the blessing and in accordance with the statutes of the Holy Mountain', as
described by the *Russian Primary Chronicle*. The monks of Xylourgou are
likely to have remained a small community until 1169, when they were
granted full title to the ruined monastery of St Panteleimon with permission to rebuild it and repopulate it. Thus was founded the monastery
which remains to this day (though now removed to a different site) the
focus of the Russian presence on Mount Athos. Xylourgou soon dwindled
to the status of a skete, which it remains.[28]

The Serbian monastery has a similar history. A Greek monastery of
Chelandarios ('of the boatman') was founded in the tenth century and is
mentioned in a document of 1015[29] as being empty and abandoned. It was
then given to the monastery of Konstamonitou and continues to appear in
Greek documents of the eleventh and twelfth centuries until 1169. By the
end of the twelfth century, as the Byzantine empire descended into political
chaos, a state of affairs that was reflected in the condition of many of the
Greek houses on Athos, the monastery was once again deserted. Meanwhile

the Serbs, who under the Nemanjid dynasty took advantage of the growing weakness of Byzantium, cultivated cultural relations with their venerable but vulnerable neighbours.

In 1193 the younger son of Stefan I Nemanya, ruler of Serbia from 1168 to 1196, went to Athos and was tonsured a monk at the monastery of Vatopedi with the name Savvas.[30] Three years later, Stefan himself abdicated and became a monk, and in 1198 he joined his son on Athos with the name Symeon. In that year Symeon and Savvas were granted by imperial chrysobull ownership of the derelict Greek monastery of Chelandarios 'to be a gift to the Serbs in perpetuity'. They founded the new cenobitic monastery of Chilandar, which was to have the same status as the Georgian monastery of Iviron and the Latin house of the Amalfitans.[31] Symeon died the following year, but the work of establishing the monastery was continued with tireless energy by Savvas. The buildings were completed on a grand scale: a *typikon*[32] was devised along the lines of that in use at the Evergetis monastery in Constantinople, large estates in Serbia were granted to the monastery, and further privileges were assigned to it by the emperor Alexios III Angelos, including the right to own a ship and to take over the abandoned monastery of Zygos. By 1204 Chilandar had ninety monks and was well established as a centre of Serbian Orthodox religion and culture. In 1208 Savvas returned to Serbia and founded the monastery of Studenica. Here too he introduced a *typikon* based on that of the Evergetis monastery and incorporating elements derived from Chilandar; this became the model for all subsequent monastic foundations in Serbia.

Similar too is the history of the Bulgarian monastery, Zographou. This house may have been founded as early as the tenth century, during the heyday of monasticism in Bulgaria; there is a story that its founders were three brothers from Ohrid, the capital of the first Bulgarian empire. It is mentioned in documents of 1049 and 1051 as the monastery 'of the great martyr George', though it may have been a Greek house at this time.[33] Like many of the smaller monasteries, Zographou was in disarray by the end of the twelfth century, just as Bulgaria was reasserting itself and throwing off Byzantine rule. It was certainly back in Bulgarian hands by about 1270, when it became a ruling monastery with estates and other privileges granted to it by Bulgarian tsars, Byzantine emperors and Serbian kings.

All three Slav houses—St Panteleimon, Chilandar and Zographou— were flourishing centres of Byzantine literary culture. All three housed scriptoria where Greek texts were translated into Slavonic and diffused to the monasteries and cities of Eastern Europe. All three attracted holy men who were anxious to be trained in the monastic life and who were sent back to their homelands to found monasteries on the Athonite model and to transmit the ideas and learning they had absorbed. In short, Athos was already operating as the spiritual heart of Orthodoxy, playing host to 'an

27 The port buildings of Zographou, the Bulgarian monastery. Though an early foundation, the monastery has no surviving Byzantine buildings, but the tower at the port dates from the late fifteenth or early sixteenth century.

alternating current of men and ideas flowing to and from the Mediterranean' which the Oxford historian Dimitri Obolensky has graphically likened to 'the pulsations of a living heart'.[34]

THE LATIN EMPIRE

The second half of the twelfth century saw a marked decline in standards of spirituality and even of discipline not only on Athos but in monasteries throughout the Byzantine empire. Archbishop Eustathios of Thessaloniki (*c.*1178–95) was so shocked by what he found that he wrote a treatise *On the Improvement of Monastic Life* in which he drew attention to some of the worst abuses in an attempt to eradicate them. His complaints ranged over such matters as the admission of unsuitable candidates (such as beggars and criminals) to the monasteries, the worldliness of monks who divided their time between hunting and the pursuit of wealthy patrons, the consequent neglect of spiritual matters, and the careless management of libraries. Eustathios was so outspoken in his criticisms that he was temporarily expelled from his see, a clear enough indication that there was a good deal of truth in what he wrote.

As usual, the state of the monasteries was a reflection of the state of the empire. The last two decades of the twelfth century witnessed a serious weakening of the imperial administration, a massacre of the Italian merchants in Constantinople, riots over the succession, the loss of Bulgaria and Cyprus, and the appearance of separatist regimes in various parts of the empire. Byzantium was already beginning to fragment when in 1204 the unthinkable happened and self-styled crusaders captured and sacked the city. Steven Runciman, a historian renowned for his balanced and sober judgement, has written of this event with uncharacteristic passion:

There was never a greater crime against humanity than the Fourth Crusade. Not only did it cause the destruction or dispersal of all the treasures of the past that Byzantium had devotedly stored, and the mortal wounding of a civilisation that was still active and great; but it was also an act of gigantic political folly. It brought no help to the Christians in Palestine. Instead it robbed them of potential helpers. And it upset the whole defence of Christendom.[35]

In an earlier book he had put it bluntly: 'The conquests of the Ottomans were made possible by the Crusaders' crime.'[36]

The immediate repercussions of this disaster on the Holy Mountain were dire. The territories of the empire were parcelled out among the conquerors, with the Venetians taking the western half of Greece and the Franks the eastern. Boniface of Montferrat, passed over for the throne of Constantinople, was installed as ruler of Thessaloniki. Throughout the empire there was an attempt to introduce the Latin rite, Greek bishops were replaced by or made subservient to Latin bishops, and monks suffered persecution and expulsion. On Athos the bishop of Sebaste, who had formal jurisdiction over the monasteries, was succeded by a Latin bishop, who promptly built a castle from which he could dispatch raiding parties to attack them. Stories are still told of the outrages perpetrated by this despotic prelate. So unspeakable were they that he had to be removed by the Latin emperor. Despite the aspirations of the pope, the chasm between the Orthodox east and the Latin west was reinforced by the atrocities committed by the Franks, and the breakdown in relations now became permanent.

Pope Innocent III was genuinely shocked not only by the sack of Constantinople but by the reports of subsequent ill-treatment of the subject churches and monasteries. The monks of Athos were so demoralized by the situation that they turned to him for protection and restoration of their rights. In a bull dated 17 January 1213 the pope declared his support for them and their way of life; he confirmed their rights, privileges and immunities, and denounced the behaviour of the former bishop of Sebaste and his thugs. Even the Emperor Henry of Flanders (1206–16) was persuaded to intervene on behalf of the monks, as a result of which there was a temporary respite in the Frankish raids. But ten years later a new pope complained that the Athonites were showing signs of disobedience and were inclined to revolt. Small wonder that the Mountain remained in a state of turmoil as long as a Latin emperor reigned in Constantinople.

4
PALAIOLOGAN ATHOS

In the wake of the sack of Constantinople and the subsequent dismemberment of the empire, a number of successor states sprang up in what had been imperial territory. The province of Epirus, together with all of north-western Greece and much of Thessaly, was united under a dynasty of rulers (so-called despots) who held it until 1318, when it came under Italian rule. In the east, another state was founded at Trebizond by the Komnenos family, who had been forced to give up the throne of Constantinople to the Angeloi in 1185. This self-styled empire extended along a strip of Black Sea coastline and survived for 250 years before falling to the Ottomans in 1461. Most successful of all was the state founded at Nicaea in north-west Asia Minor, which in 1208 became the capital of the Byzantine empire in exile. Nicaea was also the seat of the patriarch and became the centre of an administratively and financially efficient regime that lasted until the recapture of Constantinople in 1261.

As the Latin empire gradually weakened during the thirteenth century, there was a race between Epirus and Nicaea for the recovery of Constantinople. Epirus took an early lead with the capture of Thessaloniki in 1224, but was soon ousted by a revived Bulgaria, which took over most of the European territories of the Latins. These territories were in turn acquired by the emperor of Nicaea. After defeating an alliance of the despot of Epirus, the Latin prince of Achaea and Manfred of Sicily at the battle of Pelagonia in 1259, Michael VIII Palaiologos of Nicaea was free to turn his attention to Constantinople. He entered the city in triumph on 15 August 1261, thereby founding a dynasty that would rule Byzantium until its fall to the Ottomans in 1453.

The Palaiologoi began strongly. During the years in Nicaea, they had cast off most of the bureaucratic baggage that had weighed down the earlier imperial administration. They had abandoned their claims to universal dominion. They had fostered good relations with the aristocracy and the monasteries by granting them additional privileges and estates, and they had made a concerted effort to preserve their Hellenic heritage by founding schools, collecting manuscripts from monastic libraries (including those of Mount Athos), and editing texts. Once they were re-established in Constantinople, the new regime was in most respects better equipped to serve the remnants of the empire than its predecessor.

THE UNION OF CHURCHES

The emperor's first task was to restore the city itself, to repair its damaged churches and public buildings, repopulate its residential quarters and strengthen its defences. The most immediate danger was from the west, and there remained a serious threat of invasion by Charles I of Anjou. Michael VIII was a skilful diplomat who realized that the best way to secure the empire from further attack by the Latins was an ecclesiastical union with Rome; this was effected by the emperor's representatives at the second Council of Lyons in 1274. Having secured the submission of the Byzantine Church to the supremacy of Rome, Pope Gregory X agreed to honour his side of the bargain and remove the threat of attack by Charles of Anjou. Michael and his Latinizing patriarch John Bekkos won this diplomatic victory in the teeth of opposition from monks, clergy and the populace in Byzantium. The Church was the most conservative element in Byzantine society and was fiercely proud of its Orthodox traditions. To have them compromised by a 'Latin-minded' emperor was deeply offensive. The survival of the empire had been ensured, but at the cost of the loyalty of the majority of the emperor's subjects. Seeds of disaffection had been sown for which the empire would pay dearly in the years to come.

Violent persecution of those unwilling to accept the union ensued, nowhere more so than on the Holy Mountain. Stories are still told of the acts of heroism performed by Athonite fathers willing to die for their faith, though there is some confusion with similar stories relating to the attempted union of churches in the dying days of the empire in the fifteenth century. The emperor is said to have sent an expedition to Athos, which he may even have accompanied, to enforce the union on the monks and punish those who refused to accept it. At Iviron, for example, it is said that the tombs of the founders were desecrated and that some monks were drowned. At Vatopedi some monks were taken to the top of a hill and hanged; others suffered the same fate outside the monastery; and the abbot Euthymios was drowned from a rock in the bay (a cross still marks the spot).

R.M. Dawkins's *Monks of Athos* is a rich source of such accounts, though he suggests the reader approaches them with a degree of scepticism. In a chapter devoted to 'The Latinizing Persecutions' he describes the hilltop now called the Abbot's Seat, where the monks are said to have been hanged, and urges caution:

> The stories now told about this place vary. One is that an abbot of Vatopedi was hanged there. Another is that the Pope of Rome came to Athos and brought the abbot of Vatopedi up to this place and beheaded him. This story comes from the muleteer Panayotis, to whose muddled mind nothing seemed improbable. It was he who failed to find the path down to Pantokrator, and in his efforts to guide us

there from Vatopedi brought us very nearly all the way to Karyes. A matter of fact version of the legend is that an abbot after walking up the very steep hill from Vatopedi, here sat down and expired: hence the name *The Seat of the Abbot*.[1]

A particularly gruesome story is told of the monks of Zographou who resisted the Latinizers.[2] Twenty-six of them denied the papal claims, refused to flee, and locked themselves inside the tower of the monastery, whereupon the tower was burnt to the ground. Their martyrdom is depicted in a fresco in the narthex to the katholikon. The site of the tower is marked by a cenotaph in the north-west corner of the courtyard. A lamp burns continually in front of it, and an inscription tells the story of what happened on that fateful day, 10 October 1274.

Other monasteries, such as Megiste Lavra and Xeropotamou, are said to have yielded to the emperor's demands and allowed the Latin mass to be celebrated in their churches. Terrible fates overtook the monks as a result of their treachery.

What are we to make of such stories? No doubt they have been embellished with the passing of the years. There is no hard evidence to support them,[3] and suggestions that the Protaton was burned and all the monks in Karyes massacred clearly tax the limits of credulity. But rather than dismiss them out of hand, as E. Amand de Mendieta does,[4] it seems to me preferable, as so often with Athonite oral tradition, to regard them as embroideries of a fundamental truth. Michael VIII had after all accepted the union of churches; he had to make some effort to enforce it, if only to show his friends in the west that he was serious about what he said; it was inevitable that, if he did so, he would encounter opposition, not least among the defenders of the faith on the Holy Mountain. Suffice it to say that the Latinizing policies died with the emperor in 1282, and his successor, Andronikos II, repudiated the union that had saved the empire for his father, albeit with short-term traumatic consequences.

PIRATE RAIDS

For Athos, Andronikos II Palaiologos was a good king. Even Donald Nicol, who takes a pragmatic approach in his history of the last centuries of Byzantium, has to admit that it is surprising that he achieved as much as he did, given the problems with which he had to contend at the end of the thirteenth century. 'Politically and internally the Empire and the Church were divided into warring factions. There was never enough money, there were never enough troops.'[5] He was a great benefactor of the monasteries in the course of his long reign (1282–1328) and he was to die a monk himself (in

1332). But with hindsight it is unfortunate that in order to counteract the advances being made by the Turks in Asia Minor he chose to hire a band of Spanish mercenaries known as the Catalan Grand Company who fought, not under his command, but under that of their own leader Roger de Flor.

At first the Catalans achieved some success, driving the Turks out of Cyzicus and relieving Philadelphia. But after their fleet was lost in a skirmish with the Genoese and their leader was assassinated during a meeting with the emperor's son in 1305, they turned on the Byzantines, blaming them for their misfortunes. They took over the Gallipoli peninsula, declaring it Spanish territory and massacring all the inhabitants; and from there they launched devastating attacks on the coast to the west. For two and a half years, with the backing of the Bulgarians, they instigated a reign of terror throughout Thrace before moving further west. They then established themselves on the peninsula of Cassandra for two years (1307–9) from where they attacked the neighbouring peninsula of Athos. No monastery was spared. Churches were desecrated, books and archives were burnt, works of art were plundered. According to the account left by Abbot Daniel of Chilandar, his monastery resisted the attacks for almost three years. He eventually escaped to seek help from Serbia. Meanwhile the monks of the Lavra were so desperate that they appealed to James II of Aragon to deliver them. According to E. Amand de Mendieta, 'This was the most dreadful experience that the Holy Mountain had to undergo in its thousand years of existence.'[6]

Sated with hagioritic loot, the Catalans eventually moved on by way of Thessaly and Boeotia to conquer Thebes and Athens. There in 1311 they took over the duchy set up by the Franks in 1204, thus succeeding, where they had failed in Asia Minor, Gallipoli and Cassandra, in establishing a principality of their own which they ruled for nearly eighty years.

RECONSTRUCTION AND RENEWAL

After more than a century of deterioration and disorder, which encompassed periods of foreign rule and scenes of violent confrontation, the monasteries were at a low ebb. To their rescue came an emperor determined to make good the havoc created by his seditious mercenaries. Regardless of their ethnic allegiance, Andronikos made grants to all the monasteries. Their buildings were restored, their estates were extended, their numbers of monks were increased, their privileges were confirmed. Nor was all the munificence Byzantine. The tsar of Serbia, Stefan Dushan (1331–55), who had enlarged his empire to encompass much of Macedonia and Chalkidiki (including Athos), also became a benefactor on a grand scale, and not just of Serbian Chilandar, but Dochiariou, Esphigmenou, Lavra, Philotheou, Vatopedi, Xenophontos,

Xeropotamou, and Zographou all benefited from his generosity. Since its capture by the Mongols in 1240, Kievan Rus' had ceased to send monks to St Panteleimonos, and the buildings had been ransacked by the Catalans in 1307–8; but now they were repopulated with Serbian monks and the monastery received generous donations from Tsar Stefan Dushan.

In addition to this refurbishment of the existing monasteries, seven major monasteries were either founded or refounded during the fourteenth or early fifteenth century. All seven quickly established themselves as prominent institutions and all survive today. In fact, apart from the foundation of Stavronikita in 1541, the list of monasteries has not changed since the early fifteenth century.

The monastery of Grigoriou is first mentioned in documents of 1347 and 1348, though the precise date of its foundation is unknown, as is the identity of its founder. His name was Gregory, but he is probably not to be identified with Gregory of Sinai who by 1330 had left Athos to found another monastery in Thrace. In 1489 Grigoriou is described as being Serbian.

Simonopetra also was founded (or refounded if one credits the Life of Simon which describes an earlier foundation in about 1257) around the middle of the fourteenth century.[7] Prince John Ugljesa, the Serbian despot of Serres (1365–71), was given permission by the Holy Community to erect buildings 'in that empty place' (which suggests that, if there had been a monastery there before, it had now completely disappeared). Their inaugu-

28 Simonopetra seen from the west. Perched on top of a rock 300 metres above sea level, the monastery has a most spectacular location.

ration is celebrated in a royal chrysobull which he issued in 1368. He endowed it not only with magnificent buildings, treasures and works of art but also with estates and properties to provide for its income.

More is known about the monastery of Dionysiou which was founded between 1356 and 1362 by one Dionysios, a Greek from Kastoria whose brother was the metropolitan of Trebizond. As a result of this connection the monastery easily won the support of the emperor of Trebizond, Alexios III Komnenos, who, in the expectation that the monastery would be named after himself (which it never was), saw it as a means of enhancing his personal prestige. His imperial chrysobull, dated September 1374, is preserved in the monastery's archives, a magnificent document decorated with miniatures of the emperor and his empress being blessed by St John the Baptist and still retaining its gold seal. In it he endows the monastery with lavish gifts and an annual income, in return for which he and his family were to be commemorated in perpetuity at services in the church. 'For all emperors, kings, or rulers of note have built monasteries on Mount Athos for their eternal memory; and since the emperor of Trebizond surpasses many of them, he too should add a new foundation in order to live eternally in the memory of the people and to enjoy unending pleasures of the soul.'[8]

The monastery of Pantokrator was founded by two brothers, Alexios and John, who were high up in the service of the Byzantine emperor John V Palaiologos (1341–91) to whom they were related by marriage. In the confused political situation of the time, when the empire was riven by civil war, these two brothers had carved out for themselves a small principality in eastern Macedonia based on the castle of Chrysoupolis. Branded as 'adventurers' by Nikolaos Oikonomides, they obtained legitimacy for their operation by means of an imperial chrysobull granted to them in March 1357. At the same time they also acquired land on the Holy Mountain where they instigated the construction of Pantokrator, providing it with revenue and estates, half of which they retained for themselves. After the death of Alexios in 1368/9, John continued to defend his territory against the advancing Turks until 1383 when it was taken at the same time as Serres. John withdrew to Pantokrator where he died in 1386/7.

> This was the end of the adventure [writes Oikonomides]. A company of soldiers of fortune, like so many others in the fourteenth century, ended by creating a semi-independent principality—a Greek 'emirate' combining piety with aggressive greediness. The phenomenon was not unique and was too small in scale to influence the course of events. But it left a permanent legacy: the monastery of Pantokrator.[9]

29 Right: Dionysiou seen from the south. This monastery was founded in the second half of the fourteenth century with the support of Alexios III Komnenos, emperor of Trebizond.

30 The chrysobull of 1374 recording the endowment of the monastery of Dionysiou by the emperor of Trebizond. In this miniature St John the Baptist, to whom the monastery is dedicated, gives his blessing to the emperor and empress.

31 Pantokrator, another fourteenth-century foundation, seen from the south. The monastery stands on a headland overlooking a small harbour.

The monastery now known as St Paul's has its origins in the late tenth or early eleventh century when it was first set up as a dependency of Xeropotamou with the same name as its parent house. By 1035 it seems to have won its independence, and later assumed the name of an abbot named Paul. But this early foundation had long been abandoned when in the 1380s two Serbs from Kastoria, named Gerasimos Radonias and Antonios-Arsenios Pagasis, purchased the site and, with support from both the Serbian and Byzantine royal houses, created a flourishing new Serbian monastery, fully endowed with income and estates.[10]

The monastery of Koutloumousiou also was an earlier foundation, dating from the eleventh century, but by the 1360s it was seriously dilapidated. The abbot Chariton sent a plea to the voivodes of Wallachia, Alexander Basarab (1352–64) and his son John Vladislav (1364–74), who undertook the rebuilding of the entire monastery. Chariton also had played on the Wallachians' eagerness to enhance their personal prestige. According to a document preserved in the archives, John Vladislav was advised that 'he should act in the same fashion as many other rulers have acted before him, that is Serbs and Bulgarians, Russians and Georgians, who obtained the right to be commemorated and honoured in this admirable Holy Mountain, the eye of the Universe one might say, and who acquired the right to rest body and soul for their people'.[11] In return Chariton agreed to admit

32 St Paul's from the south-west. The monastery overlooks a fertile valley but is itself overshadowed by the peak of the mountain which towers over it.

Romanian monks to his monastery which for a while was known as the 'monastery of the voivode' or the 'lavra of Wallachia'. In the light of Romanian support, so generously given not only to Koutloumousiou but to numerous other monasteries, especially during the Tourkokratia, it seems one of the injustices of Athos that the Romanians have never been given permanent control of a ruling monastery.

Konstamonitou was originally an eleventh-century Greek foundation. It had been founded by a man from Kastamon in Asia Minor (or by a member of the Kastamonites family) and was therefore properly known as Kastamonitou. But the name was changed to lend credence to the myth of an earlier foundation by the emperor Constans (340–50) for which there is no evidence whatever. This monastery too was in a bad way after a fire in the 1420s when the abbot Neophytos appealed to a wealthy Serbian aristocrat and general with the name of Radic. Radic owned silver mines at Novo Brdo and poured his own money into restoring the monastery. He himself was tonsured before his death, and the monastery flourished as a Serbian house for the rest of the fifteenth century. 'The case of the Celnik [general] Radic', writes one scholar, 'indicates that Mt Athos had become a place of refuge not only for poor Christians, but also for rich aristocrats, all of whom wished to escape the warfare and pillaging which had become such a feature of life in the fifteenth-century Balkans.'[12]

THE INFLUENCE OF SERBIA

The influence of Serbia on fourteenth- and fifteenth-century Athos deserves comment. The empire created by Stefan Dushan did not long survive his death (1355): Athos was lost by 1371; and by 1389 the Serbs had become vassals of the Ottomans. But cultural, and especially ecclesiastical, contacts between Serbia and Byzantium were maintained; and Serbian rulers and feudal lords continued to support the Athonite monasteries most generously until the downfall of Serbia in 1459. When the Russian monk Isaiah visited Athos in 1489, he listed no fewer than five monasteries as predominantly Serbian (Dochiariou, Grigoriou, Dionysiou, St Paul's and Chilandar), a list that a few years earlier would presumably have included Konstamonitou as well.[13] But Chilandar was always the jewel in the Serbian crown, and the basis of its wealth was its landed property. By the end of the fourteenth century it possessed more than thirty metochia and 360 villages over which it exercised full administrative, fiscal and judicial rights so that it operated almost like a state within a state. According to the monk Isaiah, by the late fifteenth century the number of its properties had increased to 600 villages, and this included a total of 180,000 vineyards. The power that

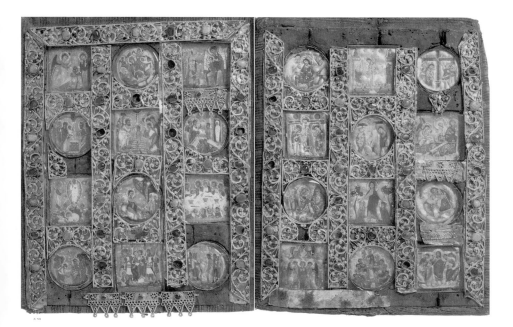

33 Left: By tradition a tenth-century foundation, the courtyard of Dochiariou climbs steeply up the hillside. The katholikon (right) was built in the sixteenth century and the defence tower is dated 1617.

34 The so-called Milutin diptych from Chilandar. This astonishing work of the late thirteenth or early fourteenth century contains twenty-four miniatures painted on parchment and encased in rock crystal, apparently in imitation of enamel, depicting scenes from the life of Christ.

Chilandar wielded, not only spiritually but economically and politically, was unequalled among Athonite monasteries at the time. 'Without exaggeration', the historians of the monastery have written,

> Chilandar may be described as the centre of medieval Serbia's spiritual life and an important intermediary and representative in Serbia's relations with Byzantium. Without its intermediary role, it is inconceivable that Serbia would have adopted Byzantine civilization and the classical heritage. As it was, the elite of the Serbian Church, literature and theology passed through Chilandar. In the eyes of Byzantium, Chilandar was a lasting proof of Serbian legitimacy, recognized and confirmed by imperial chrysobulls. Enjoying the status of a Byzantine 'imperial lavra', this rich and independent monastery was Serbia's best diplomatic mission in Byzantium.[14]

Among these imperial chrysobulls is that issued by the emperor John V in July 1351 confirming the privileges of Chilandar at the request 'of the

35 Detail of the Annunciation from the so-called Milutin diptych from Chilandar .

sublime emperor of Serbia, his beloved ... Lord Stephen'.[15] This Lord Stephen, otherwise known as Stefan Dushan, had already had himself crowned as 'emperor of the Serbs and Greeks' and variously described himself as 'lord of almost the whole Roman empire' and 'successor of the great and holy Greek emperors'. It is interesting to find him deferring to the emperor of Byzantium as the only legitimate ruler of the entire Christian Commonwealth at a time when the Holy Mountain itself was Serbian territory. As Donald Nicol remarks, Stefan Dushan 'had played cat and mouse with the Byzantine emperors for many years'.[16]

To this day Chilandar controls as much as twenty per cent of the territory of the Holy Mountain as well as a large proportion of the cells in and around Karyes. It still holds fourth place in the hierarchy; its buildings are as beautiful as those of any monastery; and its library and treasury bear witness to its former wealth and power.

EMPERORS AND PATRIARCHS

Since the tenth century Athos had been under the direct jurisdiction of the emperor. By tradition the hegoumenoi had elected their own Protos or primate, whose election and powers were then confirmed by the emperor. In an act designed to strengthen to authority of the patriarchate and to make the monks more accountable, Andronikos II Palaiologos issued a solemn chrysobull in November 1312 by which he transferred jurisdiction over the monasteries, including the appointment of the Protos, to the ecumenical patriarch. In future, every newly elected Protos was required to visit Constantinople to be ordained by the patriarch. This had the effect of weakening the position of the Protos and would have been unthinkable a century earlier.

Further threats to the independence of the Athonites came from closer at hand. Successive bishops of Ierissos attempted to capitalize on their honorific title of 'bishop of the Holy Mountain' and exercise their episcopal authority over the monasteries. After lengthy disputes the matter was finally resolved by Patriarch Anthony IV, who in 1392 confirmed the traditional rights and privileges of the Mountain and of the Protos and decreed that the bishop of Ierissos was not to enter its territory without invitation from the Protos. Furthermore the Protos was given the authority to appoint spiritual fathers and confessors.

By the end of the century problems of monastic discipline and obedience again surfaced and the emperor Manuel II Palaiologos attempted to resolve these issues by sending a delegation of bishops to issue a third typikon.[17] This charter, dating from about 1400, defined the order of precedence between the hegoumenoi and it restored some of the respect and powers of the Protos: his permision was required before the patriarch could send an exarchate to the Mountain; no bishop should exercise episcopal authority there without his consent; he had the right to confer blessings on all the hegoumenoi except that of the Lavra; he was to be honoured and respected by all; he had jurisdiction over the vicinity of Karyes; he was to be elected by the hegoumenoi, but upon his election be sent to Constantinople to be ordained by the patriarch. All the monasteries were required to commemorate the name of the patriarch during the Liturgy. Any layman who had spent three years on the Mountain was required either to be tonsured or to leave. And there were the usual exclusion orders relating to 'beardless youths' and female animals.

The emperor's own authority was tottering meanwhile. In 1383 eastern Macedonia had fallen to the Ottomans though the monasteries of Athos and their estates remained untouched by their raids, presumably because the monks had earlier done a deal with the sultan whereby in return for their submission to him they would receive his protection. Twenty years later, after the sultan's defeat at Ankara by the Mongols under Timur (Tamerlane), the area surrounding Thessaloniki and including Athos was restored to the empire, only to be conquered again in 1430. Meanwhile in 1424 a delegation of monks paid homage to Sultan Murad II in Adrianople. Despite its submission to the Turk, however, the Mountain maintained close relations with Constantinople as long as a Christian emperor reigned, and indeed a party of Athonite monks joined the emperor's delegation to the Council of Florence in 1438–9.[18]

St Gregory Palamas and the Hesychast Controversy

We have already seen that, despite the internal and external threats to the survival of the empire, the fourteenth and early fifteenth centuries were a time of physical renewal and resurgence for the Athonite monasteries. In the spiritual, intellectual and cultural spheres a similar pattern may be observed, and it is not inappropriate to speak in terms of a Palaiologan renaissance.

It was on Athos that the so-called hesychast controversy first arose which was eventually to spread throughout the Orthodox world and split the Byzantine Church. The controversy shook the very foundations of the state and probably hastened its fall. No fewer than four church councils in Constantinople were needed before it was finally settled and the interpretations of St Gregory Palamas were incorporated into Orthodoxy, reviving a tradition originating from the earliest days of monasticism.

The word 'hesychasm' derives from the Greek word for stillness or tran-

36 St Gregory Palamas (1296–1359), defender of the hesychasts, a near–contemporary portrait in the chapel of the Agioi Anargyroi at Vatopedi.

quillity (*hesychia*). It occurs in the 'Sayings of the Desert Fathers' with reference to inner tranquillity, but a hesychast could refer to someone seeking either inner or outer stillness. Hesychasm as a spiritual tradition is most fully developed by St John Klimakos in the seventh century for whom *hesychia* is a state of inner silence and vigilance, closely associated with the name of Jesus and the repetition of short prayers. The tradition was revived by St Symeon the New Theologian in the eleventh century in Byzantium and then again around 1300 by St Gregory of Sinai, whose hesychast teachings were particularly warmly received by the monks when he arrived on Athos. As Gregory travelled around the empire, so the hesychast tradition spread throughout the Orthodox world.

Hesychasts devote themselves especially to the prayer of silence, what is often referrred to as 'prayer of the heart'. This means prayer that is not merely said by the lips or thought by the mind, but generated spontaneously by the whole of one's being until it eventually takes over one's whole consciousness and repeats itself. Developing out of the invocation of the name of Jesus, this prayer of the heart became known as the Jesus Prayer: 'Lord Jesus Christ, Son of God, have mercy upon me.' Ceaseless repetition of this prayer, combined with certain breathing exercises and a particular bodily posture, induces a state of mind which enables the participant to experience a vision of divine and uncreated light such as that which was once shown to the apostles and prophets at the Transfiguration on Mount Tabor.

In the mid-fourteenth century the practices and claims of the hesychasts were challenged by a learned monk called Barlaam of Calabria. Barlaam argued that it was impossible to know or experience God in this world; he jeered at the physical contortions that the hesychasts employed to induce a state of ecstasy; and he attacked their claims to experience visions of the divine and uncreated light as shockingly materialistic. Meanwhile the hesychasts found a champion in the brilliant Athonite theologian Gregory Palamas, later archbishop of Thessaloniki (1347–59). Gregory had been tonsured at Vatopedi and had lived at the Lavra before becoming abbot of Esphigmenou, but he had abandoned that office for a life of asceticism as a hermit near Verria.

In his principal contribution to the debate Gregory stressed the bodily presence of Christ in the sacramental life of the Church (which was questioned by Barlaam) and thus linked his defence of the hesychasts with a defence of the Gospel itself:

> Since the Son of God, in his incomparable love for men, did not only unite his divine Hypostasis with our nature, by clothing himself in a living body and a soul gifted with intelligence...but also united himself...with the human hypostases themselves, in mingling himself with each of the faithful by communion with his Holy Body, and since he becomes one single body with us and makes us a tem-

ple of the undivided Divinity, for in the very body of Christ dwells the fullness of the Godhead bodily, how should he not illuminate those who commune worthily with the divine ray of his Body which is within us, lightening their souls, as he illuminated the very bodies of the disciples on Mount Tabor? For, on the day of the Transfiguration, that Body, source of the light of grace, was not yet united with our bodies; it illuminated from outside those who worthily approached it, and sent the illumination into the soul by the intermediary of the physical eyes; but now, since it is mingled with us and exists in us, it illuminates the soul from within.[19]

Gregory took a moderate line in his explanation of the uncreated light of Tabor and in drawing distinctions between the divine energies (which we do know) and the divine essence (which we do not) and was thus able to reconcile hesychasm with traditional Orthodoxy. But there were extremists on both sides and a dispute which had initially involved only monks and theologians rapidly escalated into a controversy in which the whole population became embroiled. After a synod in Constantinople in 1341 at which his attacks were deemed to be unsubstantiated, Barlaam returned to Calabria. Still the dispute rumbled on; a second council, later in 1341, came to a similar conclusion and it took a third council in 1347 and a fourth in 1351 before Gregory's teaching was finally vindicated, a vindication that was sealed by his canonization in 1368, just nine years after his death. Bishop Kallistos, the historian of the Church, concludes his discussion of the controversy on a positive note: 'Certainly Gregory Palamas was no revolutionary innovator, but firmly rooted in the tradition of the past; yet he was a creative theologian of the first rank, and his work shows that Orthodox theology did not cease to be active after the eighth century and the seventh Ecumenical Council.'[20]

The victory of the hesychasts had profound repercussions throughout the Orthodox world, for there were few subjects that engaged the Byzantine mind more than theology, and in the Byzantine world theology and politics were frequently intertwined. Socially and politically the dispute had divided the Byzantines into two factions. On the Palamite side were the aristocrats, the landowners, the rich, and of course the monks. On the opposing side were the poor, the landless, the intelligentsia, and the common people. The victory of the monks represented a victory for the forces of conservatism. Louis Bréhier, the historian of the empire, reaches a more sobering conclusion:

The victory of the hesychasts over the humanists perpetuated the triumph of monasticism. In the fifteenth century, the monks were among the largest landowners; they have control of the Church, and the upper ranks of the hierarchy are selected solely from their numbers. They have enormous influence among the people, which they use to arouse anti-western feeling, and they obstruct imperial policy by opposing all friendly advances towards Rome. They ended by controlling the Church, and by ruining the State.[21]

A less speculative, more judicious statement is offered by Steven Runciman: 'In the outcome Palamism triumphed, partly because it had the approval of the majority of the Greek clergy, partly because it had the political support of John Cantacuzenus, and partly because of the personality and intellect of Palamas himself.'[22] But there can be no doubting the fact that the tradition of hesychasm was now deeply embedded in the Holy Mountain and that as a result the monks acquired an unprecedented degree of influence and authority over the development of spirituality throughout the Orthodox world. As Dimitri Obolensky writes,

> Byzantium, Bulgaria, Serbia, Rumania and Russia were all affected by this new cosmopolitan movement: monks, churchmen, writers and artists, travelling from country to country—'wandering for the sake of the Lord', as a fourteenth-century writer put it—found themselves in a similar spiritual and cultural environment; and through this 'Hesychast International', whose influence extended far beyond the ecclesiastical sphere, the different parts of the Byzantine Commonwealth were, during the last hundred years of its existence, linked to each other and to its centre perhaps more closely than ever before.[23]

Nor did the influence of the hesychasts come to a halt in 1453. Far from it: Bishop Kallistos believes it was the hesychasts—'those who emphasized the inner, spiritual values of the Greek Christian inheritance'—who provided the oppressed Greek Church with the strength to survive the long, dark centuries of Tourkokratia. It was they who provided the inspiration for the compilation of the great anthology of spiritual texts known as the *Philokalia*, first published in Venice in 1782.[24] Moreover it is hesychasm that provides the spiritual basis of the monastic revival that is taking place on the Holy Mountain today.

St Maximos of Kafsokalyvia

Prominent among the generation of ascetics that upheld the traditions of hesychasm on the Holy Mountain around the time of the controversy is the name of St Maximos Kafsokalyvitis ('of the burning hut'). Like many Athonites, St Maximos was an eccentric character: his name, we are told, derives from his habit of regularly changing his abode, which was never more than a temporary hut made of branches, and this he always burnt before seeking another resting place. He spent much of his life wandering in the desert of Athos, at the southernmost tip of the peninsula, near where the skete of Kafsokalyvia (founded in the eighteenth century) now stands: the skete is named after the saint.

Four lives of St Maximos survive, of which two have been published.[25] One was written by St Niphon, who had shared a cell with St Maximos towards the end of the latter's life. It is not a work of great literary merit, but it contains a great deal of anecdotal information and seems to be grounded in historical fact. The other, by Theophanes, hegoumenos of Vatopedi, is a more polished account, based partly on Niphon's life but also containing information from other sources. 'These two biographies', writes Bishop Kallistos, 'despite their shortcomings, provide a relatively detailed "icon" of the saint, indicating how his life and personality were remembered by his friends in the years immediately following his death.'[26]

We are told that from an early age St Maximos, whose baptismal name was Manuel, was attracted to the life of the holy fool, the fool in Christ (*salos*). Such fools in Christ occupy a respectable if unconventional place in the spiritual tradition of the Christian east.[27] 'To his parents and to everyone he pretended to be an imbecile', writes Theophanes of the young Manuel, though at the same time he already exhibited a particular devotion to the Mother of God. At the age of seventeen he became a monk on Mount Ganos in Thrace and after further wanderings as a homeless vagrant he finally moved to Athos, where he settled for a while at the Great Lavra. One day, when he was standing in the church, he saw a vision of the Mother of God calling him to climb to the peak of Athos. The vision appeared three times and the third time, on Whitsunday, he obeyed. At the summit there is a chapel dedicated to the Transfiguration, and there Maximos remained alone for three nights, despite violent storms and demons that were sent to dislodge him. At last the Theotokos appeared to him again, gave him her blessing, and fed him with heavenly bread.

Feigning madness to cloak his humility, Maximos now embarked on a nomadic existence, wandering in the desert from cave to cave, burnt-down hut to burnt-down hut, clothed in a single garment and sustaining himself on a diet of nuts and berries. He kept this up for about ten years; then, after a meeting with St Gregory of Sinai, he occupied a fixed abode for a further fourteen years, though never relaxing his ascetic way of life: 'his cell was altogether bare of possessions', writes Theophanes; 'he did not possess even a needle or a spade or two garments; he had no bread, no wallet, not a single coin.' Finally, assailed by demons, he bequeathed his cell to Niphon and moved closer to the Lavra, so that he could hear the monastery's bells. Here he died, we are told, at the age of ninety-five, some time between 1365 and 1375.

Why does this eccentric character merit our attention? Some of his contemporaries dismissed him as not so much a fool in Christ as simply a fool. But others esteemed him as a prophet and miracle-worker. He was said to be able to cast out demons, and Theophanes claims that he saw him fly through the air. Like other Athonite ascetics both then and now, many visitors came to speak with him as his fame spread abroad. According to both Niphon and Theophanes, these included the emperors John V Palaiologos and John VI Kantakouzenos, who travelled together (presumably around

1350) specially to visit him. Having given them the benefit of his advice, he predicted (correctly) that Kantakouzenos would be tonsured as a monk, and later sent him symbolic gifts of dry bread, garlic and onion as an indication that this would in due course be his diet.

But Maximos's spiritual gifts went deeper than this. More than once his biographers refer to him as being transfigured by supranatural light, describing the light in Palamite terms as 'non-material' and 'divine'. They do not discuss the nature of the light, but their descriptions are consistent with the interpretation of St Gregory Palamas that this light, whether manifested externally or experienced internally during prayer, is to be identified with the uncreated energies of God, the divine glory that Christ reflected at his Transfiguration on Mount Tabor. 'Is it not evident', wrote Gregory Palamas, 'that there is but one and the same divine light: that which the apostles saw on Tabor, which purified souls behold even now, and which is the reality of the eternal blessings to come?'[28] Palamas always maintained that the theories he propounded were not based on his own personal opinions but on the living, shared experience of the hesychast monks of Athos, a claim that is supported by the accounts of St Maximos.

Equally significant is Theophanes's account of Maximos's meeting with St Gregory of Sinai which we have already mentioned. In the course of their conversation St Gregory asked Maximos if he possessed 'inner prayer', to which Maximos replied 'Yes, I have possessed it from my youth.' He went on to tell him of a time before he became a hermit when he was praying to the Mother of God that he might receive the grace of inner prayer:

> And when with longing I kissed her most pure icon, suddenly I felt within my chest and in my heart a great warmth, not burning me up but filling me with refreshment and sweetness and deep compunction. From that moment my heart began to say the prayer inwardly; and at the same time my reason, together with my intellect, holds fast to the memory of Jesus and of my Theotokos, and it has never left me.

Here is a clear reference to the Jesus Prayer that St Gregory had already been teaching for some years on the Mountain and that had always been central to hesychast practice. While saying it, Maximos goes on, he often passed into a state of ecstasy, and as a result of this grace he felt compelled to leave the monastery and move into the desert in search of greater stillness (*hesychia*).

In acknowledging the sources of his inspiration for the defence of hesychasm, Gregory Palamas cites not only previous generations of scholars but also contemporary ascetics and holy men who were known to him personally and from whom he had received first-hand instruction.[29] For him the living oral tradition was no less important than the ancient written record. Bishop Kallistos concludes:

There is no evidence that Palamas had ever met Maximos or even knew of his existence, and yet with good reason he might have included the Kapsokalyvite among the contemporary authorities to whom he appealed. Much more than an eccentric or an extremist, Maximos of Kapsokalyvia is a true witness to tradition—to that continuing tradition of living, experiential theology which today, as in the fourteenth century, constitutes the inner reality of the Holy Mountain of Athos.[30]

ARTISTS AND MUSICIANS

Most of the Byzantine art that survives on Athos dates from the Palaiologan period (1261–1453). Most of what was done in the earlier centuries, especially in the form of fresco, was either covered over by later artists or destroyed. Isolated examples of earlier art survive. In mosaic there are the eleventh-century representations of the Annunciation high up on the piers of the katholikon at Vatopedi and a Deesis (a representation of Christ between the Virgin and St John the Baptist), better preserved and easier to see, over the entrance to the narthex; at Xenophontos there are two mosaic icons dating from the eleventh and twelfth centuries, and one of the Virgin at Chilandar from the twelfth century. In fresco nearly everything has been painted over, though superb examples of what lies underneath have recently been revealed in the katholikon at Vatopedi; otherwise there are fragments from the decoration of the old refectory at Vatopedi and a few examples of apostles in the kellion of Rabdouchou. There are more, but still not many, icons that date from the early centuries; the best of them at the Protaton, Megiste Lavra, and Vatopedi. Legend would have us believe that there are many more, but most of them can be shown by other criteria to date from later periods.

Byzantine artists did not usually sign their work and as a result very few are known to us by name. The exception is Manuel Panselinos, an artist of the front rank from Thessaloniki who worked on Athos in the late thirteenth and early fourteenth centuries. Dionysios of Phourna, a monk, painter and writer whose *Painter's Manual* (written on Athos in about 1730–4) presents a paradigm of Byzantine iconography, acknowledges Panselinos as the source of his inspiration in the prologue to his treatise:

> I urged myself to increase the slight talent that the Lord had given me, that is to say the little art that I possess, which I learnt from my youth, studying hard to copy as far as I was able, the master of Thessalonica, Manuel Panselinos, who was compared with the brilliance of the moon; this painter, having worked on the Holy Mountain of Athos, painting holy icons and beautiful churches, shone in his profession of painting so that his brilliance exceeded that of the moon, and he obscured with his miraculous art all painters, both ancient and modern, as is shown most clearly by the walls and panels that were painted with images by

37 St Phokas, a fresco of 1312, recently uncovered beneath a layer of
eighteenth–century overpainting, in the katholikon of Vatopedi.

38 The paintings in the nave of the katholikon at Vatopedi, dating from 1312, are arranged in three bands. In the top band are scenes from the life of Christ (here in the north choir the lamentation at the tomb); in the second band are scenes from the life of the Virgin (here the presentation in the Temple); in the lowest band full-length portraits of saints and further scenes (here Christ explaining the meaning of the washing of the disciples' feet).

him; and anyone who participates to some extent in painting will understand this very clearly when he looks at them and examines them carefully.[31]

Panselinos's greatest monument is the decoration of the church of the Protaton in Karyes, a building which, as we have already noted, dates from the first half of the tenth century and is the only basilica on Athos. There is evidence on the south wall to suggest that by the end of the thirteenth century the building was in a ruinous condition. At this time it was rebuilt on the more usual cross-in-square plan at ground level, though the upper levels retain the form of a timber-roofed basilica. After this reconstruction Panselinos was invited to paint the walls following the usual iconographic programme. The paintings belong to what is known as the Macedonian

Ο Α ΙΩ ΘΕΟ
ΛΟΓΟ

Ο Α ΓΡΌΧΟΡΟC

39 'In the beginning was the Word.' St John dictates the opening words of his Gospel to his disciple Prochoros, a fresco in the church of the Protaton painted by Manuel Panselinos c.1300.

School of painting, other examples of which may be seen in the churches at Ohrid, Prizren, Studenica and Staro Nagoricino. Nothing else on Athos, except for a fragment from the Lavra, appears to be by the master's hand, but there are works by other painters of the Macedonian School at Vatopedi and Chilandar. The paintings in the Protaton are arranged in four horizontal bands. The top and bottom bands are occupied by full-length depictions of saints—warrior saints and martyrs, prophets and ascetics—while the central bands contain scenes from the life of Christ and the Virgin in a continuous frieze, together with depictions of the four evangelists which would in a domed church fill the pendentives. The striking realism of the figures portrayed—the serene expressions of the youthful martyrs, the intense spirituality of the ancient ascetics—the brightness of colour and the elegance of drapery are features that distinguish these paintings from the more linear traditions of Byzantine art and have led many commentators to draw comparisons with the contemporary work of Giotto. All are agreed that they are masterpieces in their own right and that together they represent the most important example of Byzantine art of this period.

40 The Virgin Hodegetria, an icon of *c*.1260–70 from Chilandar. The Virgin's sad gaze is thought to foreshadow the future events of Christ's Passion.

41 The Presentation of the Virgin is the patronal feast of Chilandar. In this early fourteenth-century icon the Virgin's parents Joachim and Anne present the diminutive Mary to the priest Zacharias.

42 Right: Christ Pantokrator, an icon of *c.*1360 from Vatopedi. It was originally one of a group of icons that graced the iconostasis in the monastery's katholikon.

Three other examples of work of the Macedonian School survive on Athos, though they are probably not by the hand of the master himself. The first is the outer narthex of the katholikon at Vatopedi, where the original painting dates from 1312, though some of it has been covered by later work. The excellent state of preservation and recent cleaning of these frescos give an idea of what may yet be achieved at the Protaton when the projected con-

43 A mosaic icon of the Crucifixion from Vatopedi, *c.*1300. The crucified Christ is flanked by the Mother of God and St John. The icon's silver frame, contemporary with the icon itself, illustrates the twelve great feasts of the Church's year

44 The Annunciation, an icon of *c*.1400 from Vatopedi. 'Do not be afraid, Mary, for you have found favour with God' (Luke 1: 30).

45 St John Koukouzeles, maestro of Athonite music in the late thirteenth and early fourteenth centuries. From the fly-leaf of Iviron cod. 1250, *c*.1670.

46–49 Minor Art of the Palaiologan period. Above is the so-called Pulcheria Paten from the monastery of Xeropotamou, fourteenth century. The iconography, carved in green steatite, represents the Divine Liturgy, but the association with the empress Pulcheria (fifth century) is fanciful.

47 The cover of a gospel book from the monastery of Dionysiou, c.1400. The enamel panel depicting the Crucifixion is a western import from Limoges.

48 The cross of the empress Helena, wife of Emperor Manuel II Palaiologos, from the monastery of Dionysiou, fifteenth century. The silver decoration in high and low relief depicts (on the front) the Crucifixion and (on the back) Christ standing beside the Jordan.

49 A wooden lectern from the monastery of Vatopedi, fifteenth century. The 24 carved
panels depict scenes from the Akathist Hymn sung to the Virgin during Lent. Vatopedi has
two such lecterns, rare survivals of Byzantine woodcarving.

servation programme is eventually put into effect. The second example is the katholikon at Chilandar, where a complete programme was painted in about 1320, though much of it was unfortunately overpainted in the nineteenth century. The third example is to be found in the tiny chapel of St Basil on the Sea, a fortified cell which was once an independent monastery but became a dependency of Chilandar in the fifteenth century. Here the figures of Christ the Saviour and the Virgin Hodegetria either side of the iconostasis are clearly reminiscent of other work of the Macedonian School; since their recent cleaning they have been securely dated to the second quarter of the fourteenth century.[32]

Other frescos of the Palaiologan period are to be found in the katholikon of the monastery of Pantokrator, dating from the time of the foundation around 1360, and also in the chapel of the Agioi Anargyroi at Vatopedi and the chapel of the Archangels at Chilandar, though these have been mostly overpainted. Worthy of special mention, however, is the portrait of St Gregory Palamas standing beside St John Chrysostom in the Vatopedi chapel. Here the overpainting has been removed to reveal a figure that was painted in 1371, just three years after Gregory's canonization and twelve years after his death, which makes this the next best thing to a contemporary portrait. The inscription is particularly revealing of the regard in which he was held by the monastery: 'The most holy Archbishop of Thessaloniki Gregorios and New Chrysostom the Wonder-Worker'.

The portable icons of the Palaiologan period form a particularly important collection, though many of them are as yet unpublished.[33] Icons are among the things most revered and most treasured by the monks: often they are associated with stories of the monastery's foundation; some are regarded as miracle-working, others are linked with imperial donations made in Byzantine times. The fact that they are portable makes them particularly vulnerable, though it also makes them easier to conceal when the monastery is under attack. It also means that they can be imported from elsewhere and many are of a quality to lead one to suspect that they derive from major studios in centres such as Constantinople and Thessaloniki. Especially notable are the sequences of apostles at Chilandar and Vatopedi, and the mosaic icons such as the St Nicholas at Stavronikita, the Crucifixion at Vatopedi, and the St John the Evangelist at the Lavra, which may be the work of Panselinos himself. But if one were to single out just one icon for special mention it might be the Annunciation at Vatopedi, which dates from the late fourteenth or early fifteenth century and occupies a prominent place in the katholikon of that monastery whose patronal feast it is. It attracted the attention of iconographer Efthymios Tsigaridas, who regards it as truly representative of the finest productions of the Palaiologan period. He compares it, in terms of physiognomy and style, with the Hospitality of Abraham (an icon of the Trinity also belonging to

Vatopedi) and above all with the icon of the same subject (dated 1425–7) by the Russian artist Rublev. He concludes:

> To sum up, it is our opinion that the high artistic quality of the icon, with its slender figures, the idealised faces, this aristocratic tone and the delicacy of the painting put it among the masterpieces of the aesthetics, associated with the court, of the Late Palaeologue period and, more specifically, at the turn of the 14th to the 15th century. On the other hand, the close artistic connection which we have noted between the icon of the Annunciation and the icon of the Holy Trinity by Rubliev indicates the models which influenced the artistic development of this great Russian artist of the first quarter of the 15th century.[34]

The visual arts are the aspects of the Palaiologan renaissance that are most obvious to the Athonite pilgrim because they are all around him and strike the eye with an awesome impact. But equally striking, for those who stop to listen, is the impact on the ear during services in the katholikon. If St John of Damascus is regarded as the father of Byzantine liturgical music, then St John Koukouzeles is justifiably honoured as its 'second source'. Tonsured a monk of the Great Lavra early in the fourteenth century, Koukouzeles was enormously influential in his capacity as a maistor, composer, hymnographer, scribe, editor, teacher, and theorist of music. He (and others around him) cultivated a distinct personal style in his compositions of multiple settings of psalms and hymns, writing in a new 'beautified' or 'kalophonic' style which called for virtuoso rendering of melismatic passages and vocalizations on nonsense syllables ('teretisms'). Although he did not invent the style, which had existed for half a century or more before his time, he brought it to maturity and was responsible for its subsequent wide dissemination. His work established the stylistic parameters for Greek Orthodox chant, echoes of which are still to be heard every day in the churches and chapels of the monasteries of Mount Athos. As the musicologist Grigorios T. Stathis has written,

> The chants of the Athonite fathers, from the simplest and unsophisticated of falterings to the highly artistic and kalophonic compositions, take flight on wings of fear and longing from the thirst for God. They aspire to make contact with supracelestial spheres, those so distant but at the same time so near, under the painted domes of the Byzantine churches, both great and small, on the Holy Mountain. These chants, which are the most suitable medium for the beauty of and for preparation for the worship of God, are treasures . . .[35]

No less treasured are the gold-embroidered ornaments, the exquisite miniature works of art, enkolpia (pendants worn 'on the breast') in jewelled frames, reliquaries and sacred vessels of silver and gold, painted enamels, ivory book covers, and illuminated manuscripts, so many of which date from the spectacular cultural flowering that coincided with the total disin-

50 A chalice, known as the 'Jasper', from the monastery of Vatopedi, second half of the fourteenth century. The cup is carved from a single piece of jasper; the base and handles are gilded silver relief work. The decoration combines elements of Gothic and late Byzantine inspiration.

tegration of the Byzantine state. Every monastery has a treasury bursting with such priceless items. The doors are kept locked lest the contents take the fancy of the ungodly as they did so often in the past. It is impossible to imagine the sumptuous splendour that the monasteries would have presented to a fourteenth-century pilgrim's eyes and ears, but thankfully enough of it survives for us to appreciate what a debt is owed to this last great Byzantine renaissance. Athos, no less than Constantinople, was at the heart of it.

Decline and Fall: the Idiorrhythmic Movement and the Union of Churches (again)

Today every ruling monastery on the Holy Mountain is a coenobium in which monks lead a common life following the traditions of Stoudite monasticism as brought to Athos in the tenth century by St Athanasios. But as recently as the 1960s no fewer than nine of the twenty monasteries were still following the idiorrhythmic way of life according to which individual monks were allowed to set their own pattern, were not bound by the vow of poverty or the vow of obedience to an abbot, and lived in separate apartments, often with their own servants and their own worldly goods, neither eating together nor contributing to a common purse. This apparent denial of all the monastic norms in a monastic context was essentially a phenomenon of the Tourkokratia and it will feature more largely in the next chapter, but it had its origins in the Byzantine period and must therefore be given some space here.

Numerous factors played a part in bringing about this fundamental change in the interpretation of the monastic way of life which by the end of the seventeenth century had overtaken not only every monastery on Athos but many others elsewhere in the Orthodox world. Humanism (i.e. scholarship that was independent of the authority of the Church) was obviously one of them. Dangerously liberal new ideas were being promoted by intellectuals in Constantinople and even more so in the Byzantine satellite state of Mistra in the Peloponnese. These were the intellectual descendants of those who had supported Barlaam in the hesychast controversy of the first half of the fourteenth century. Now they gathered at the feet of the philosopher Gemistos Plethon (*c.*1360–1452), who had taught in Constantinople until about 1410 when he was banished by the emperor Manuel II Palaiologos for corrupting the young with his ideas. These ideas were based on a revived Platonism that had no room for the Christian religion. He preached a form of ancient paganism and expounded his unorthodox views on religion in a book *On the Laws* of which only fragments survive. After his death the text of this unpublished work was sent to Constantinople, where it was examined by George Scholarios, now the Patriarch Gennadios.

> The Patriarch [writes Steven Runciman], as he read the pages in which God was usually called Zeus and the Trinity consisted of a supra-essential Creator, the Mind of the world and the Soul of the world, and maybe in which doctrines more shocking still were aired, decided, rather reluctantly but not surprisingly, that the manuscript must be burnt.[36]

We have no evidence of intellectual exchange between Mistra and Athos, though contact there certainly was. The famous jasper cup which is still one of the most prized treasures of Vatopedi was a gift to the monastery from Manuel Kantakouzenos, despot of the Morea from 1349 to 1380. Plethon himself ultimately had more lasting influence in Italy than in his native land, but at all events the intellectual climate of the day encouraged a desire among men for more personal freedom and this no doubt had some impact on the minds of the better-educated monks. Other factors that had some bearing no doubt included the political instability of the empire, the unbridled increase in the wealth of the monasteries, and the emergence of an 'aristocracy' among the monks that gradually began to assume some of the powers and privileges traditionally reserved to the abbot.

The patriarchate was not slow to condemn the first signs of idiorrhythmic practices. In a letter of April 1396 Patriarch Anthony advised the abbot of Pantokrator to set an example to his monks by living a godly and ascetic life; he reminded the monks of their duty to obey their abbot and to follow the cenobitic rule in every detail, adding: 'Any monk who owns any article or property (movable or immovable) in accordance with idiorrhythmic practice, will at the Last Judgement be condemned as an unrighteous man who has disgraced the Church.' His advice seems to have been ignored. In June 1406 the emperor Manuel II Palaiologos felt obliged to intervene with another *typikon*, published in the form of a chrysobull.[37]

This fourth *typikon* contains the usual reminders about beardless youths and female animals ('no monk should ever be defiled by the sight of any female creature'). Monks are reminded of their vows, to renounce everything to God and to obey their superior. Monks are forbidden to move from one monastery to another, to leave Athos, and to join societies with laymen. Each monastery is to be governed by its abbot, assisted by a council of fifteen elders. Gifts of precious items must be placed in the sanctuary; gifts of food must be handed to the refectory. The secretary is to keep accounts of all expenditure. Farms and estates are to be managed by monks selected by the abbot and his elders who, if they allow themselves to be influenced by partiality or greed, will cause discontent, the ruin of the monastery and the loss of souls. No monk who has any private property at the time of his being professed is to be accorded any privilege on this account. Even if he objects to this rule, or if he wishes to follow the idiorrhythmic way of life, a monk can never demand the return of things that he has dedicated to God. Nevertheless, a monk who enjoys an income from his private property may do so for life but on his death he must leave it to his monastery. This is already the custom at the Lavra and the emperor sanctions the practice, even though he believes it to contravene the ideals of monasticism and of the cenobitic way of life.

Thus did idiorrhythmic practices receive imperial sanction, albeit grudgingly. The emperor could scarcely do anything else without incurring the charge of hypocrisy, for the monks were acting largely in self-defence. Since 1371, after the Ottoman defeat of the Serbs and conquest of Macedonia, the empire had lost so much of its territory that the monasteries actually controlled more land than the emperor. In order to counteract this intolerable situation and obtain some land with which to reward the army, Manuel, who at the time was still despot of Thessaloniki, risked the enmity of the monks and of the Church and shamelessly confiscated half of the monasteries' estates. The monks now found themselves stripped of their many immunities and liable to pay tax on their estates and produce in order to provide funds for the defence of the empire. It is scarcely surpising that fifteen years later they willingly submitted to the sultan. They still had to pay tax on their remaining estates, but at least their ownership of them was not threatened. And this was the same Manuel who in 1404 dared to tell them to remember their vows of poverty and obedience. Who can blame them for wanting to safeguard their property by whatever means seemed appropriate to them? Ironically Manuel himself died as a monk in 1425.

By now the reprieve granted to Byzantium by the Mongols had ended and the Turks were once again threatening the survival of the empire. As we have seen, the Athonites had already bowed to the inevitable and acknowledged their allegiance to the sultan at Adrianople in 1424. The new emperor John VIII Palaiologos (1425–48) was prepared to clutch at any straw in order to hold on to his throne. The historian George Sphrantzes (1401–77/8), who had been in the service of the emperor Manuel and who wrote a history of his own times down to the year 1477, records a conversation that he overheard between Manuel and his son, the future emperor John, in which the older man offers his son some wise thoughts on the subject of the union of churches:

The infidels are very worried that we might unite and come to agreement with the Christians of the west; for they sense that if this occurred it would be very harmful to their own interests. Therefore my advice with regard to the holding of a council is this: go on studying and investigating the project as long as you can, especially when you have need of something to frighten the Turks. But do not really try to put it into practice; for in my opinion our people are not in the frame of mind to discover a way of uniting with the Latins or to put themselves out to create an atmosphere of peace, concord and mutual understanding, unless it were through the hope that the Latins would revert to the position in which we all found ourselves originally. But this is a virtual impossibility; and I fear that if we are not careful a worse schism may come about and then we shall be left defenceless before the infidel.[38]

Unfortunately John did not heed this advice. In 1438–9, in a last-ditch attempt to save the empire from destruction, John himself participated in the Council of Ferrara-Florence, together with a delegation of monks from the Holy Mountain. Though the basic issues were not properly resolved, the act of union was eventually signed by the pope Eugenius IV and the emperor John on 6 July 1439. Among the other signatories were priest-monk Moses, the official representative of the Lavra, and priest-monk Dorotheos, the official representative of Vatopedi. Needless to say, the 'peace' that had been signed in Florence provoked storms in the Orthodox world. The Church in Constantinople officially repudiated the terms of the union shortly after the fall of the empire in 1453. Meanwhile the majority of the Athonites, who were already the sultan's subjects, declared themselves to be the 'Champions of the Faith of our Fathers' and knuckled down to Ottoman rule.

5
OTTOMAN ATHOS

Unlike the Byzantines, who had been ruling the eastern half of the Roman empire for more than 1100 years, the Ottomans were new-comers to empire. Originally a Turcoman tribe from Central Asia, they had been pushed westwards into Anatolia by the advancing Mongols. Here they took over from the disintegrating Seljuk state and by the early fourteenth century had established themselves in the north-west corner of Anatolia. Their progress was rapid: they took Brusa in 1326 and made it their capital; five years later they captured Nicaea, formerly capital of the Byzantine empire in exile; in 1354 they won their first toehold in Europe, at Gallipoli. Having defeated the southern Serbs at Marica in 1371, they made further advances into the Balkans and consolidated their gains with a crushing vic-tory over the Serbs and Bosnians at Kosovo in 1389. By now all that remained of Byzantium, apart from the satellite states of Mistra and Trebizond, was the area immediately surrounding the city of Constantinople, to which the Ottomans laid siege in 1396. A Mongol attack on Ankara in 1402 distracted the assailants, giving the Byzantines their last half-century of freedom before the final capture of the city in 1453.

But the Ottomans did not stop there. There was to be further dramatic expansion in the first half of the sixteenth century: Syria and Palestine were conquered in 1516, Egypt in 1517, rapidly followed by the rest of North Africa. In 1534 they took Mesopotamia, in 1543 Hungary, and soon they were also masters of the Arabian peninsula. In an amazingly short space of time the Ottoman state had become one of the most powerful in the world. The secret of their success was their military expertise, fired by religious zeal. Bolstered by their devotion to Islam and their loyalty to the sultan they were practically invincible. Having conquered this vast swathe of territory they then had to find a means of governing it.

The secret of the Byzantines' survival had been diplomacy. They were pastmasters at creating alliances and setting their enemies against one another, and these strategies accounted for the empire's survival during its last two centuries. As subjects of the sultan they would now need all their diplomatic skills to retain their cultural identity.

The Sultan and the Patriarch

The Ottomans had to come to terms with the fact that the vast majority of their newly conquered subjects were adherents of another religion, Orthodox Christianity. And the Orthodox Byzantines were as deeply devoted to their faith as were the Muslim Ottomans to theirs. The highly organized Orthodox Church, with its hierarchy of parish priests serving area bishops serving metropolitans serving patriarchs, might have presented a serious obstacle to the smooth administration of the empire if the Church had been antagonized.

However, it had long been the practice for Muslim rulers to treat Christian minorities within their realm as *milets*, or nations, allowing them to govern themselves and maintain their own customs and religious practices under the supervision of their own religious hierarchy, which in turn ensured allegiance to the supreme power of the Caliph. When Mehmet II took Constantinople he found the patriarchal throne vacant since the abdication of Gregory Mammas in 1451 when he fled to Italy. The sultan looked for a suitable candidate and hit upon George Scholarios, now known as the monk Gennadios, who had been the leader of the anti-unionist party and was therefore deeply respected by the Orthodox for his piety as well as his learning. Gennadios was enthroned in January 1454 and was presented with the insignia of his office by the sultan who pronounced these words: 'Be Patriarch, with good fortune, and be assured of our friendship, keeping all the privileges that the Patriarchs before you enjoyed.' After his consecration in the Church of the Holy Apostles (Hagia Sophia having already been converted into a mosque) the new patriarch rode in procession around the city, mounted on a fine horse which the sultan had given him together with a generous gift of gold.[1]

The terms of the partnership between the sultan and the patriarch seem not to have been committed to writing. But according to the historian Sphrantzes, the patriarch received guarantees of his own personal inviolability, immunity from taxation, freedom of movement, security from deposition, and the right to confer these privileges on his successors. The patriarch, together with the Holy Synod, was to have authority over the entire ecclesiastical establishment, over all bishops, all churches, all monasteries and their possessions, and also over all matters of dogma. But in addition to his control of the Church, a similar authority over the Orthodox laity was also vested in the patriarch. He was responsible for the maintenance of law and order, for the collection of taxes, and the administration of justice. The patriarch himself continued to be elected officially by the Holy Synod, and his election was then confirmed by the sultan, as before it had been by the emperor. The officers of the Church retained the titles that they had borne in Byzantine times, but their responsibilities were enhanced. Metropolitans and bishops were similarly charged with the administration of justice in the provinces.[2] As Ottoman rule expanded during the sixteenth century, the empire acquired dominion over the patriarchates of Alexandria, Antioch and Jerusalem. The traditional rights and privileges of these patriarchs were confirmed, but in practice they were subservient to the patriarchate of Constantinople. The same was true of the Slav Churches of the Balkans which were incorporated into the Ottoman empire.

The powers granted to the patriarch by the sultan, which went far beyond those he had enjoyed under the Byzantines, ensured the integrity of the Orthodox *milet*. The patriarch had in effect regained control over all the territory that had once been Byzantine, territory which was now once again united and, within the limits imposed by the Ottoman state, was permitted to govern its own affairs and flourish. The unionists, who would have subjected the Orthodox Church to Roman supremacy in order to retain no more than a fragment of imperial territory, were confounded. As Steven Runciman has written, 'the integrity of the Church had been preserved, and with it the integrity of the Greek people.' But he goes on to point out the risks involved in this new dispensation:

51 The monastery of Stavronikita from the south-east. 'I appointed an abbot there and made good arrangement that there should be a cenobitic monastery', wrote the founder, Patriarch Jeremiah I, in his Will.

52 Overleaf: Stavronikita from the west. The aqueduct was built in the seventeenth century at the expense of the Phanariot prince of Wallachia, Sherban Cantacuzino (1679–88).

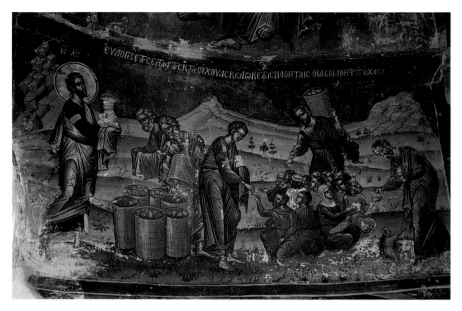

53 The Feeding of the Five Thousand, a fresco in the refectory of Stavronikita, painted in 1546 by a monk known as Theophanes the Cretan, one of the principal representatives of the post-Byzantine Cretan School of painting.

The Byzantine Empire had been, in theory at least, oecumenical, the holy Empire of all Christians, regardless of their race. Its decline had reduced it to an empire of the Greeks; and the Orthodox *milet* organized by the new constitution was essentially a Greek *milet*. Its task as the Greeks saw it was to preserve Hellenism. But could Hellenism be combined with oecumenicity? Could the Patriarch be Patriarch of the Orthodox Slavs and the Orthodox Arabs as well as of the Greeks? Would there not inevitably be a narrowing of his vision? The events of the following centuries were to show how difficult these problems were to be.[3]

THE SULTAN AND THE MONKS

The Athonites, like the Byzantines, were skilled diplomats. They had anticipated the collapse of the empire and ensured their own survival by making overtures to the Ottomans, first in 1383 before the fall of Thessaloniki and again in 1424 before the fall of Constantinople. By so doing they saved not only their lives but their property, their political autonomy and their religious freedom. They had to pay tribute, but then they had been taxed by the Byzantines too, and we have seen that their estates were not immune from confiscation by the tottering imperial regime. The very year the city fell to the Ottomans, the Athonites sent a delegation to Sultan Mehmet II, who

54 The Annunciation, painted in 1546 by Theophanes the Cretan on the doors to the sanctuary in the katholikon of Stavronikita. The same artist, assisted by his son Symeon, painted a complete cycle of icons to decorate the entire iconostasis of the church.

55 The Transfiguration, an icon from the monastery of Stavronikita attributed to
Theophanes the Cretan, 1535–45. Examples of his work are also to be found in the
monasteries of the Meteora.

agreed to protect their rights and safeguard their independence.[4] But how
did the new dispensation with the patriarchate affect the monks?

It had not escaped the notice of the Ottomans that the Athonite
monasteries were among the richest and most powerful institutions in the
ecclesiastical establishment of the empire they had now acquired. They were
conscious of the high regard in which the monks were held in Byzantine
society and of the extent to which the monasteries operated as centres of
intellectual and spiritual excellence. As in their dealings with the patriarchate,
the Ottomans saw fit to tread lightly. An early violation had occurred in 1433,
when Sultan Murad had laid hands on the monasteries' ships and other property, but the monks had managed to buy them back. After that, at least until

56 The Ladder of St John Klimakos, a sixteenth-century icon from the monastery of Pantokrator. The idea of the spiritual ladder which monks must climb to reach heaven was devised by St John of Sinai, Abbot of St Catherine's monastery. Various scenes connected with Mount Sinai are depicted on the left side of the icon.

the second half of the sixteenth century, the monks enjoyed the active support of successive sultans, who went out of their way to protect them from exploitation by officials and tax collectors and to preserve their independence. It has even been suggested that the Ottomans may have been in awe of the monks' supernatural powers and the efficacy of their prayers. One document states: 'Athos is a place where the name of God is invoked continuously. It is a place of refuge for the poor and homeless.'⁵ Athonite support was considered essential to the success of a candidate for elevation to the patriarchate.

An indication of the continuing prosperity of the Mountain is the foundation of another monastery, Stavronikita, in 1541. The last of the twenty ruling monasteries, it was established by the Ecumenical Patriarch Jeremiah I. He endowed it with his own money and is portrayed as the founder on the wall paintings of the katholikon, which were done in 1546 by the renowned artist Theophanes the Cretan and his son Symeon. Despite this early prosperity, Stavronikita has since remained the smallest and poorest of all the ruling monasteries.⁶

There was a more serious violation of the Mountain in 1568, when Sultan Selim II attempted to confiscate all ecclesiastical and monastic estates throughout the empire. With generous support from the rulers of Moldavia and Wallachia together with loans at extortionate rates of interest from the moneylenders of Thessaloniki, the Athonites were once again able to buy back their property. From then on their estates were regarded as *waqf*, which gave them a charitable status and made them theoretically inalienable. But this did not mean an end to assaults on the property of the monks, and as time went on, these grew more intense and more destructive.

A further encroachment on the autonomy of the Athonites was the introduction in 1575 of a Turkish aga or governor who resided in Karyes as the sultan's representative. Condemned to temporary celibacy, he was expected to keep order with the assistance of a small garrison; it was not a sought-after posting and did not attract applicants of the highest calibre.

IDIORRHYTHMIC RULE AND THE *TYPIKON* OF 1573

We have already remarked on the change to the idiorrhythmic way of life that had begun to affect the monasteries before the end of the Byzantine period. The change was a gradual one, and it did not take place unopposed. The reduction in the term of office of an abbot from life to just one year had weakened the role of the abbot and the cenobitic system as a whole. It was a short step to the election of a pair of elders who took office for a year and administered the monastery by committee. Following the relaxation of other rules, monks were now permitted to retain possession of their private property, to receive remuneration for their labour, and to prepare their own meals. It was still possible to lead a life of considerable austerity according to the idiorrhythmic system, as many did, but the changes seem more often than not to have led to a relaxation of moral and spiritual standards and so to have provoked a response among adherents of the traditional cenobitic way of life.

These traditionalists included a monk called Pachomios, who in the sixteenth century wrote a pamphlet attacking the idiorrhythmic practices of his fellow monks.[7] Pachomios recognized three categories of monks: eremitic, cenobitic and idiorrhythmic; the last he branded as 'half-monks' and likened them to women who disobey their husbands and seek divorce. He rebuked them for repudiating their vows of poverty and obedience and for indulging in luxury and ostentatious forms of dress. Successive patriarchs also chastized the monks for abandoning the laws and traditions of cenobitic monasticism and encouraged them to return to the Stoudite rule as proclaimed by St Athanasios and to adhere to the old *typika*. In 1498 Patriarch Joachim I threatened the hegoumenoi and their monks with divine retribution if they did not abandon their careless and idle ways and return to the cenobitic rule.[8] Such was the state of degradation by the second half of the sixteenth century, when the monasteries were seriously in debt, monks were indulging in commercial activities outside the Mountain, beardless youths were to be found in the monasteries, cows in the fields, nuns in the *metochia* and scandal was rife, that there were even protests from among the Athonites.

As Patriarch Jeremiah II was passing through Thessaloniki at Christmas 1573, he was met by a delegation of hegoumenoi who asked him to intervene to save the Mountain from the spread of wanton practices that threatened to destroy it. Jeremiah invited Patriarch Sylvester of Alexandria to institute an inquiry and draft a new *typikon* in consultation with the Protos, the bishop of Ierissos, and the hegoumenoi. The resulting document was ratified by Jeremiah in September 1574.[9] Among its requirements were that monks were to live a communal life, in peace and harmony, according to God's commandments; youths were banned from entering Athos; domestic animals other than male animals needed by the monasteries were to be driven off the peninsula; monks were forbidden to distil and drink raki ('the source of every evil'); nuns were not allowed to live in cells and farms off the Mountain, even as 'spiritual sisters' of the monks; monks were not to gossip about their neighbours. Also prohibited were the forging of business documents, the sowing of wheat and barley, the export of nuts for sale, and dealing in monastic clothing for profit. The fact that these misdeeds were specified means of course that they were all being practised.

The principal purpose of this *typikon*, the Mountain's fifth, was to check the spread of the idiorrhythmic system and to raise standards of morality on the Mountain. In that the Lavra and Vatopedi reverted temporarily to the cenobitic rule the *typikon* may be said to have achieved some limited success. But by the end of the sixteenth century every monastery was idiorrhythmic and remained so until the late eighteenth century. It is conceivable that monasticism might not otherwise have survived at all, since the idiorrhythmic system allowed individual monks greater freedom of action and helped the monasteries to cope with the changing economic climate. We may conclude that it was a necessary evil.

The Emergence of the Sketes

The earliest surviving sketes on Athos were founded in the second half of the sixteenth century as a result of the monasteries' adoption of the idiorrhythmic system. The word skete (deriving from *asketerion*, a settlement of ascetics) was not new and had been used in Egyptian contexts (as the equivalent of *lavra*) as early as the fourth century and in Athonite documents from the fourteenth century. These idiorrhythmic sketes (which are to be distinguished from the cenobitic sketes which developed later and were a Slav phenomenon) take the form of a monastic village, a group of huts or small houses gathered around a central church (or *kyriakon*). They are very similar to the ancient Egyptian or Judaean lavras except that each of them is dependent on a ruling monastery. Their founders sought to establish settlements where it would be easier to practise a truly ascetic life than in the monasteries, where standards of asceticism were often falling as a result of the adoption of the idiorrhythmic way of life.

Each skete is ruled by a prior (*dikaios*) who is usually a priest, by two or three counsellors, and by an assembly of elders. The prior is elected by the

57 St Anne's skete from the south. The terrain is very steep in this part of the peninsula but there is enough water to make terraced cultivation possible.

elders and holds office for one year. The counsellors are elected at the same time, but half of them are appointed by the skete's ruling monastery. Each house (or *kalyva*) in the skete is ruled by an elder who is responsible for the rhythm of that house, which may contain between two and five other monks. In most cases they live by a very strict rule of life.

The first such monastic village to be established was St Anne's, a dependency of the Lavra founded in the third quarter of the sixteenth century.[10] The present church was built in 1680, when the skete was enlarged by Patriarch Dionysios III. Its chief treasures are a miracle-working icon of St Anne and a relic of the saint's left foot. It has about fifty houses. St Anne's is near the southern point of the peninsula where the terrain is at its steepest, near the so-called desert of Athos. This has always been the area most favoured by ascetics and anchorites searching for complete isolation from the world.

Not far from St Anne's is another skete, Kafsokalyvia, which occupies a steep and narrow ravine cut out of the southern face of the mountain itself. Its name (which means 'burnt huts') derives from the activities of the hermit Maximos, who lived a nomadic existence in this area in the fourteenth century when there were only a few huts there.[11] Towards the end of the seventeenth century another ascetic, by the name of Akakios, took up residence

58 The Romanian skete of Lakkou ('of the Ravine') lies on the east-facing slopes of the Mountain, though it is a dependency of St Paul's monastery to the west.

in what had once been Maximos's cave. Akakios was famous for the austerity of his life: he rarely slept and he lived on a diet of herbs mixed with crushed stones, he breathed fire when he prayed, and he had prophetic powers. Gradually other ascetics came to live around him and so the skete was established. In 1725, when the Russian pilgrim Vasily Barsky visited him in his cave, Akakios was the best-known ascetic on the Mountain. Three of his disciples died as martyrs.[12] Another dependency of the Lavra, this skete has long been famous for its woodcarving.

There are two other surviving sketes in this southern part of the peninsula, both of them founded in the eighteenth century as dependencies of St Paul's monastery. The skete of the Theotokos, otherwise known as New Skete, lies on the west coast to the north of St Anne's; here some thirty huts cluster around an ancient tower. The other is the skete of St Demetrios of the Ravine, or Lakkou for short. This skete was founded in 1760 by two monks from Neamt monastery in Moldavia and has always been reserved for Romanians. It lies high up on the east-facing slopes of the Mountain in a verdant valley which leads steeply down to the lonely tower of the Amalfitan monastery.

Elsewhere on the Mountain there are four other surviving idiorrhythmic sketes: that of St Demetrios, which is a dependency of Vatopedi; the skete

59 The central church (*kyriakon*) of the Romanian skete of Lakkou has a grand marble
iconostasis reminiscent of that at St Paul's.

of the Prodromos (or St John the Baptist), which belongs to Iviron; that of St Panteleimon, which belongs to Koutloumousiou; and the skete of the Annunciation, which is a dependency of Xenophontos.[13] Apart from St Demetrios, which has recently been deserted, all still operate as monastic villages where monks have the opportunity to live in greater seclusion than in the monasteries, in more intimate groups, often as disciples of a charismatic elder. Many of them are located in inhospitable parts of the Mountain and often the monks resort to handicrafts in order to support themselves.

EXTERNAL SUPPORT FOR THE MOUNTAIN

As early as the fourteenth century, as we have earlier remarked (p. 78–81), the monastery of Koutloumousiou was supported by the rulers of the Danubian principalities of Moldavia and Wallachia. As the Tourkokratia wore on, several other monasteries found themselves in difficulties for one reason or another: in addition to general wear and tear, fire and earthquake were recurrent hazards, and monastic buildings often fell into disrepair as a result. Now that there was no longer a Christian emperor in Constantinople, the monks had to look elsewhere for sources of support. The Danubian principalities were nominally part of the Ottoman empire but they enjoyed a large measure of self-government. Their rulers were Orthodox Christians with substantial resources at their disposal who were proud of their Byzantine culture and, as the only self-governing Orthodox rulers in southeast Europe, were keen to support the faith throughout the Balkans. They were especially sympathetic to the plight of the Athonites, but monasteries in Bulgaria and Serbia were also recipients of their generosity.

Consider, for example, the history of Simonopetra in the second half of the sixteenth century.[14] In about 1566 the Great Postelnik at the court of Wallachia, Gheorma, and his wife Caplea gave Simonopetra the newly built monastery of St Nicholas in the Palcov suburb of Bucharest. This was an immensely well-endowed monastery, but it was on a poor site described as 'pestilent and wholly marshy'. This problem was overcome by a young nobleman who on a neighbouring hill built

> another *metochi*, greatly superior . . . and another church, decorous and prominent, in the name of the great Nicholas, and having ascribed this *metochi* to the venerable monastery of Simonopetra, he built kellia around it in great number . . . and further dedicated both sacred vessels and silver and gold decoration of every kind; moreover, he added to these things villages, together with their serfs . . .[15]

Meanwhile, on Athos, the port building (*arsanas*) of Simonopetra was completed in the year 1567 and, according to the surviving inscription, was paid

60 The Presentation of the Virgin in the Temple, an embroidery in coloured silks from the monastery of Grigoriou, *c.*1500. This is Moldavian work and is the gift of Stefan the Great of Moldavia who is commemorated as one of the 'founders' (i.e. major benefactors) of the monastery.

for by 'the most worshipful lord Oxiotis Agas', who was an official at the court of the ruler of Wallachia. When in 1580 the monastery itself was totally destroyed by fire, the surviving monks moved temporarily to Xenophontos. They were back home by 1586, but vast sums were still need-

61 St Nephon II, Patriarch of Contantinople (1486–9 and 1497–8), and Voivode Neagoe Basarab, Prince of Wallachia (1512–21), a sixteenth-century icon from the monastery of Dionysiou. St Nephon was the spiritual father of Neagoe as well as being a monk of the monastery which Neagoe supported by building its tower and aqueduct.

ed to complete the rebuilding of the monastery, and for this purpose the abbot Evgenios travelled to Wallachia and remained there from 1587 to 1592. By good fortune his visit coincided with that of the Patriarch Jeremiah II, who was passing through Wallachia on his way back from Russia. The patriarch was therefore able to give his seal of approval to the gift of the new *metochi* of St Nicholas, which together with the property and land of the old one had just been donated to Simonopetra. The donor was Michael, shortly to become prince of Wallachia (1593–1601), who is known to both Greeks and Romanians as Michael the Brave.

The monastery of Xenophontos, which agreed to accommodate the monks of Simonopetra after the fire of 1580, owes a similar debt to the rulers of Wallachia, without whose support it might not have survived the sixteenth century.[16] Two seventeenth-century documents, of the princes Matthew Basarab (1635) and Mihnea III Radu (1658), give a tally of their predecessors' benefactions to the monastery. Estates in Wallachia were first given in the early decades of the sixteenth century, followed by an annual cash subsidy. The wall paintings of the old katholikon (1544) and its narthex (1563) were carried out at the expense of the princes of Wallachia. In 1607 Prince Radu-Serban provided further generous subsidies, in return for which he was to be commemorated in perpetuity as a 'new founder' of the monastery. In the course of the seventeenth century a good deal of building work and decoration of the monastery was carried out and its fortifications were strengthened, all thanks to the generosity of the Danubian rulers. Matthew Basarab, prince of Wallachia (1632–54), and his wife Eleni are depicted in the wall paintings of the exonarthex of the katholikon as 'founders', holding a model of the church which had evidently been restored at their expense.

Nearly every monastery acknowledges a similar debt to the rulers of the Danubian principalities.[17] But they were not the only ones to help the Athonites to survive the demise of the Byzantine empire. The monks of Iviron, for example, turned to the Orthodox princes of Georgia, with whom that monastery had always maintained close links.[18] With their support the defences of the monastery were strengthened, the walls were repaired, a tower was built complete with a cannon, the katholikon was restored, a hospital was provided, and the miracle-working icon of the Portaïtissa was given a new revetment. In the mid-seventeenth century a copy of this same icon, which is the monastery's most valued treasure, was taken to Moscow at the request of Tsar Alexios, whose daughter was grievously ill. The girl recovered and her grateful father presented Iviron with the wealthy monastery of St Nicholas in the heart of Moscow. A century earlier Tsar Ivan IV Vasilyevich ('the Terrible') had made generous gifts to the monasteries of Chilandar and Vatopedi. Monks from these monasteries were given permission to make regular visits to Russia and raise funds from the faithful. Meanwhile, the Russian monastery of St Panteleimon, which had begun to receive Russian novices again after the withdrawal of the Mongols in 1497, was in such a bad state by 1591 that Tsar Fyodor Ivanovich issued a chrysobull to Abbot Gregory of Chilandar charging him with the responsibility of restoring the Roussikon.[19] Serbian bishops, priests and laymen supported Chilandar with gifts of money and chattels. But the deterioration of the Roussikon was not arrested for long: on his first visit to the monastery in 1725 the Russian pilgrim Barsky found just four monks, two Russians and two Bulgarians; on his second, in 1744, he recorded that the monastery was now in Greek hands, that it was idiorrhythmic and that its buildings were in serious disrepair.[20] He found Russian monks 'wandering hither and thither about the hills, living by manual labour, eating scraps and being despised by all'. He felt sorry for them, 'for foxes have holes and birds their nests, but the Russians have nowhere to lay their heads', but he suggested that they had only their laziness to blame: 'for in Russia, where all labour is carried out by dedicated Christians, the monks live in great ease and comfort.'[21]

62 Right: The port building (*arsanas*) of the monastery of Simonopetra. The tower was completed in 1567 at the expense of yet another prince of Wallachia.

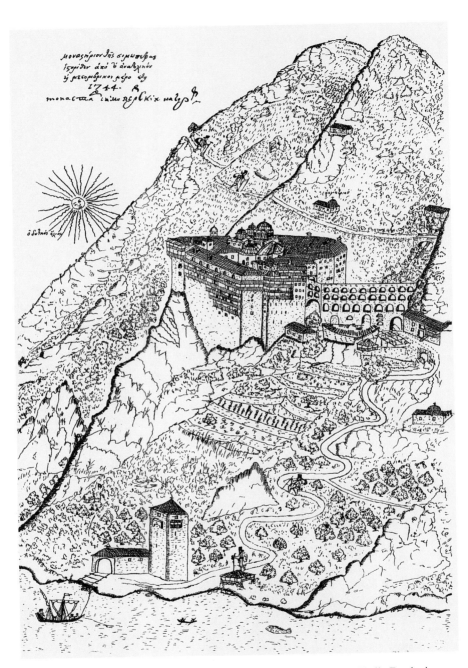

63 The monastery of Simonopetra as depicted by the Russian pilgrim Vasily Barsky in 1744 on his second visit to the Mountain. Barsky's drawings are valued especially for the accuracy of their architectural detail in an age before photography.

DESTITUTION AND DECAY IN THE SEVENTEENTH CENTURY

Thanks to the remarkable generosity of the other Orthodox nations, and particularly the rulers of the Danubian principalities of Moldavia and Wallachia, and not forgetting the single donations of individual pilgrims, most monasteries managed to preserve at least a façade of prosperity for most of the sixteenth century. By 1600, however, the Ottomans had begun to tighten their grip and every monastery started to feel the pinch. The tax burden had by now become intolerable, and while initially some of the richer monasteries were able to help some of the poorer ones, in 1661 every monastery was ordered to pay its own way. Few could afford to do so; most succumbed to a spiral of debt which took the best part of two centuries to pay off and several were reduced to such extremity that they were driven to borrow from the Jews of Thessaloniki, who charged extortionate rates of interest. Barsky reports that by the early eighteenth century the monks of Xenophontos owed 15,000 *leva*, mostly to the Jews, and that they had been forced to pawn their sacred vessels as surety for their debt. As a result many had left the monastery and no more than three or four Slav-speaking monks remained to care for the place.

Meanwhile, troubles in the Danubian principalities prevented the monks from drawing income from their properties there and made it harder for the rulers to send money. Barsky found Simonopetra in an even worse position than Xenophontos. On his first visit, in 1725, he reported finding a fair number of monks; but by 1744 he writes:

> the monastery was in a state of considerable confusion because of its great poverty and its debts, which exceeded 50,000 *leva*. For this reason its creditors seized many valuable items as pledges. Of the monks, being unable to pay the Turks the intolerable taxes, some departed to other, richer monasteries, while others roamed in the world in search of alms. There were only five of them left there.[22]

By 1762, according to a document in the archives, a Serb spiritual father arrived with a brotherhood of 35 monks, intending to take over the monastery and care for it. But this he was unable to do: 'rather he left it and departed to Moldavia; and on his departure the monastery was closed up and the Great Mese had authority over it.'[23] In fact this 'Serb' was the famous Russian elder St Paisy Velichkovsky, who in 1757 had founded the skete of the Prophet Elijah. After his departure the Holy Community sold several of the monastery's *metochia* to pay off its debts, but in 1765 it bought them back and started to function again as a monastery.

Economic hardship came from a variety of quarters: the Ottomans raised their taxes further in order to pay for the costly war in Crete (1645–69); the Venetians were still masters of the seas and could impose an additional levy on the monasteries, and the monks suffered constantly from pirate raids that went unchecked because of the war. Some of the bigger monasteries, such as Vatopedi, Iviron and Chilandar, were strong enough to ride out the economic storm. But the Lavra was reduced to five or six monks by 1623, all of them living in abject poverty, and the Protaton had its share of troubles too. The position of the Protos had become increasingly weak until it was eventually abolished around 1662. At the same time the lavra of the Protaton was forced to close because of the bankruptcy of its cells. From now on, the administration of the Mountain was vested in the Holy Community, which consisted, as now, of twenty elders, each of whom was elected to serve for a year as the representative of his monastery. The representatives of the first four monasteries in the hierarchy—Lavra, Vatopedi, Iviron and Chilandar—formed a permanent executive committee known as the Holy Epistasia which dealt with most everyday business. Plenary sessions of all twenty members were only convened when matters of great moment were scheduled for discussion.

Hard on the heels of economic decline followed intellectual decline and even to some extent spiritual decline, though standards of asceticism were maintained and vows were strictly observed despite the apparent laxity of the idiorrhythmic system. Libraries were the most conspicuous casualties. Few acquisitions were made and most collections were totally neglected. Thousands of manuscripts were sold off to collectors from western countries, often for trifling sums; many were given away to Orthodox benefactors and other dignitaries; others were simply left to rot. Librarians, if they existed at all, were utterly ignorant of their responsibilities; others took advantage of the situation for their personal profit.

Senior monks were aware of the problem. The Society of Jesus, founded in 1540, had established schools at various points in the Ottoman empire, and those in Constantinople were particularly successful. On a visit to Rome in 1628 Ignatios, abbot of Vatopedi, proposed that such a school be established on Athos for the training of monks, and in 1635 a school was duly opened in Karyes. But the Ottomans were alarmed by the introduction of western ideas on the Mountain and forced the school to move to Thessaloniki in 1641, where it soon closed.[24]

THE SEEDS OF RENEWAL

For practical purposes, in the seventeenth century Athonite scholarship was dead. But not quite. There were always a number of monks, particularly in the larger monasteries such as Vatopedi and Iviron, who maintained a tradition of learning. The hermit Agapios Landos, who lived in a cave at the settlement of Little St Anne, was notably prolific. He was the author of many works of hagiography and moral theology of which the most popular, entitled *The Salvation of Sinners*, was first published in Venice in 1641 and is still read today. Better known is the eighteenth-century writer Constantine Dapontis (1714–84), who was tonsured as monk Kaisarios and joined the monastery of Xeropotamou in 1757. He was immediately sent on a mission to Moldavia, Wallachia and Constantinople with two other monks to raise funds for the restoration of the buildings which were in serious disrepair. By their return in 1765 they had enough money to rebuild the monastery. Kaisarios devoted the remainder of his life to writing and produced a large number of popular works in both prose and verse including the *Garden of the Graces* (repr. Paris, 1891), which carries an idyllic description of life on the Holy Mountain.

> You are tired of your cell? Go out and take a walk through all the many beauties of the wilderness. Go to the fountain; go to the shore; it is full of fairness, a great joy to behold. Go to the caves; go to the cells of the hermits of old, divine palaces . . . You see a mountain? A field? Marvel at the wisdom of the Creator and at His almighty power. Through woods and groves you walk; ravines and valleys; think upon the holy men of old and make yourself like them.[25]

Other works of Kaisarios include a chronicle of the Balkan wars of his time (*Dacian Ephemerides*) and a geographical history of the world (unpublished). His style is light and humorous, not quite what one would expect of a monk, though there is no doubt of his serious devotion to Athos, this 'paradise of delight' as he calls it. Not dissimilar is the work of another monk, Cyril of the Great Lavra (d. 1809), who wrote a *Description of Russia* and an *Ecclesiastical and Political History*; he also compiled a book of prayers for his monastery and was the first to attempt to put its archives in order.

Such writers did not necessarily advance the cause of scholarship. Their aims were more modest, though it could be said that their collective achievement was infinitely more important, for they served to keep alive the traditions of Hellenism in the dark age of the mid-Tourkokratia. As long as men continued to write in Greek, to retell the stories on the ancient world, to elucidate the mysteries of Orthodoxy for the benefit of their contemporaries, or just to describe the pattern of everyday events, then there was a chance that the culture of the Greeks would survive and one day be revived. Without such writers, and without the real efforts made by the monks of the Holy Mountain, there is a strong likelihood that Hellenism would have perished and the movement for independence never have been born.

As the eighteenth century progressed, Athos grew increasingly receptive to intellectual and spiritual currents from the outside world. From the early years of the century monks had gone out into the world to preach and teach among their fellow countrymen. Some worked in schools, others in parishes and dioceses. Wherever they went, they assumed positions of leadership and helped to maintain the pride of the Greeks in their cultural and spiritual heritage. At the same time they came into contact with intellectual movements from the west and by the mid-eighteenth century they had begun to bring back aspects of the new secular learning to Athos. The foundation of the Athonite Academy in 1749 is a striking demonstration of what must have been a more general trend.

THE ATHONITE ACADEMY AND EVGENIOS VOULGARIS

By 1748, when Cyril V came to the patriarchal throne, the school on Patmos, which had been a great centre of Orthodox education, was in decline and there was a need for a new school to provide religious and philosophical education for the Orthodox subjects of the sultan. But it was the initiative of Vatopedi, which under its prohegoumenos Meletios was then the leading monastery on the Holy Mountain, that led to its foundation on Athos. The patriarch and the Holy Synod gave their blessing to the enterprise and imposing buildings were duly erected at the monastery's expense on high ground overlooking the bay of Vatopedi. The school was intended to become the principal centre for higher education for all Greek-speaking people and its first director was the monk Neophytos of Kafsokalyvia. But in 1753 the patriarch appointed the eminent scholar Evgenios Voulgaris (1716–1806) to succeed him and provide instruction in Greek and Latin literature, rhetoric, philosophy and mathematics as well as theology, logic and ethics. The school was to operate as a fully fledged university, open not only to the monks of Vatopedi but to all Athonites who had the blessing of their hegoumenos, and to any Orthodox priest or layman who wished to study there; according to its charter the school was to provide 'a complete course of classical learning'. It was, in short, to be a vehicle for the revival of Hellenism.[26]

To all appearances, Voulgaris was a brilliant appointment. Born in Corfu and ordained a deacon, he had studied in Ioannina and at the university of Padua, where he had acquired a knowledge of Latin, Italian and French. In the 1740s he had taught in Ioannina and Kozani and gained a great reputation as both a theologian and a philosopher. But he was a controversial figure and his lectures, which introduced the ideas of such western thinkers as Descartes, Leibniz and Locke into the study of the ancient philosophers, aroused a good deal of opposition in conservative circles in Ioannina. Notwithstanding his reputation, this was the man chosen by the patriarch to head his academy for the revival of Hellenism in the heart of ultra-conservative Athos.

Initially the confidence of the patriarch in his appointee was shown to be well placed. Numbers attending the school leapt from twenty to 200 during the six years of Voulgaris's tenure (1753–9). Students came not only from

64 The ruins of the Athonite Academy overlooking the monastery of Vatopedi. Though its success was short-lived, it represents a serious attempt by the monks to restore their spiritual and intellectual well-being in difficult times.

neighbouring parts of the Ottoman empire but from Italy and Russia, drawn by the reputation of the school's flamboyant director, by the thirst for knowledge that marked the eighteenth century in general, and no doubt also by the attractive location of this new academy. They included Athanasios Parios, Iosipos Moisiodax and Kosmas the Aetolian, all of whom would earn high reputations as scholars. In a letter to a colleague in Constantinople in 1756 Voulgaris writes enthusiastically about the progress of the academy and its delightful situation. Of the subjects taught he mentions Homer, Herodotus, Thucydides, Demosthenes, Plato and Aristotle among the ancients and 'the French, the Germans and the English' among the moderns (presumably a reference to Descartes, Leibniz, Wolff and Locke). There is no mention of religious instruction. More basic teaching of subjects such as grammar was provided by Neophytos, who stayed on for a while after ceasing to be director, and Panayiotis Palamas.

As had happened in Ioannina, Voulgaris's teaching soon attracted opposition. This was not because he was disrespectful of Athonite traditions: he was an admirer of hesychastic theology and he himself received a miraculous cure from a serious illness from the Virgin of the Akathist in 1758. Opposition came in the first instance from the monks, most of whom regarded the teaching at the academy as novel, dangerous and incompatible with their own monastic traditions. They saw the new syllabus as an attack on Orthodoxy, the very system of belief they were pledged to defend. Opposition also came from Voulgaris's students, the followers of Panayiotis Palamas, who took exception to his philosophical teaching. The trouble had started as early as 1756, when Voulgaris appealed to his patron, Patriarch Cyril, for help 'for we are greatly storm-tossed and all but lost'. The next year the patriarch himself was unseated and retired to Athos, where he proceeded to meddle in the affairs of the academy. Having been the patron of Voulgaris, Cyril now became his most vigorous opponent and succeeded in setting everyone on the Mountain against him. Assailed on all fronts, by colleagues, students and even the former patriarch, Voulgaris had no alternative but to resign, which he did with some bitterness in January 1759. Leaving Athos shortly afterwards, he fled to Constantinople and resumed teaching there.

For practical purposes this was the end of the academy. A successor was appointed, Nikolaos Zerzoulis, a Newtonian philosopher from Metsovo, but his teaching was no more acceptable than was his predecessor's and following the deposition of his patron, Patriarch Seraphim II, in 1761, Zerzoulis returned to Metsovo. The remaining students followed Voulgaris to Constantinople and the Athonite Academy was closed. Visiting his *alma mater* in 1765, Iosipos Moisiodax referred to it as a 'nest of crows'.[27]

Various abortive attempts were made to revive the school. An effort by the former patriarch Seraphim II in 1769 was rejected by the monks of Vatopedi. In 1782 the school was re-endowed by Patriarch Gabriel IV; Kaisarios Dapontes reports that it was operating in the 1780s and there are references in the archives of the Protaton to the 'school at Vatopedi' in the 1790s. A major initiative in 1800 from Patriarch Kallinikos V received support from communities throughout the Greek-speaking world including those of the diaspora and even from Adamantios Korais in Paris, the greatest scholar of the Greek enlightenment. Though no particular friend of the Holy Mountain, Korais proudly announced the foundation of 'a university on Athos' as proof of the final triumph of civilization over barbarism in Greece.[28] But despite the best efforts of so many, nothing came of this initiative; the school closed for the last time in 1809; its buildings were soon engulfed in flames fanned, if not lit, by the hands of vengeful monks determined that what they saw as a satanic den of free-thinking secularism and atheistic doctrine should never again open its doors on Athos. Its ruins, clearly visible from Vatopedi, still pose the question of what might have happened if the regime had moderated its stance and the monks had been able to tolerate the existence in their midst of an institution which promised to be the intellectual and spiritual centre of the entire Greek world.

The Kollyvades Movement and the *Philokalia*

Despite their rejection of the opportunity to become the intellectual leaders of the Greek world, the monks retained their obsessive devotion to all aspects of their faith and what they regarded as its correct practice. Throughout the Tourkokratia they remained ardent adherents of the hesychastic tradition. But a new dispute arose on Athos in the second half of the eighteenth century which threatened to divide the Orthodox world in much the same way as hesychasm had in the fourteenth. This focused on whether it was lawful to hold memorial services not only on Saturdays, as was traditional, but on other days too; it was later widened to include other questions such as how often holy communion should be taken, and out of the dispute there grew a widely influential movement for religious conservatism and the preservation of Hellenic identity.[29]

Kollyva is a cake made of boiled wheat mixed with flour, herbs, nuts and raisins and coated with sugar. During the Divine Liturgy it is blessed as an offering with which to commemorate the dead or a saint and thus it acquires a symbolic and sacred quality through which it represents the resurrection of the body. In Athonite monasteries it is consumed by the monks either at the end of the Liturgy or, more often, at the end of the meal in the refectory. Traditionally this rite had been observed only on Saturday, the day on

65 An eighteenth-century icon depicting all the principal Athonite fathers, from the Protaton in Karyes. The icon (and the feast associated with it) was the brainchild of St Nikodimos of the Holy Mountain, one of the leaders of the Kollyvades movement.

which special prayers are said for the deceased. But Saturday was incon-venient for a variety of reasons: many monks needed to attend the weekly market in Karyes and in the world laymen were only free to attend church on Sunday. There was therefore a move to allow memorial services to take place on Sunday. This change was vigorously opposed by traditionalists, who were given the name *Kollyvades* to indicate their association with the consumption of *kollyva* and the commemoration of the dead on Saturday, keeping Sunday as a day of rejoicing. The dispute lasted for seventy years and was only resolved by a council held at Constantinople in 1819. Meanwhile the ecumenical patriarch was forced to intervene on several occasions to urge the monks to live in peace.

After one such intervention, in 1776, the leaders of the movement at the time, Athanasios Parios, Makarios Notaras and Nikodimos of the Holy Mountain, left Mount Athos and began to spread their ideas in other parts of Greece. Their chief concern was to bring about a return to the authen-tic fonts of Orthodox tradition and their motives were twofold: first, to counteract the spiritual decline that was evident not only in the Athonite monasteries but elsewhere in Greece too, and secondly to prevent their compatriots from falling under the influence of the western Enlightenment sweeping through Europe. They believed that the only way to regenerate the Greek people was not by adopting the secular ideas about nationalism currently fashionable in the west but by returning to the roots of the Orthodox faith and rediscovering their liturgical traditions and patristic theology.

Among the leaders of the movement it was Athanasios Parios, former pupil of Evgenios Voulgaris, who became the most bitter opponent of the Enlightenment. He wrote numerous attacks on the French Revolution and the ideas it spawned and urged his fellow Orthodox to keep as far away as possible from western Europe if they wished for salvation. His supporters also tried to prevent the teaching of western ideas in Greek schools.

But without doubt the greatest achievement and most influential product of the Kollyvades movement was the publication by Makarios Notaras and Nikodimos of the Holy Mountain of the *Philokalia* (Venice, 1782), a vast anthology of ascetic and mystical texts ranging in date from the fourth to the fifteenth century and running to over 1200 folio pages. The work focuses in particular on the theory and practice of prayer from the heart and was aimed at the Orthodox laity in the world as well as monks. Nikodimos issues a gen-eral invitation to the reader in his preface with these enticing words:

> Draw near, all of you who share the Orthodox calling, laity and monks alike, who are eager to discover the kingdom of God that is within you, the treasure hidden in the field of the heart, which is the sweet Lord Jesus. Released from enslavement to things below and from the wanderings of your intellect, your heart cleansed from the passions through the awesome and unceasing invocation

of our Lord Jesus and through all the other interconnected virtues that are taught in this present book, you can in this way be united within yourselves and also with God, as the Lord said in His prayer to the Father: 'May they be one as we are one.'[30]

The initial impact of the *Philokalia* was limited and it was not reissued in Greek for more than a century. But a Slavonic translation, published in Moscow in 1793, made a significant contribution to the nineteenth-century revival of spirituality in Russia and more recently it has attracted wide attention not only among the Greeks but among western readers too. To quote its most recent translator into English, 'the *Philokalia* has acted as a spiritual "time bomb", for the true "age of the *Philokalia*" has not been the late eighteenth but the late twentieth century.'[31]

The Kollyvades would no doubt today be labelled 'fundamentalists' and clear links may be traced from them to the modern movement for Orthodox fundamentalism. But they were none the worse for that. They had identified a serious flaw in the spiritual life of their contemporary Athonites and they were genuinely concerned to preserve the purity of their common Hellenic culture uncontaminated by ideas emanating from the west. They were not unsuccessful in their attempts to counter what they saw as the unacceptable tendencies of their time. They produced (among other editions of patristic texts) a monument of mystical wisdom in the *Philokalia*. Not for nothing was Nikodimos dubbed 'an encyclopedia of the Athonite learning of his time'.[32] Their ideas were ultimately sanctioned by the council held at Constantinople in 1819, and all three of the most prominent figures were subsequently canonized.

St Kosmas the Aetolian and the New Martyrs

Another Athonite defender of the faith in the eighteenth century was St Kosmas the Aetolian, though most of his work was conducted off the Mountain. Born near Arta in 1714, he became a student at the Athonite Academy and then served for twelve years as a priest-monk at the monastery of Philotheou. But he could never forget the sufferings of his fellow countrymen under the Turkish yoke and, realizing that his vocation was to minister directly to them, he applied for permission to leave the monastery and become an itinerant preacher. In this capacity he travelled throughout Greece, preaching in demotic Greek and drawing vast crowds. He placed equal importance on the Orthodox faith and the Greek language as the bastions of Hellenic identity, and he established schools to teach both wherever he went. 'My beloved children in Christ,' he said, 'bravely and fearlessly preserve our holy faith and the language of our Fathers, because both of these characterize our most beloved homeland, and without them our nation is destroyed.'[33] In addition to preaching the usual Christian virtues of repentance and forgiveness, prayer and fasting, humility and love, the saint transmitted the Athonite practice of the Jesus Prayer to the common people. He also predicted the liberation of Greece within three generations of his own, and although he gained admirers across religious divides, he inevitably aroused the suspicion of the Turkish authorities. While travelling in southern Albania he was seized by agents of the local governor and hanged on 24 August 1779. 'Thus', his disciple and biographer Sapphiros Christodoulidis wrote, 'the thrice-blessed Cosmas, that great benefactor of men, became worthy of receiving, at the age of sixty-five, a double crown from the Lord, one as a Peer of the Apostles and the other as a holy Martyr.'[34]

St Kosmas inspired a whole school of itinerant preachers who brought about a spiritual revival among the Greek people that sustained them in their coming fight for national independence. Though not formally canonized until 1961, he has long been revered as one of the so-called 'New Martyrs of the Turkish Yoke'. The term Neomartyr had been in use since the eighth century, when it referred to those who were persecuted for their Orthodox beliefs regarding the veneration of icons; more recently it has been used in Russia of those who suffered under communist rule for their Orthodox faith. During the Tourkokratia such martyrdoms more often than not occurred as a direct result of forced conversion to Islam and many apostates went to Athos to recant. Athelstan Riley tells the story of St Agathangelos:

> The other relics [in the katholikon at Esphigmenou] . . . are the head of St Agathangelos, who won the crown of martyrdom in Smyrna about the commencement of the present century. Agathangelos had apostasized in his childhood, but at the age of nineteen, overcome by remorse, he fled to Mount Athos and embraced the monastic life in Esphigmenou. Here he devoted himself to penance for his fall and adopted the Great or Angelic Habit. But all his mortifications were powerless to assuage his deep remorse, and finally, being warned of God in a dream that he should seal his contrition with his blood, he resolved to return to Smyrna, where he had formerly denied his Master, and then openly publish his return to Christianity. He went, accompanied by a priest, whom his convent sent to comfort him in his last hour with the Holy Sacraments, for all knew that he was going to certain death. Standing before the governor of Smyrna, he announced his rejection of the Mohammedan religion and declared that he would die in the faith of the Crucified One. For days the furious infidels employed every means to turn him from his purpose, but in vain; and finally he suffered death by decapitation.[35]

In such circumstances penitents were strongly discouraged by their spiritual fathers from seeking martyrdom, but for the unfortunate few there appeared to be no other way of regaining their lost identity. The Church did not keep an official register of Neomartyrs, but St Nikodimos of the Holy Mountain made a collection of Lives which was published in Venice in 1799 as the *New Martyrologion*. His main purpose in compiling it was to stem the tide of apostasy by encouraging his readers, as he wrote in the Preface, 'to burn from divine love, so that they also in turn may be ready to endure the martyrdom for Christ'.[36]

ATHONITE REFORM AND THE GREEK REVOLUTION

During the eighteenth century many of the monasteries had fallen into debt, and some into considerable disrepair too. There was a clear disparity between the five most senior monasteries (Lavra, Vatopedi, Iviron, Chilandar and Dionysiou), which prospered thanks largely to Romanian support and had assumed control of the whole Mountain, and the rest, which grew steadily poorer, weaker, and more depleted in numbers. Patriarch Gabriel IV (1780–5) saw the need for reform and in 1783 he published a new *typikon*, the sixth, which made the government of Athos more democratic and reorganized the central administration into the form that still exists today.[37]

The centrepiece of his legislation was the reform of the Holy Epistasia, a permanent committee of four, elected annually on 1 June from the Holy Community and responsible for executing the decisions taken by that body. In order to select them, the twenty monasteries were divided into five groups of four; the groups rotated and each monastery would be represented on the Epistasia every fifth year. The dominance of the five senior monasteries survived to the extent that one of them was included in each group of four and its representative normally chaired the meetings of the committee. The members of the Epistasia were housed in a single dwelling in Karyes. They were provided with a secretary who took minutes of their meetings and kept accounts. They held office for a year, at the end of which period they must submit accounts to the Holy Community for the approval of the patriarch. A new seal was made for the Holy Community and the Holy Epistasia, divided into four parts. Each member of the Epistasia held one part of the seal; and every edict of the Holy Community or the Epistasia was to be stamped by the whole seal to indicate the agreement of all four members. If they failed to agree, they had to refer the matter to the Holy Community, and if there was still no agreement the matter was then referred to the Great Church in Constantinople.

The Holy Community was to be the central governing body of the Mountain. It consisted of the twenty representatives of the twenty ruling monasteries, each of them elected to serve for one year. In special cases a

matter of supreme importance affecting the whole of Athos would be referred to a double *synaxis* of the twenty representatives and the twenty hegoumenoi.

In order to relieve the burden of debt, the new *typikon* required all the monasteries to come to the assistance of any house that found itself in serious and unexpected difficulties. And any individual monks who had assets available for investment (a state of affairs that could only obtain in an idiorrhythmic community) were directed to lend them to the monasteries at an agreed low rate of interest. This ruling suggests that not only was there great finanacial disparity between the monasteries but also between individual monks and that this was cause for resentment. Finally, the number of shops in Karyes had become unacceptable, giving the place a worldly and commercial air, and their number was to be restricted to four.

As a result of Gabriel's reforms several monasteries reverted to the cenobitic rule: Xenophontos in 1784, Esphigmenou in 1797, Konstamonitou in 1799, Simonopetra in 1801, St Panteleimonos in 1803, Dionysiou in 1805, Karakalou in 1813. Subsequently St Paul's ceased to be idiorrhythmic in 1839, Grigoriou in 1840, Zographou in 1849, and Koutloumousiou in 1856. After that there were no further changes until the latter half of the twentieth century, when all remaining idiorrhythmic houses became coenobia. Other signs of revival in the first two decades of the nineteenth century included the paying off of debts, the restoration of the monasteries' build-

66 Left: Edward Lear, *The Monastery of Karakalou.* Lear spent three weeks on Athos in 1856 and made drawings of all the monasteries. He was inspired by the scenery and the buildings but did not appreciate the monastic atmosphere.

67 A nineteenth-century silver and gilt incense casket in the shape of a church from the monastery of Dionysiou. The exuberance of the decoration is symptomatic of the spirit of euphoria and optimism that prevailed in the mid-nineteenth century.

ings, the repopulation of the sketes, and the revitalization of many cells. All the monasteries prospered and all enjoyed an income from their extensive estates in other parts of Macedonia, Thrace, Asia Minor, the Aegean islands, the Danubian provinces, Georgia and Russia.

This revival in the fortunes of Athos was temporarily interrupted by the Greek War of Independence, which broke out in 1821. The monks were divided as to how they should respond to the call to arms. Many of the younger ones, perhaps influenced by agents of the revolutionary Friendly Society (Philiki Hetairia), were in favour of supporting it: they saw it as their Christian duty to enlist; both the peninsula and the monasteries were easy to defend, the Greeks had command of the sea and the Turkish aga in Karyes was unpopular. Many of the older monks urged caution: the monasteries had mostly been well treated by the Turks and their privileges had been respected; the security of the Mountain would be put at risk if they joined the rebellion, whereas nothing would be lost if they remained neutral.[38] Their wise counsels were overruled.

In the event the hegoumenoi of the most belligerent monasteries, Lavra, Vatopedi, Iviron and Chilandar, agreed to support the revolt and a large number of monks joined the rebels in Macedonia. They were defeated and withdrew to defend the isthmus, but they disagreed among themselves and abandoned their position. A few monasteries prepared for armed resistance, but most did not, and the Mountain voluntarily submitted to the Turks. A Turkish garrison of 3000 troops entered the peninsula unopposed and proceeded to occupy all the monasteries. The Holy Community confirmed the unconditional surrender of the whole Mountain to the sultan, but it was too late to escape punishment. The occupying force remained until the war ended in 1830; severe fines were imposed on the monasteries, and much looting took place. As a result large numbers of monks left the Mountain, including most of the younger ones, and between 1821 and 1826 the population fell from 2980 to 590. Many of those who left took away manuscripts and other treasures. This at least saved them from depredation by the Turks and many were recovered after the end of hostilities.[39]

The events of the 1820s dealt a serious blow to the monasteries and represent one of the darkest periods in their history. They were to remain subject to the Ottoman empire for a further eighty years or more. But they received some support from the newly independent Greek state, and after 1830 their fortunes began to recover with remarkable speed.

THE RETURN OF THE RUSSIANS

There were exceptions to this trend. When St Panteleimonos, the Russian monastery, became a coenobium in 1803 it had been entirely Greek for eighty years. This remained the case even after the Greek War of Independence, and by 1835 the monastery was bankrupt. The Greek monks, under their abbot Gerasimos, decided that the only course of action open to them was to invite the Russians, described by the itinerant Russian Athonite monk Parfeny Aggeev as 'the ancient inhabitants of this house', to return.[40]

There had been Russians on the Holy Mountain probably since the eleventh century, though before the nineteenth century their numbers had never exceeded a few hundred. Their first monastery, Bogoroditsa Xylourgou (now the skete of Bogoroditsa), lay south-east of Vatopedi and was founded about 1030. In 1169 they were permitted to occupy the monastery of St Panteleimonos, then located at a considerable distance inland from its present site. Little is known of its early history and it seems that the monastery's links with Russia were broken during the Mongol period. Before the end of the fifteenth century they were restored and in 1561 there were said to be an abbot, fifteen priests, seven deacons and a total of 170 brethren in residence.[41] But for most of the next two centuries

68 Right: The *kyriakon* (central church) of the Prophet Elijah skete, a massive and sumptuous structure typical of late nineteenth- and early twentieth-century Russian work on Athos. The iconostasis alone cost 17,000 roubles to build.

69 Overleaf: The katholikon of the monastery of St Panteleimonos, built between 1812 and 1821 when it was a Greek house. Russian monks arrived from 1839 onwards and the interior of the church was later frescoed in the Russian style.

the story is one of poverty and decline and of Russians frequently being in the minority. We have already noted that when Barsky visited in 1744 he found that the monastery was now in Greek hands and its buildings in a state of disrepair. In 1765 these already dilapidated buildings were destroyed by fire and the monks moved to a new site by the sea. Even though it contained no Russians at the time, the monastery continued to be known as the 'Roussikon'.

By the start of the nineteenth century the financial position of St Panteleimonos was giving cause for concern and it came close to being closed down by the Holy Community. This was the moment when Iviron ceased to be a Georgian monastery. In 1801, after Georgia signed its unification treaty with Russia, the Georgian monarchy was no longer able to provide the monastery with the necessary spiritual and financial protection to maintain its Georgian status and it became a Greek house.[42] The Roussikon came close to suffering the same fate but it was rescued by a member of the wealthy Kallimachis family, which had supported the monastery since the sixteenth century and now provided funds to keep it afloat and for a new katholikon to be built. In 1821 most of the brotherhood left the Mountain (apparently for the Peloponnese) and their benefactor was beheaded by the Turks. Those who returned after 1830 were faced with a serious financial crisis.

The only sizeable community of Russians that existed on Athos in the early nineteenth century was the brotherhood at the Prophet Elijah skete. As noted above, this community was founded in 1757 by St Paisy Velichkovsky, a learned Russian monk who did much to revive the traditions of hesychasm on the Mountain. Though originally a hermit, St Paisy acquired numerous disciples and was held in equally high regard by both Greek and Slav monks as an elder. The house became the first cenobitic skete on Athos and within five years it contained sixty monks. In 1798 it was given 540 acres of woodland by its parent monastery, Pantokrator, an unusually large area of land to be owned by a skete and indicative of the good relations that then obtained between the two, and its numbers grew rapidly. After 1821 they dispersed and in 1830 a handful returned to find the place in considerable disarray. A decade of instability followed and in 1839 the skete was deprived of its lands, but its existence was confirmed by a declaration of the Holy Community and its fortunes swiftly revived after the installation of Prior Paisy II (1841–71).

A first attempt to attract a Russian brotherhood to the monastery of St Panteleimonos failed. But in 1839, when an internal dispute in the Prophet Elijah skete resulted in the expulsion of a group of Great Russians led by the deposed prior Fr Pavel, the Greeks of the Roussikon were quick to invite them to join their monastery. This they did and the Greeks welcomed them as saviours, for Russians had a reputation for great wealth at the time. By chance, only two years earlier a wealthy Russian abbot had arrived on Athos

70 St Panteleimonos from the west. Its buildings, many of which are now ruinous, cover a vast area and at the start of the twentieth century accommodated nearly 1500 monks.

and announced his intention to purchase an impoverished Greek monastery and Russify it. He failed, but his tactless remark not only gave the Great Russians a bad name but sowed the seeds of future discord between Greeks and Russians on Athos. Meanwhile Abbot Gerasimos of St Panteleimonos ordered the Greeks and the Russians to follow the cenobitic rule and perform their monastic duties together; he assigned the latter their own living quarters and their own places of worship. 'The monastery was thus physically divided', writes Nicholas Fennell.

> Gerasimos was also undermining his own authority by appointing Pavel as father-confessor and *de facto* leader of the Russians. Above all, the Russians were vastly more wealthy than their impoverished brethren . . . In the short term, the Russians' wealth saved the monastery from debt and decay. But riches and the monastic life do not go together; and when the well-off live in close proximity with the poor, envy, greed and pride are bound to flourish.[43]

From now on the Russians at St Panteleimonos went from strength to strength. As a result of missions to Russia the monastery became rich and famous, and large numbers of Russian pilgrims visited the Holy Mountain. In 1845 Grand Duke Konstantin Nikolaevich, a son of Tsar Nicholas I, vis-

71 The skete of St Andrew from the air, looking south-east. Its church, consecrated in 1900, was the largest in the Balkans after the Alexander Nevsky Cathedral in Sofia.

ited the monastery, to be followed in 1867 by Grand Duke Aleksey Aleksandrovich, son of Tsar Alexander II. Meanwhile in 1860 there had been an outrageous attempt to Russify the monastery of Koutloumousiou. Senior members of the Holy Community were bribed, the doors of the monastery broken down and the abbot was expelled by force. The anarchy was only brought to an end and order restored by the intervention of an Ottoman official. The fact that the declaration of Romanian independence in 1859 and the confiscation of Athonite properties on the Danube had deprived the monasteries of one of their most important sources of funding served to increase the influence of the Russians and of the monasteries and sketes that they supported.

The changes at St Andrew's in Karyes should also be recorded in this context. In 1841 it was a small cell inhabited by a handful of monks and dependent on Vatopedi when two Russian monks arrived. Soon they were joined by others; and in 1845 Grand Duke Konstantin Nikolaevich came to lay the foundation stone of a new church. At the same time he tried to have the cell recognized as a cenobitic skete, but this move was blocked by the Greeks in the Holy Community. A similar attempt in 1849, supported by generous donations to the Holy Community, the Holy Epistasia and the monastery of Vatopedi, was successful and Patriarch Anthimos VI not only proclaimed it a cenobitic skete but gave it stavropegic status (i.e. directly dependent on the patriarchate, even though it remained a dependency of Vatopedi) and conferred on its prior Theodorit the title of hegoumenos (hitherto reserved for abbots of the ruling monasteries). The new skete now had a higher status not only than the Prophet Elijah skete but than all the Greek sketes on the Mountain, another cause of grievance among the Greek monks. In 1867 Grand Duke Aleksey Aleksandrovich laid the foundation stone of the central church at St Andrew's. The Greeks were appalled to see the size and ornate grandeur of this church, which had no equal on Athos, but they passed no comment out of respect for the visitor's high rank.[44] This 'respect' did not prevent the skete becoming known as the Serai, or palace, for the imperial splendour of its buildings, a soubriquet it bears to this day.

By the 1870s the Russians on Athos possessed three very substantial houses: the monastery of St Panteleimonos and the sketes of St Andrew and the Prophet Elijah. All three were flourishing: their numbers were increasing rapidly; their buildings were eloquent (if not aggressive) reminders of their wealth; and they were greedy for power, land, and recognition. Inevitably the Greeks became not only jealous but worried. Tensions grew; relations deteriorated; wild stories began to circulate: that the tsar had designs on the throne of Constantinople; that he was using the Holy Mountain as a stepping stone towards the realization of his political ambitions; that the cellars of the Russian houses were stocked with arms; that most of the Russian monks were crypto-officers of the imperial army. Nineteenth-century histories of Athos by Greek writers proclaim the truth of the rumours and some are still in circulation today.[45]

RUSSIAN EXPANSION AND THE LIBERATION OF ATHOS

In 1874 the Russians at St Panteleimonos began to assert themselves. They now numbered over 400 monks while the Greeks were fewer than 200, and the two communities were at each other's throats. The abbot was Greek and the Greeks believed that the monastery was still Greek property, but in 1875 the abbot died. Both sides appealed to Constantinople. The verdict of the the patriarch was that 'the Russians cannot be denied a monastery on Athos.'[46] Furthermore, by patriarchal decree, the Russian candidate was appointed abbot, thereby ensuring the ascendancy of the Russians within the monastery. His enthronement was attended by representatives of all the monasteries except Grigoriou, Konstamonitou and Esphigmenou. St Panteleimonos was finally re-established as a Russian house with the endorsement of a large majority of the other monasteries. But the Greeks had suffered a humiliating defeat at the hands of an aggressive people who now seemed destined to dominate the Mountain. The calm of Athos had been disturbed and its international status had been put to the test in a very public manner.

Calm was restored, at least for a while. By means of its publications St Panteleimonos became a centre of enlightenment and as a focus of spiritual revival it attracted generous financial support from all sectors of Russian society. Most of the money was used to strengthen the Russian houses, though other monasteries benefited too: Simonopetra was rebuilt after its disastrous fire in 1891 largely thanks to Russian donations.[47] Large numbers of Russian pilgrims were also attracted to the Mountain and by the start of the twentieth century there were as many as 25,000 visitors each year. They could stay as long as they wished, but the recommended minimum period was two months and as a result guest houses were fully stretched.

During the Russo-Turkish war of 1877–8 the Ottomans accused the monks of pan-Slav agitation in Macedonia and sent a delegation to search the monastery. But as one of the most anti-Russian of Greek newspapers reported, 'no weapons were found in the monastery other than ecclesiastical books . . . no ammunition other than beans, cabbage, courgettes, and olives.'[48] The position of the Russians on Athos was strengthened by Russia's victory in this conflict.

The Englishman Athelstan Riley, visiting the Mountain in 1883, described the Russian monastery as 'a go-ahead colony' and recounts the observations of a 'well-known professor of the University of Athens':

> . . . now the original inhabitants of the Holy Mountain, being fully roused, have entered into a solemn compact never again to sell a foot of ground to the intruders . . . Thus they [the Russians] are obliged to make the most of what they have already, and consequently at their two great stations, Russico and St. Andrew's, they are hard at work with stones and mortar. Many are the tales told of lights seen at night on the mountain moving between these two communities, the evidence of secret communications carried on under the cover of darkness. The bitterness of feeling between the two parties may be imagined from the fact that the Greeks attribute the frequent fires which have taken place in their monasteries during the last fifty years to Russian incendiaries . . .

Riley continues:

> I give these stories chiefly for the sake of showing the bitterness of the struggle now undoubtedly going on at Athos, though there is great reason for believing that these tales are only exaggerations of the truth. It is quite possible, and even probable, that the Greeks are jealous of the greater number of Russian than Greek pilgrims to the Holy Mountain (caused by the deeper religious feeling that exists amongst the lower orders of Russians than amongst the Greeks)—pilgrims who make the journey, I believe, entirely from religious motives. Yet that the Russian authorities both at home and at Athos are scheming for important polit-

72 The Ottoman governor of Athos with the insignia of his office in Karyes. As the Ottoman occupation neared its end, relations with the monks were often poor and for obvious reasons the governorship was not a popular posting.

ical ends I see no reason to doubt; but that munitions of war are being stored up at Russico, as has been asserted, is very improbable, and I saw nothing to confirm this statement.[49]

Nicholas Fennell, who has made a study of the (now lost) archives of the Prophet Elijah skete, takes a different line: 'It was only later in the twentieth century . . . that official Russian intervention on Athos, so long dreaded by the Greeks, became a reality. Until then all the Russians could be accused of was unbridled zeal and tactlessness.'[50] Yet he is hard put to it to account for the sudden and dramatic expansion that occurred:

> There is no single explanation for the meteoric rise of the Russian population . . . Nothing that happened in the seventy years of growth was due to the isolated actions of a single government or of individuals . . . What is clear about the Russians on Athos is that they never intended to seize power and territory in a political sense: even the worldliest, most uncouth kelliot built his great stone edifices with pious if misguided intentions.[51]

Whatever the motives for it may have been—and it seems not unreasonable to assume a combination of religious zeal and patriotic fervour—there was indeed phenomenal growth in the Russian population. In 1902 Gerasimos Smyrnakis, later to become abbot of Esphigmenou, reported that there were 3496 Russians on the Mountain and 3276 Greeks.[52] The largest Russian concentrations were 1858 at the monastery of St Panteleimonos and its dependencies, roughly 500 at the Serai and 400 at the Prophet Elijah skete. The rest lived out in the cells, some of which housed as many as 100 monks. The Russians repeatedly attempted to convert the cenobitic sketes into monasteries as a means to gain a louder voice in the Holy Community, but every such request was turned down. The cells grew to the size of monasteries, though the behaviour of some of their inhabitants left much to be desired. The Greeks felt threatened by this alien people that had suddenly gained a majority on *their* Holy Mountain. The Russians were frustrated because despite their numerical superiority they never had more than a single vote in the Holy Community.[53] Meanwhile the political situation in the Balkans became increasingly unstable.

Greece had acquired Thessaly in 1881 but Macedonia still remained in Ottoman hands. While the Ottomans were distracted by an Italian attack on Libya, an alliance of Greece, Serbia and Bulgaria attacked the Ottoman forces in Europe on 18 October 1912 and was quickly successful. On 8 November, the feast of St Demetrios by the old calendar, Greek forces entered Thessaloniki, a matter of hours ahead of the Bulgarians, who also laid claim to Macedonia, and the Greek navy swiftly assumed control of the Aegean. On 15 November Athos was liberated without a struggle and the Turkish aga vacated his office in Karyes, bringing to an end 488 years of Ottoman rule over the Holy Mountain. Bells were rung in every belfry; the flags of the Balkan nations were flown; guns were fired all night long; there was wild rejoicing and shouting of the Easter greeting 'Christ is risen! He is risen indeed!'

6
TWENTIETH-CENTURY ATHOS

I n 1912 Athos for the first time in its history became Greek territory. Until then, whether ruled by Byzantines or Ottomans, it had belonged to the worldwide ('ecumenical') dominion of Orthodoxy. It had been a theocratic republic, a monastic enclave, where monks acknowledged no sovereign except the Mother of God, and where even the jurisdiction of the ecumenical patriarch was carefully circumscribed. This was the basis of its much-vaunted supranational status. Suddenly it seemed to be in danger of losing this special position, of becoming simply a monkish extension of the secular Greek state—ironically at a time when Greeks on the Mountain were themselves in a minority. Athos had been liberated by Greek forces in the name of King George I of the Hellenes. When the initial jubilation subsided, the Athonites had to do some hard thinking about how to regain their autonomy and their *raison d'être*. And it was not long before the patriarchate had to answer similar questions about its own future.

THE RUSSIAN BUBBLE BURSTS

The Slavs posed the most serious and immediate threat to the stability of the Mountain. Eleven days after the liberation, seventy Bulgarian troops landed on Athos and took up positions in Zographou and Chilandar, ostensibly to protect Bulgarian property and Bulgarian interests. Seven months later, on the eve of the outbreak of the Second Balkan War, when Greece and Serbia took arms against Bulgaria, they were still there. Greek troops, assisted by large numbers of armed monks, laid siege to the two monasteries concerned and the Bulgarians surrendered. The crisis was averted, but tensions between Greeks and Bulgarians persisted.

Nor was there any lessening of the tension between Greeks and Russians, even though (or perhaps because) the former were now in a position of authority. Greek customs officials treated Russian monks and pilgrims alike in an unmannerly and insolent fashion. Despite their political superiority, the Greeks still felt inferior to the Russians and remained intensely jealous of their wealth. Relations deteriorated further and the problem seemed intractable.

In 1913, when the attention of the Greeks was distracted by hostilities in

73 The Holy Epistasia (or Executive Committee) of the Holy Community 'in the year of the liberation of our holy place 1912–13'. The presence of Greek police in ceremonial costume attests to the reality of Greek rule.

the Balkans, an extraordinary episode took place on Athos that fortunately affected only the Russians. Early in the year groups of monks in two of the Russian houses were incited by rabble-rousers to become involved in a theological controversy concerning the name of God. This controversy had been sparked off a few years earlier by monks in Russia who contended that the name of God was the Lord Himself and that God could not be separated from His all-holy name. They became known as the Glorifiers of the Name and at the time they were regarded as heretics by most other Orthodox, including the patriarch. The question of whether the teaching was indeed heretical exercised Russian theologians for some time; one pointed out that at least the debate proved that the Russian monks on Athos were genuinely interested in spiritual matters.[1] But in fact the majority of those monks were simple peasants, incapable of understanding the intricacies of theological argument, and they were being incited by demagogues.

On Athos the rebels seized control of the Serai and expelled the prior and fifty monks amid ugly scenes. They also established themselves at St Panteleimonos, though they failed by a narrow margin to win a vote of confidence at a meeting of the brotherhood. The Russian authorities in St Petersburg were informed of the situation and decided to act quickly. When the rebels ignored an appeal from the Russian Synod to step down, three

Russian warships were sent to Athos in June 1913 together with a detachment of troops who besieged the Serai. The operation was conducted with dispatch and 833 monks were swiftly arrested and deported to Russia. But the Russian Synod admitted that many bystanders had been wounded in the action, and the patriarch was understandably outraged that the Russian navy had used violence against Athonite monks.[2] The episode was a considerable embarrassment to the Russians and could have had serious international repercussions.

In 1914 the Russian Athonites, assisted by A.A. Pavlovsky, who was now installed as the permanent Russian diplomatic representative on the Holy Mountain, made a concerted effort to unite and make a case for recognition. In a memorandum put out in the name of all three houses and 34 leading cells they asked that the sketes be made into monasteries and the larger cells into sketes; in view of their numbers they asked to be given an equal voice in the Holy Community or permission to divorce themselves from it.[3] After the conclusion of the Balkan Wars in 1913 the reallocation of Turkey's European territories was administered by the great powers. The position of Mount Athos, however, was not defined beyond an agreement that it should have an independent, neutral autonomy. This raised a question over Greece's sovereignty and the presence of Greek troops on the Mountain. The Russians began to press their case harder than ever, but

74 All that remains of the Russian monks at the Serai is their skulls, displayed in neat rows in the charnel house. A much smaller Greek brotherhood has recently occupied the skete.

negotiations were interrupted by the outbreak of the First World War, and after the 1917 revolution there was no likelihood of their being resumed. Greece's sovereignty over the Mountain was eventually given international recognition.

As the war progressed, the situation of the Russian Athonites deteriorated. Greece was divided by the so-called national schism: Prime Minister Venizelos was eager for Greece to enter the war to support Serbia, while King Constantine insisted that Greece remain neutral. In 1916 Venizelos set up a separatist government in Thessaloniki for which the Holy Community declared its support, but the political situation of Athos remained uncertain, and it was only after the Russian Revolution of 1917 that the Greeks were sufficiently confident to assert their authority. At this point the Russians on Athos were suddenly cut off from all contact with their fatherland. They lost access to their substantial bank deposits and they received no more visitors and no more novices from Russia. At the same time the Greeks imposed heavy taxes on the Russian monks who remained and on any goods that they imported into Athos. Almost overnight the position of the Russians was reversed, from near domination of the Mountain to almost total subjection. They have never recovered. As

75 The Serai's buildings were left to rot after the last of the Russians died in the 1970s. Restoration of the tower is now in hand and the bells have been taken out for safety reasons.

76 The First World War made little impact on the life of the monks, but in order to counter the rumour that some monasteries were assisting the Germans a small detachment of French troops was sent to Karyes in 1917.

the monks grew older and fewer, they lost more and more of their properties. The cells were abandoned, the sketes were Hellenized, and the Russian monastery itself, once home to close on 1500 monks, became so depopulated that it was nearly forced to close. But in fact it never has, and the revival of monasticism in Russia itself has brought a gleam of hope, though the Greek authorities have ensured that the influx of novices is nothing more than a trickle.

Fennell concludes his study on an optimistic note:

The situation on Athos on the eve of the First World War was precarious. The Holy Mountain was the scene of ethnic quarrels fuelled by greed, jealousy and even violence; it was becoming overcrowded; monastic humility and other-worldliness were being forgotten: all this was a far cry from the hesychastic revival of the eighteenth century. The will of the individual on Athos was proved to be powerless. God's will prevailed: the Russians were humbled, made destitute and brought back to their senses. Let us pray that the Holy Mountain will continue to be the centre of Pan-Orthodoxy as it was in St Paisy's day and as St Nikodemos saw it.[4]

THE POLITICAL SETTLEMENT

After the First World War the Russian state took no further interest in Mount Athos. It was therefore left to the western allies to establish a settlement with Turkey in which the legal status of the Holy Mountain was agreed. The Treaty of Sèvres (1920), ratified by the Treaty of Lausanne (1923), recognized Greece's sovereignty over Athos. But it included an important clause that protected the rights and liberties of the non-Greek monastic communities on the Mountain according to the provisions of Article 62 of the Treaty of Berlin (1878). At the same time Greece undertook to prepare a new charter that would take account of recent developments while safeguarding the traditions of the centuries-old regime by constitutional means. The outcome of this inquiry was the Mount Athos Charter, which was approved by the Holy Community in 1924 and ratified by the Greek state in 1926. This charter includes clauses to protect the privileged status of Athos which remain in force today. Since they are fundamental to the legal situation of the Mountain, it is worth recording its main provisions.[5]

(1) The Athos peninsula, extending beyond Megali Vigla and constituting the region of Mount Athos in accordance with its ancient privileged status, is a self-governing part of the Greek state, whose sovereignty over it remains intact. Spiritually Mount Athos is under the jurisdiction of the Ecumenical Patriarchate. All persons leading a monastic life there acquire Greek citizenship without further formalities upon admission as novices or monks.

(2) Mount Athos is governed in accordance with its regime by its twenty holy monasteries among which the entire Athos peninsula is divided; the territory of the peninsula is exempt from expropriation. Administration of the Mount Athos region is exercised by representatives of the holy monasteries constituting the Holy Community. No change whatsoever is permitted in the administrative system or in the number of monasteries of Mount Athos, or in their order of pre-eminence or in their position to their subordinate dependencies. Heterodox or schismatic persons are prohibited from dwelling there.

(3) The determination in detail of the regimes of Mount Athos and the manner of operation thereof is effected by the Charter of Mount Athos which, with the co-operation of the state representative, is drawn up and voted by the twenty holy monasteries and ratified by the Ecumenical Patriarchate and the Parliament of the Hellenes.

(4) Faithful observance of the regimes of Mount Athos in the spiritual field is under the supreme supervision of the Ecumenical Patriarchate, and,

in the administrative, under the supervision of the state, which also is exclusively responsible for safeguarding public order and security.

(5) The afore-mentioned powers of the state are exercised through a governor whose rights and duties are determined by law. The law likewise determines the judicial power exercised by the monastic authorities and the Holy Community, as well as the customs and taxation privileges of Mount Athos.

In addition to these main provisions the charter defines in legal terms and makes allowance for every form of monastic life that obtains on the Mountain, and it provides for the peaceful coexistence of cenobitic and idiorrhythmic communities. It also specifies a number of restrictions relating to rights of establishment. Any male, regardless of nationality, may settle on Athos as a monk or novice so long as he is a member of the Orthodox Church (with the corollary that if he leaves the Orthodox faith he ceases to be Athonite and must leave the Mountain). Monks may not leave the Mountain without written permission from their monastery. Monks who do not belong to a monastery and are found wandering on the Mountain are to be expelled by the Holy Epistasia, as are laymen who create a disturbance. Every visitor to the Mountain (whether layman, clergyman, or non-Athonite monk) must first obtain a permit (*diamonitirion*) from the authorities in Karyes giving him the right to travel on the peninsula and to seek hospitality from the monasteries. Anyone wishing to consult the libraries and archives of the monasteries must first obtain a letter of introduction from the Ecumenical Patriarchate or the Greek Ministry of Foreign Affairs. Females, whether women or animals, are forbidden from entering Athos. In Greek law any woman who sets foot on the Holy Mountain will receive an automatic prison sentence of between two and twelve months.[6]

This was the first time that the prohibition of women had been explicitly stated. Before 1924 it was simply taken for granted since it had always been in force and was never questioned. In 1975, International Women's Year, a member of the Greek Parliament proposed the lifting of the ban. Parliament rejected the proposal for two reasons: first, because the ban had always been in place and so constituted one of the traditional and internationally protected rights of the Mountain; and secondly, because it was specifically mentioned in the charter which could only be amended by the Athonites themselves. It has been questioned again more recently with similar results.[7]

The charter of 1924 was a summing up of all the traditions and customs that had accumulated in the course of a millennium of monasticism on the Holy Mountain. It incorporated all the rules and regulations that had been laid down over the past ten centuries in Byzantine *typika* and imperial chrysobulls, in patriarchal edicts and Ottoman firmans. The charter defined the relationship of the Mountain with both the state and the Church. It provided for the administration of justice and the appointment of a civil governor who reports to the Ministry of Foreign Affairs in Athens and who, together with his deputy, resides in Karyes. It spelt out once and for all the role of the Holy Community and the Holy Epistasia. It protected the rights of the non-Greek minorities. In short, it provided the administrative, political and judicial apparatus that enabled the Mountain to operate as a self-governing entity within the modern Greek state. The fact that its provisions have simply been adopted more or less unchanged in all subsequent Greek constitutions is a testament to the trouble that was taken to get it right. Its promulgation was a major achievement, perhaps the most important event in the history of Orthodox monasticism in the twentieth century.

THE ISSUE OF THE CALENDAR

When the western Church adopted the Gregorian calendar in 1582, the Orthodox Church refused to comply, regarding the change as a unilateral break with tradition and with the paschal calendar of the First Council of Nicaea. In 1923 Patriarch Meletios convened a pan-Orthodox council which recommended a number of liberal reforms including the adoption of the Gregorian calendar. The next year, on 10/23 March 1924, Archbishop Christodoulos, backed by the patriarchate and the Greek government of Nicholas Plastiras, imposed the change on the Church of Greece. It was accepted by the vast majority of the clergy and by most of the laity, though pockets of (mostly lay) resistance held out against it and continue to do so. It is estimated that the so-called Old Calendarists in Greece today number as many as 150,000.

The monks of Athos have never accepted the change and to this day continue to use the Julian calendar, which places them thirteen days behind the rest of the world. Some were so affronted by the patriarchate's imposition of the new calendar in 1924 that they broke communion with the reformers, ceased to commemorate the name of the patriarch in their church services, and declared themselves 'Zealots'. Traditionally these monks lived out in the cells and sketes, but more recently they have taken control of the monastery of Esphigmenou.

In the 1960s, in defiance of the charter of 1924, several monasteries stopped commemorating the name of the patriarch because of Athenagoras's involvement in the ecumenical movement and his gestures of reconciliation towards Roman Catholics and Anglicans. By 1970 as many as eleven monasteries (including Lavra, Iviron, Stavronikita, St Paul's, Simonopetra, Dionysiou, and Grigoriou) were not commemorating the

77 'Orthodoxy or Death'—a stark choice proclaimed by the Zealot monks of Esphigmenou from an upper balcony of the monastery.

patriarch by name. When Patriarch Demetrios was elected in 1972, he took steps to restore the monks' confidence and all but one of the monasteries resumed the practice of commemorating the patriarch. The exception was the Zealot monastery of Esphigmenou. The other nineteen monasteries of the Holy Community voted to expel Esphigmenou's representative, and since then the monks of Esphigmenou have been out of communion with the rest of the Mountain in both church and refectory. Their stance is symbolized by a banner suspended from a high balcony overlooking the sea which reads 'Orthodoxy or Death'.[8]

MID-CENTURY DECLINE

St Panteleimonos was not the only monastery to suffer decline after the First World War, though its fall was perhaps the most dramatic because it had started from such a peak of prosperity. All the non-Greek houses experienced similar problems for similar reasons: lack of men and lack of money. Zographou's difficulties were exacerbated by the fact that the Church of Bulgaria, re-established in 1871, was not formally recognized by the Ecumenical Patriarchate until 1945. The Romanian sketes also suffered from a serious shortage of recruits. Numbers at Chilandar held up longer, no doubt because of Greece's improved relations with the newly created state of Yugoslavia. But the Greek monasteries too were forced to tighten their belts. All their overseas estates had now been confiscated, and in 1922, after the Asia Minor disaster when an ill-judged Greek thrust into Anatolia was repulsed by the Turks and the entire Christian population of Turkey was forced to flee the country, their remaining estates in Macedonia, Thrace and the islands were requisitioned by the Greek government to provide homes for the influx of refugees. The government tried to make up for the losses suffered by the monasteries by giving them an annuity of three million drachmas, but this never matched the income they had received from their estates and its value was quickly eroded by inflation and devaluation of the drachma.

The Second World War made little impact on Athos. The German occupation of Greece was savage and oppressive, but though most of the Athonites supported the Allies they suffered few reprisals.[9] In fact the Mountain operated as a link in one of the main escape routes for British, Australian and New Zealand soldiers, and many monasteries sheltered and fed the fugitives. Some soldiers stayed for months in isolated hermitages in the forest until they could be got away by sea, often in monkish disguise. A few were still there when the war ended, though none is known to have taken monastic vows.

78 Fr Pavlos Pavlides of the Great Lavra, photographed in 1968 seated in front of his voluminous diary.

W. B. Thomas, a young New Zealander wounded in Crete and captured by the Germans, in a semi-autobiographical thriller entitled *Dare to be Free* writes endearingly of his sojourn at the Great Lavra (which he calls St Lawrence) in 1942 and of the monks who helped him to escape:

'I have thought over the whole thing,' said Pavlides, the quietly spoken and cultured monk-doctor of St Lawrence, 'and I will have some suggestions to make to you later. In the meantime, let us enjoy the meal that God has provided.'

We were seated at a small table in the good doctor's quarters, and in front of us was arrayed a tasty meal of macaroni and white cheese. I had been in the monastery for over ten days, and this was the first time I had been 'invited out' for a meal, normally being required to live and eat in the monastery hospital. The monks of St Lawrence differed from St Denys [Dionysiou] in that they lived *monos* or to a great degree singly [i.e. idiorrhythmically]. Thus, they did not dine together as a community. On the other hand, they were permitted two great privileges. First, they were permitted, in between fasts, to eat red meat, and, secondly, they could bring into the monastery, and still retain, their worldly wealth. This enabled some of them to live in well-furnished quarters, with paid lesser monks for servants.

'Well now, Pavlides,' I tackled him when we had finished our meal, 'what is the news you have for me? What are the suggestions you mentioned which will help me in my one great desire, to get to Egypt?'

Dr Pavlides proceeded to outline his plan for the young soldier's escape which involved making use of the substantial fortunes that only idiorrhythmic monks could lay their hands on. The story continues:

> We rose from the small table, for it was getting late. I started to make my farewells and thanks. Pavlides, however, was in no hurry to retire. He drew me out on to a small balcony.
> 'This is the most restful place in my apartment,' he smiled. 'Here I work on my hobby of book-binding when it is not too cold. Don't you think it is a beautiful view for an old man to look on for his last years?'[10]

Old man or not, Dr Pavlides continued to enjoy the view from his balcony for a good many more years. He was still there, writing a copious diary and carefully binding its volumes, when Bishop Kallistos first visited the monastery in the early 1960s.

More serious for Athos was the devastating civil war that Greece endured immediately after its liberation. The fighting was especially fierce in Chalkidiki and the peasants were allowed to drive their flocks, mostly goats, on to the Mountain to preserve them from the guerrillas. As many as 70,000 animals are said to have been involved and they proved too great a temptation to a raiding party in December 1948, which included twenty-five women who flouted the law excluding them. The insurgents advanced as far as Karyes, where they encamped for the night and exchanged fire with the local police. They withdrew the next day, taking with them precious stocks of food and 200 animals. When the war ended in 1949, the remaining animals were driven off the Mountain, but not before they had done great damage to crops and trees.[11]

By far the most serious problem, however, faced by all the monasteries after the Second World War was the persistent decline in the numbers of monks, and especially the numbers of novices. According to Smyrnakis,[12] in 1903 there was a total of 7432 monks on the Holy Mountain, of whom 3496 (47%) were Russians and 3260 (43.9%) lived in the monasteries (as opposed to the sketes and cells). By 1956 the total figure had fallen to 1862, of whom 814 (43.7%) were resident in the monasteries. In 1965, when the total number was 1491, there were only 62 Russians (4.2%). By 1968 the total was down to 1238 with only 518 (41.8%) in the monasteries. In 1971 the total reached a low of 1145. The following table shows the numbers for each monastery, including monks living in the dependencies:[13]

Monastery	1903	1959	1968	1971
Lavra	1187	459	406	378
Vatopedi	966	129	83	74
Iviron	456	101	68	57
Dionysiou	131	53	40	42
Chilandar	385	63	55	54
Koutloumousiou	214	107	68	57
Pantokrator	548	118	84	76
Xeropotamou	106	43	36	30
Zographou	155	21	15	11
Dochiariou	60	29	16	16
Karakalou	130	42	30	30
Philotheou	133	44	36	24
Simonopetra	108	27	18	27
St Paul's	250	115	111	96
Stavronikita	219	35	26	31
Xenophontos	195	66	43	38
Grigoriou	105	53	34	30
Esphigmenou	91	46	25	33
St Panteleimonos	1928	61	27	24
Konstamonitou	65	29	17	17
Total	7432	1641	1238	1145

Bare statistics fail to demonstrate other relevant factors. As the monks grew fewer, so they also grew older. They were less able to work, and as they also grew poorer, they were unable to employ the same amount of labour as in the past. The drop in numbers of monks meant that less accommodation was required, and so large parts of monasteries were abandoned and buildings fell into disrepair. With fewer mouths to feed, the monks needed fewer acres to cultivate, and so once-fertile fields, vineyards and orchards reverted to waste land. Church services were less well attended, choirs were depleted in numbers, and standards of liturgical practice, chanting, and spirituality inevitably began to decline. Monasteries assumed a desolate and decadent appearance. At best they were nostalgic reminders of departed splendour. Visitors such as John Julius Norwich were driven to predict the worst:

The fundamental, unanswerable fact is that Mount Athos has become an anachronism, and one which modern Greece is no longer able to indulge. Ironically enough, it is in the communist countries of Eastern Europe that the call of the Holy Mountain seems most clearly heard. In 1964 the Soviet Government agreed to release a few Russian novices—the first since the Revolution—to St Panteleimon, and Marshal Tito has done the same for

Chilandar—following this gesture, according to a recent report, with the gift of an electric generator. But such recruits, welcome as they may be, cannot hope to buttress the whole community against the onslaught of a hostile age. Unless a miracle happens—a great nation-wide religious revival, nothing less—the Holy Mountain is doomed.[14]

A few years later Emmanuel Amand de Mendieta was equally pessimistic:

The authorities of every monastery, and the Holy Community and the Patriarchate at Constantinople, must be aware how near some houses are to complete closure. St. Paul may have been helped, in recent years, by its reputation for vigorous intellectual life, and for some years the monastery published a small journal, which has now ceased. But it is distressing to see that two of the oldest and once largest monasteries, Vatopedi and Iviron, are so greatly reduced. Vatopedi's reputation as the monastery which has always been most receptive to up-to-date ideas, has not been able to attract recruits, nor has the reputation of Dionysiou for a strict observance of the monastic code assisted it.[15]

Philip Sherrard was one of the twentieth century's most astute and devoted observers of Athonite affairs. He could not deny the ever dwindling numbers and the paucity of new recruits which he attributed to two factors: a spirit of intolerance to the monastic way of life in Greece as a whole, and the determination of the Greek state to restrict the entry of non-Greek nationals as part of its aim to destroy the pan-Orthodox traditions of the Mountain. But he knew that Athos had recovered from downturns in its fortunes in the past, and he did not exclude the possiblity of recovery again:

The answer, in part at least, depends on the monks themselves. At the end of a thousand years they are in possession of a constitution which enshrines and secures, in so far as a paper constitution can enshrine and secure anything, the privileges and independence of the Holy Mountain. The geographical and political boundaries of the Mountain are clearly defined. There is an administrative organization fit for the preserving of internal order and stability. There are what one might describe as adequate conditions for the pursuit of the monastic life. With a consciousness of the principles of this life, and the resolution to pursue it, the monks of Athos may yet frustrate the forces which aim at the destruction of their community.[16]

There were of course exceptions to the trend. Amid the gloomy predictions and diminishing population statistics a number of luminaries continued to uphold the torch of Athonite spirituality. The Elder Silouan, who lived on Athos from 1892 to 1938, is a shining example. His early years at the monastery of St Panteleimonos were darkened by fits of depression until one day he received a vision. His disciple, Fr Sophrony, takes up the story:

That same day, during vespers in the Church of the Holy Prophet Elijah (adjoining the mill), to the right of the Royal Doors, by the ikon of the Saviour, he beheld the living Christ.

In a manner passing all understanding the Lord appeared to the young novice whose whole being filled with the fire of the grace of the Holy Spirit—that fire which the Lord brought down to earth with His coming . . .

There is no describing how it was with Brother Simeon [later Fr Silouan] at that moment. From his words and from his writings we know that a great Divine light shone about him, that he was lifted out of this world and in spirit transported to heaven, where he heard ineffable words; that he received, as it were, a new birth from on high.[17]

Even in later life he was still persecuted by demons. Fr Sophrony recounts another famous incident in his life:

It was fifteen years after the Lord had appeared to him, and Silouan was engaged in one of these nocturnal struggles with devils which so tormented him. No matter how he tried, he could not pray with a pure mind. At last he rose from his stool, intending to bow down and worship, when he saw a gigantic devil standing in front of the ikon, waiting to be worshipped. Meanwhile, the cell filled with other evil spirits. Father Silouan sat down again, and with bowed head and aching heart he prayed,

'Lord, Thou seest that I desire to pray to Thee with a pure mind but the devils will not let me. Instruct me, what must I do to stop them hindering me?'

And in his soul he heard,

'The proud always suffer from devils.'

'Lord,' said Silouan, 'teach me what I must do that my soul may grow humble.'

Once more, his heart heard God's answer,

Keep thy mind in hell, and despair not.[18]

Fr Silouan was a simple, uneducated monk from a peasant background, but his meditations and writings, based on his personal experience of Christianity and his tireless inner striving, have been edited and translated into many languages and have inspired countless readers. He was canonized in 1988.

In the same context we should celebrate the life and work of Fr Gabriel, former abbot of Dionysiou, who died, aged ninety-eight, on 25 October 1983 after more than 69 years on Athos and half a century as abbot. By sheer strength of character he rose to be the unelected representative of the Holy Mountain in all its dealings with both the external world and with the Athonites themselves. He was known as 'the abbot of the abbots', the 'father' of all the Athonites, and the 'grandfather' of all the young monks whom he attracted to the Mountain. Of the many stories told of his qualities as a spiritual father and guide to the young, one must suffice here:

In 1982 a young monk came to pay him a visit at the infirmary of Dionysiou where he was lying in the bed next to Father Arsenius. After having given his blessing, the patriarch of the Athonites said to the young monk:

'Come, dear Father, this is the last time that we shall see each other. I am departing.'

'No, Elder, I'll come to see you again.'

'You won't have time for it. I'm dying.'

'If you depart this life, the All-Holy Mother of God will surely receive you with open arms. For, look, you've served her "garden" faithfully for seventy years.'

The old man looked at him with tears in his eyes:

'My child, we judge altogether too easily, we men. But God, He has His own judgement of us.'[19]

The Millennium in 1963

Amid all the gloomy prognostications for their future the monks of Athos had somehow to find the energy and the enthusiasm to celebrate their millennium in 1963. Megiste Lavra, founded in 963, the oldest of all the surviving ruling monasteries, was a thousand years old. A major celebration was called for.[20]

Representatives of Church and state congregated in Karyes in large numbers. The Ecumenical Patriarch, Athenagoras I, was there with a large entourage, as were patriarchs and divines from many other Christian churches, both Eastern and Western. King Paul of the Hellenes and his son, Crown Prince Constantine, also came, as did several Greek government ministers. The hospitality was lavish—too lavish for some monks, who absented themselves from what they considered to be inappropriate displays of extravagance. One banquet had to be postponed because the king was ill; it was rearranged for a fast day, a fact that had escaped the notice of the organizers, and as a result there was no suitable food; when some was found it was no longer fresh because of the high temperatures, and the consequences were most unfortunate.

It was of course an occasion for speech-making. The patriarch took the opportunity to emphasize the need for new recruits regardless of their nationality. He also supported an extension of the ecclesiastical school that had been founded in Karyes ten years earlier with full state recognition and government funding. And he called for the setting up of an academy of Byzantine Christian studies as well as retreat houses and conference centres on Athos. The king responded by saying that his government was prepared to do everything that was necessary to ensure that Athos remained a spiritual beacon for those outside the limits of Greek Orthodoxy. Despite these fine words, the seriousness of which was not to be doubted, many observers commented that the celebrations marked not so much the triumph of Athonite monasticism as its funeral or even its requiem. It was widely believed that the Mountain, whose past stretched back for a thousand years and more, had no future at all.[21]

79 Patriarchs and hierarchs from all over the Orthodox world assembled in Karyes for the celebrations to mark the millennium of Athos in 1963.

One superficially insignificant prelude to the events of 1963 was the construction of a road, the first in modern times, from the port of Daphne up to the town of Karyes. This no doubt facilitated the journey for the many dignitaries who were to visit the Mountain in the course of the celebrations. With it of course came the first motorized vehicles ever seen on Athos.[22] Such concessions to modernization were deeply shocking to many of the monks. And they were right to suspect that the trend would not stop there.

SEEDS OF RENEWAL

Numbers of monks continued to fall throughout the 1960s and it was only in the early 1970s that the trend was finally arrested. In 1972 the population rose from 1145 to 1146—not a spectacular increase, but nevertheless the first to be recorded since the turn of the century. Since then the upturn has been maintained in most years and the official total in 2000 stood at just over 1600. The following table shows the numbers for each monastery including novices and those living in the dependencies:

Monastery	1972	1976	1978	1980	1982	1986	1988	1990	1992	2000
Lavra	380	355	348	325	326	329	309	317	345	362
Vatopedi	71	65	60	54	50	48	55	50	75	142
Iviron	54	63	52	52	51	53	53	61	61	78
Chilandar	57	64	69	43	48	52	45	46	60	75
Dionysiou	42	37	35	54	56	59	59	59	50	58
Koutloumousiou	61	61	66	57	80	75	73	73	77	95
Pantokrator	80	71	63	63	62	69	57	66	50	70
Xeropotamou	30	26	22	47	46	37	38	40	34	40
Zographou	12	9	13	11	16	12	11	15	11	20
Dochiariou	14	13	11	32	29	31	31	32	32	27
Karakalou	28	16	13	18	20	16	16	19	26	37
Philotheou	28	80	81	63	66	79	82	79	74	70
Simonopetra	23	59	61	60	72	79	78	80	78	73
St Paul's	95	91	87	81	87	116	85	91	85	104
Stavronikita	37	35	43	40	41	40	40	28	33	45
Xenophontos	37	26	39	41	46	47	50	57	46	48
Grigoriou	22	40	57	63	71	62	72	70	77	86
Esphigmenou	38	49	41	35	48	38	40	42	56	101
Panteleimonos	22	29	30	30	31	23	32	35	40	53
Konstamonitou	16	17	16	22	29	20	26	30	27	26
Total	1146	1206	1217	1191	1275	1285	1255	1290	1337	1610

These figures tell us a great deal about the current revival and we shall examine them in some detail shortly. But what they do not tell us is that the revival did not in fact start in the monasteries themselves but in the cells and hermitages, down at the southern tip of the peninsula, in the most inhospitable environment of all, the so-called desert of Athos. There in the middle decades of the twentieth century a number of gifted teachers and holy men took up residence, where many had been before for centuries, and they began gathering around them groups of disciples. While the monasteries were in some cases near to closing for lack of novices, places like New Skete were bursting with new life and new vocations. But one should be careful when using the word 'new' because really there was nothing new about it. It was the way the Mountain had always regenerated itself. Near St Paul's, for example, overlooking the sea and overhung by a sheer cliff, is the cell where the great Russian *starets* Fr Sophrony, whom we have already met as the disciple of St Silouan, lived during the Second World War. He is perhaps best remembered for having founded the monastery of St John the Baptist at Tolleshunt Knights in Essex which is the most dynamic centre of Orthodox spirituality in Britain today. Fr Sophrony's cell is ruinous

80 The cell of Fr Sophrony near St Paul's monastery. The great Russian elder lived here for only a few years during the Second World War but his memory is kept alive by means of some photographs and icons.

at the time of writing; but there are plans for its restoration and it may not be empty for much longer.

During the 1950s a particularly dynamic brotherhood gathered around the renowned desert father Elder Joseph the Hesychast (also known as the Cave Dweller). After many years living in conditions of extreme privation at St Basil's, Elder Joseph had eventually settled at New Skete, where he earned fame as a teacher and spiritual father. His teaching was based on St Paul's injunction, 'Pray without ceasing' (1 Thess. 5: 17), and on the cultivation of inner stillness (*hesychia*) and prayer of the heart; this has been the direction followed by all the leaders of the current Athonite revival. He died in 1959, but no fewer than six Athonite monasteries have been revived by his spiritual children, who include Fr Ephraim, subsequently to become abbot of Philotheou, Fr Charalambos, subsequently abbot of Dionysiou, and Elder Joseph of Vatopedi, who was one of the leading lights in the revival of that house and remains its principal spiritual father.[23]

Another figure worthy of special mention is Fr Vasileios Gontikakis. He had studied in Western Europe and had become aware of the more liberal approach to monasticism that had sprung up recently in the Roman tradition. By the 1960s he was living as a hermit in a cell attached to Vatopedi at the time when the monastery of Stavronikita was so short of monks that it

81 The settlement of Katounakia near the southernmost point of the peninsula. Here the renowned Elder Daniel (1846–1929) lived for 50 years surrounded by disciples who learned the lessons of pure Orthodoxy in the 'university' of the desert.

was threatened with closure. When John Julius Norwich visited Stavronikita in 1964, he had found only eight monks, living a miserable existence according to the idiorrhythmic system. In 1968, when the site had actually been abandoned, the civil governor of the Mountain invited Fr Vasileios to take charge of the monastery. He accepted the invitation on condition that the monastery reverted to the cenobitic rule and that he was appointed abbot by the Holy Community. This was agreed, and with the approval of the ecumenical patriarch Fr Vasileios became abbot of Stavronikita later in 1968. He brought with him a group of disciples and together they revived the monastery. Fr Vasileios is author of many books, perhaps the best known being a study of liturgy and life in the Orthodox Church entitled *Hymn of Entry*. In his Foreword to the English edition Bishop Kallistos has written that it 'offers nothing less than a fresh vision of theology, the church and the world—a vision that is both original and yet genuinely traditional'.[24] 'Both original and genuinely traditional' are words that might be applied to the monastic revival that began at Stavronikita in 1968. Although Fr Vasileios has since moved on to Iviron, the brotherhood at Stavronikita, as a result of his influence, is more intellectual than most and places a greater emphasis on academic study.

Two other monasteries were revived in 1973, as is indicated by the

82 Elder Joseph the Hesychast shortly before his death in 1959. As a young man he had attached himself as a disciple to the Elder Daniel.

increase in numbers in the table above. Philotheou, like Stavronikita, had become very depleted in numbers and was still following the idiorrhythmic way of life when Fr Ephraim from New Skete, a former disciple of Elder Joseph the Hesychast, was invited to become abbot and bring his group of disciples to repopulate the monastery. Archimandrite Ephraim has since moved to North America, where he has founded a great many monasteries in recent years. But his influence remains strong at Philotheou, where the brotherhood is regarded as strict and sees itself as upholding the purest form of Orthodoxy. For this reason they require non-Orthodox pilgrims to progress no further than the narthex during services in the katholikon and to wait until the monks have finished before eating in the refectory.

83 The chapel of St John the Baptist at Little St Anne where Elder Joseph the Hesychast and his companion Fr Arsenios lived in caves from 1938 to 1951. They were short of space but from 1947 they were joined by a growing group of disciples.

Regulations of this sort would never have been imposed in the 1960s and are among the less attractive features of the current revival.

The other monastery to enjoy revival in 1973 was Simonopetra, but its 'new blood' came not from within Athos but from Meteora in Thessaly. Cenobitic monasteries had flourished there since the fourteenth century, but as in other parts of mainland Greece they were unprotected from the scourge of tourism. In 1973 the monks of the monastery of the Transfiguration could bear it no longer. To a man, they packed their bags and

84 New Skete from the west, to which Elder Joseph the Hesychast and his brotherhood moved in 1951 after they were forced by ill health to leave the caves of Little St Anne. The elder's spiritual children went on to become leading lights in the subsequent renewal.

decamped to Athos, together with their spiritual father, the charismatic Fr Aimilianos, to whom they were entirely devoted. The beetling heights of Simonopetra's location—quite the most spectacular of any Athonite house—have often been compared with the remarkable physical setting of the monks' previous abode. The monastery is now full and, despite the recent addition of a new wing to accommodate more monks, there is a waiting list for novices. Spiritually and intellectually, this is the most dynamic community on the Mountain today. Several of the monks are theologians of international renown whose works may be read in many languages. The Simonopetra choir has played a major role in the revival of Byzantine chant and their disciplined voices have been recorded on CD and cassette.

The trend gathered pace. In July 1974 it was the turn of Grigoriou to receive an influx of monks from Euboea (Evia) led by Fr George Kapsanis, an academic theologian who had been a professor at the University of Athens. The next year another band of monks left New Skete, this time settling at Koutloumousiou with their elder, Fr Christodoulos. And in 1976 a second group migrated from Meteora, moving to Xenophontos under the leadership of Fr Alexios. In 1979 Dochiariou abandoned the idiorrhythmic system and received an influx of young monks from off the Mountain. The next year, 1980, saw no fewer than four monasteries being revived. Both Xeropotamou and Konstamonitou received their new blood from Philotheou, whose num-

85 Elder Joseph of Vatopedi. Formerly a member of the brotherhood of Elder Joseph the Hesychast at New Skete, this Elder Joseph has been the principal spiritual father at Vatopedi since its revival as a coenobium in 1990.

bers can be seen to drop from 81 to 63 in that year. Dionysiou also took in a group of new monks from within the Mountain, led by Fr Charalambos, another disciple of Elder Joseph the Hesychast. Most significant of all, the Lavra abandoned the idiorrhythmic system on its own initiative.[25]

DECLINE OF IDIORRHYTHMIC LIFE

By the start of the 1980s it had become evident that a revival was taking place.[26] But it was not simply a fact that numbers were rising again for the first time for many years. Far more important than sheer numbers were the changes taking place in the Athonite way of life. Most of the new recruits were young men; quite suddenly the majority of beards were black rather than white and the average age of monks was soon brought down to a much healthier level. Most of them also were well educated, and many were university graduates. This represented a marked change from the traditional community where the majority of monks had been drawn from a peasant background and had received little or no formal education. The newcomers were attracted by the presence on the Mountain of so many gifted and charismatic teachers and holy men, men such as Elder Joseph, Fr Ephraim and Fr Vasileios. They came to sit at their feet and learn, but they also came to devote themselves to a life of service to God in strict obedience to their abbots. What appealed to them was the fully fledged monastic ideal of the cenobitic way of life in its purest, most hesychastic form. Not for them the *laissez-faire* lifestyle of the idiorrhythmic houses.

During the 1980s several of the grander monasteries still clung to their idiorrhythmic ways, and as long as this comfortable way of life remained a realistic option, the monks were resistant to change. But the fact was that, unlike their cenobitic neighbours, they were not receiving any novices at all and the differences soon became apparent. Their earlier grandeur now gave way to a rather squalid decadence, and one by one they were forced to accept the inevitable demands of the newcomers and abandon the idiorrhythmic life. As we have seen, the Lavra made the change, in name at least, as early as 1980 but it has to be said that the change has never been fully implemented there. Many of the monks, while paying lip-service to the cenobitic ideal, have continued much as before. As a result the community has not seen very much growth and the monastery still presents a somewhat sad and vacant appearance. By contrast, Vatopedi and Iviron, both of which made the change in 1990, have gone from strength to strength and are homes to exemplary cenobitic brotherhoods. Last, and most reluctant, to change was Pantokrator. In 1992 a new cenobitic brotherhood was introduced on the orders of the patriarchate and it too now bears all the hallmarks of a truly revived monastery.

86 Prior to its revival in 1992 the idiorrhythmic fathers of Pantokrator kept pigs. Such practices would be strictly forbidden today.

Thus ended a system that had been in place intermittently on the Mountain for 700 years. Grudgingly given imperial sanction when the Byzantine empire was fighting for its life, the idiorrhythmic system undoubtedly contributed to the survival of Athonite monasticism at crucial moments during the Tourkokratia. By the second half of the twentieth century, however, it had lost its appeal[27] and become unworkable. Scorned and rejected by a new generation of monks, the idiorrhythmic system has retreated to the sketes and cells to which it is best suited and where it flourishes alongside many of the humbler traditions of the ascetic way of life.

CONSEQUENCES OF GREEK MEMBERSHIP OF THE EUROPEAN UNION

Greece joined the European Community (as it then was) in January 1981. The next two decades saw a transformation of Greece's economy, its domestic political system and its standing in the world. The change is most evident in the countryside, where living standards have improved visibly, stemming the depopulation of rural areas. The position of the democratic government that has been in place since 1974 has been stabilized and Greece has also acquired greater credibility in global affairs in general and among its Balkan neighbours in particular. How, if at all, have these developments affected Athos?

Superficially, EU membership has had little impact on the Mountain, certainly in respect of the three areas in which Greece as a whole has most benefited. If increased tourism has improved the country's economy it has had the opposite effect on Athos, where the tradition of free hospitality makes it a drain on the monasteries' resources. Whereas Greece as a whole has had a stable democratic government only since 1974, the monks lay claim to an unbroken democracy that is more than a thousand years old. Meanwhile the international standing of the Mountain is indeed enjoying a higher profile but one that is restricted to spiritual affairs and is in no way connected with worldly politics. It cannot be denied, however, that membership of the EU has had a considerable impact on Athos in more subtle ways.

First of all, the economy of the monasteries has indeed improved. The monastic revival has brought demands for increased accommodation and improved facilities and these have had to be funded. At first the monks tried to boost their income by exploiting their forests and exporting timber. But this could never supply enough for their needs, and it also upset the conservationists. Designation of the Mountain as a World Heritage Site has made the monasteries eligible to apply for substantial grants and these have been forthcoming, largely, if indirectly, from EU sources. Monks tend to be wary of accepting largesse direct from the EU since they believe that it rarely comes unencumbered and they have no wish to see their abode turned into a theme park. Once grants are filtered through the Athens government, however, they have no such qualms. They point to the number of occasions over the centuries on which their estates have been confiscated by their political masters with little or no compensation and thus they feel entirely justified in accepting money from the Greek government with no strings attached.

Secondly, the legal status of the Holy Mountain has been given greater protection as a result of Greece's membership of the EU. The Final Act of Agreement relating to Greece's accession includes a joint declaration about Mount Athos which reads:

> Recognising that the special status granted to Mount Athos, as guaranteed by Article 105 of the Hellenic Constitution, is justified exclusively on grounds of a spiritual and religious nature, the Community will ensure that this status is taken into account in the application and subsequent preparation of provisions of Community law, in particular in relation to customs franchise privileges, tax exemptions, and the right of establishment.[28]

In theory at least, monks may draw comfort from this declaration that their special status and privileges are now guaranteed not only by the Constitution of Greece but also in European law. In reality of course monks are not so complacent. History has taught them never to relax their vigilance.

Thirdly, there is no doubting the fact that the profile of the Mountain has been raised just as much in the secular as in the spiritual sphere. In Byzantine times the two were arguably indistinguishable but today that is clearly not the case. Nowadays the visit of a European Commissioner or government minister or foreign prince is given at least as much attention as that of a bishop or metropolitan or patriarch. The fact that the former do come and come quite often is due at least as much to Greece's acquisition of a global voice in recent years as it is to the Mountain's regaining a spiritual one.

These are generalizations, and they apply, in as much as they are accurate, to the monasteries. Many of the monasteries in recent years have developed a more worldly outlook. With their adoption of new technology has come access to the worldwide web and greater knowledge of the outside world. With the improvement of facilities has come an appreciation of certain creature comforts. With their enhanced income there has had to come a greater understanding of financial affairs and an extension of networking in the commercial sector. There is nothing wrong with any of these things and, given controlled exposure, they perform a vital function in underpinning the monastic revival. But life outside the monasteries is much less susceptible to influence from the outside world. Monks in the sketes and cells are, not surprisingly, often scornful of what they see happening inside the grander revived houses. To them many of the developments of recent years seem contrary to the monastic ideal. They are less convinced of the need to modernize and some have even gone so far as to equate the European Union with the Antichrist.

Changing Fortunes of the Non-Greek Houses

Initially the revival was confined to the Greek monasteries. Numbers of monks were rising; funds were flowing in quite freely; everywhere there were signs of restoration and renewal. This was not the case in the non-Greek monasteries. St Panteleimonos had never recovered from the events of the second decade of the twentieth century. Monasteries in the Soviet Union were in dire straits and no monks were allowed to leave their homeland. Even if they had been, the Greek civil authorities would not have let them in. It was therefore a major concession when in May 1966 all the authorities concerned agreed to the admission of five Russians to St Panteleimonos. Four priest-monks duly arrived, but this was scarcely enough to stem the tide and the monastery came dangerously close to having to close. But from the 1970s small numbers began to trickle in, the pop-

87 Fr Stefan (centre right), prior of the Romanian skete of Lakkou, with some of the members of his brotherhood.

ulation steadily rose, and the threat of closure receded. The Greek authorities, however, persisted in their policy of issuing very few permits, and repeated requests by St Panteleimonos for the admission of just a few monks fell on deaf ears.[29] But in 1988 there seemed to be a slight softening of attitudes on both sides and as many as thirty new monks, many of them priests, were admitted to the monastery from Russia.[30] Since the downfall of the Soviet regime there has been a remarkable flowering of monasticism within Russia itself and many formerly deserted monasteries have been repopulated. It is likely that the Greek authorities will continue to limit the intake of Russian monks to the Holy Mountain, but numbers continued to rise steadily throughout the 1990s and a good deal of repair work has been carried out on some of the buildings; whether there is a concomitant spiritual revival among the monks is open to question.

The situation of Zographou over the same period was no better. Despite a concession in 1966 which resulted in the arrival of three Bulgarian monks, there were few new recruits and numbers in the monastery were often reduced to single figures. Bishop Kallistos was once informed by a lay worker in the guest house that there was not a single monk in the monastery at the time. Nor has Bulgaria seen any monastic revival comparable to that taking place in Russia. A hopeful sign was the election in 1997 of a new young abbot who succeeded in attracting a group of energetic novices. At last the

88 The iconostasis inside St George's *kellion* at the Romanian settlement of Kolitsou. The church dates from 1613.

89 Elder Dionysios of Kolitsou. Now blind and frail, this Romanian elder has been on the Holy Mountain since 1924.

monastery began to look less desolate and there was even a buzz of youthful activity about the courtyard.

Numbers of monks at Chilandar remained at a consistently higher level throughout this recent period, though a good many of them did not reside in the monastery. Unlike the other non-Greek houses, it remained idiorrhythmic until the 1980s, though the buildings continued to look well maintained, services were well attended, and fields and orchards immaculately cultivated. But inevitably the brotherhood was affected by the political problems in Serbia itself and it is to be hoped that the recent changes there will result in a greater stability that will be reflected in increased prosperity for the monastery.

As for the Romanians, they never succeeded in acquiring a monastery and for many years their position seemed to be the most depressed of all. Monasteries flourished in Romania itself and there was no shortage of young men wishing to join the communities on Athos. The Greek monasteries and the Holy Community made it clear that they would be welcome, but for some unaccountable reason the civil authorities in Athens would not give them entry permits. A few years ago the patriarch of Romania applied for permission to send twelve monks to each of the two Romanian sketes on Athos, but permission was refused by the Ecumenical Patriarchate on the grounds that there were 'already enough Romanians on the Holy Mountain'. It is not only the Greek government but also the Patriarchate that would like to Hellenize Athos.[31] 'Why should the Romanians be treated in this fashion?', asked Bishop Kallistos in a recent article.

> What possible threat do they present to the Greek government? The Romanian monks have never created any disturbances on the Holy Mountain; and Prodromou enjoys excellent relations with the Great Lavra, the ruling monastery on whose territory it stands. It is clear that the opposition to the recruitment of non-Greek monks, whether Romanian or otherwise, does not come from the Greek monasteries or from the holy community at Karyes . . .
>
> One thing is beyond dispute. The exclusion of non-Greeks is directly contrary to the international treaties governing the Holy Mountain. It is contrary to the constitutional charter of Athos, and to the principles of the European community, of which Greece is a member. It is contrary above all to the idea which has inspired the monastic republic of Athos ever since its foundation more than a thousand years ago. The Mountain has always been supra-national, never an ethnic enclave, never the exclusive preserve of one national group. It has always been a centre of *ecumenical* Orthodoxy, and may it always remain so.[32]

Gradually the position of the Romanian skete of Prodromou improved under the inspired leadership of the much-admired prior Fr Petronios, though persistent requests for it to be upgraded to a monastery were ignored. But despite its extensive buildings, now restored to good order, and excellent relations with its parent monastery, Megiste Lavra, numbers never rose much above twenty or so. Meanwhile at Lakkou, the other skete reserved for Romanians, numbers dwindled to four in 1975 and just one in 1977. Then in 1985 a dynamic new prior arrived, Fr Stefan Nutescu, and with him a group of a dozen young monks eager to bring life back to this eighteenth-century settlement that was on the verge of collapse. Subsequently others came to join them and they have succeeded in reviving the skete, despite great poverty and very difficult circumstances. There is a third settlement of Romanians at Kolitsou, a group of cells dependent on Vatopedi, where the famous (and blind) Elder Dionysios has lived for many years and gathered around himself a number of devoted disciples. Vatopedi is one of the most cosmopolitan houses on Athos today and within the monastery at the time of writing there were a further thirteen Romanian monks, including three novices. From having been the smallest and the most persecuted of all the minorities, the Romanians have become the most numerous, with over 100 monks now on the Mountain.

THREATS TO THE PAN-ORTHODOXY AND AUTONOMY OF ATHOS

Apart from the ups and downs (mostly downs) experienced by the non-Greek houses, there have been other, more insidious threats to the ancient pan-Orthodox traditions of the Mountain and to its autonomy. In May 1992 the entire brotherhood of the Prophet Elijah skete was brutally expelled by a delegation of bishops from the Patriarchate in Constantinople. Since its foundation in the mid-eighteenth century this had been a Russian house, and since 1957 its monks had refused to commemorate the ecumenical patriarch. They were therefore technically in an irregular canonical position, but that is no excuse for the violent manner of their expulsion and the absence of any due process of law. The Patriarchate claimed that this episode was not motivated by anti-Russian sentiments, a claim that is not borne out by the facts.[33] The house has since been repopulated with Greek monks from the skete of Xenophontos.

In February 1994 a similar delegation of bishops arrived unannounced on Athos and expressed its intention of presiding at the meeting of the Holy Community planned for the next day. This was opposed by a majority of the representatives, though a minority of six were willing to accept the intervention. The immediate response of the delegation was to depose for no good reason the abbot of Xeropotamou and the representatives of Dionysiou, Philotheou and Simonopetra. As it happens, the deposed fathers were among the most outspoken on the subject of minority rights. The monks saw this as an unacceptable interference on the part of Constantinople in their traditional autonomy. Protests were published in the British and Greek press, and at Easter the depositions were finally retracted by patriarchal fax. But relations between the Mountain and the Patriarchate were badly damaged, and the split in the Holy Community between the majority and 'the six' was to fester for some time.

In 1995 there was yet another incident involving the most senior monastery, Megiste Lavra. Lavra had been one of 'the six', the group of monasteries willing to support the Patriarchate's interventions, but there were signs that it was wavering and might join the other side. This would have given the necessary two-thirds majority to the group that contested the attempts by Constantinople to undermine the autonomy and the pan-Orthodox traditions of the Mountain. In March another delegation was sent from Constantinople and this time due notice had been given to the Holy Community. But after a token reception in Karyes the bishops went straight to Lavra where they instituted a 'trial' behind locked doors. The outcome was that the abbot should remain in place but that three of his staunchest supporters (senior members of a group who had formed the cenobitic nucleus of the brotherhood at Lavra and who were believed to be traditionalists) should leave the monastery and return to their previous home at the skete of St Anne. This in effect ensured the loyalty of Lavra to the Patriarchate and the bishops regarded the crisis as solved. The Holy Community in Karyes, however, was understandably enraged at this interference in its domestic affairs and reserved its right not to accept the results.

Nevertheless the interference continued. The Patriarchate already reserved the right to grant (or withhold) blessings not only to non-Orthodox clergy who wished to make a pilgrimage to Athos but also to non-Greek Orthodox priests. Now it proposed to 'approve' the elections of abbots and of representatives to the Holy Community. It expressed a wish to vet the applications of non-Greek novices to the monasteries and to have the final say in the tonsuring of non-Greek monks. Shocked by these developments, the Holy Community asked, 'Why should only the non-Greeks be vetted by Constantinople before a monastery can accept them as novices? The Greeks too should be scrutinized; otherwise how could one reasonably deny the charge of racism?'

In addition to numerous incidents of novices being expelled from the non-Greek monasteries, it was by no means uncommon for parties of Slav or Romanian pilgrims either to be turned back at the border or to have their passports stamped with a visa that specifically excluded their entry to Athos. One such episode had occurred in the spring of 1994, when a boat bringing a group of Bosnian Serb students to visit Chilandar for a few hours was turned back by Greek officials. It elicited the following statement from the Holy Community:

These episodes, which have taken place repeatedly, not only at the expense of Orthodox foreigners, but also of Greeks from abroad and distinguished non-Orthodox foreigners, friends of the holy monasteries, are a flouting of the inalienable right of hospitality of the twenty ruling monasteries, which alone are the hosts on the Holy Mountain. In this way, the ancient self-governing status of the Holy Mountain is circumvented, its religious and spiritual mission is hindered, its universality and international repute are undermined, and Greece is discredited as an Orthodox and democratic country abroad.[34]

Embarrased by their powerlessness to repudiate these challenges to their autonomy, the fathers resorted to appealing for support from other Orthodox Churches, other Christian Churches, the European Union, and the Friends of Mount Athos. The latter responded by publishing an article in *The Times* on Easter Monday 1995, signed by their President, Sir Steven Runciman, which stated:

For their part, the Foreign Ministry and the Patriarchate declare unswerving loyalty to the constitutional guarantees, and to the self-governing status of Athos in particular, 'so long as these are interpreted correctly', though what is meant by 'correctly' has never been clearly stated. Yet it is manifestly clear that the Ecumenical Patriarchate, steered by the Foreign Ministry that cannot itself afford to be accused of ethnic cleansing or constitutional violation, has exceeded its mandate of spiritual supervision of the mountain.

Sir Steven went on to emphasize the importance of the traditionalist position:

The [Holy] Community realises that the very heart and strength of Athonite monasticism is its ecumenical profile. As a federation of monastic houses, its belief in supranational parity is not a separatist movement but simply a traditional reality. The fathers' common Orthodox faith transcends and conquers ethnic differences. Mount Athos should not be the bugbear but the boast of modern Greece. As a member of the multinational EU, Greece alone can point to this unique republic under God—a paradigm of harmonious collaboration among different peoples striving for a common cause. The Ecumenical Patriarchate in Turkey, itself a persecuted entity, should rejoice in this most valuable adornment in its spiritual jurisdiction.[35]

The extent to which such protests carry weight in the corridors of the Phanar can never be known. We should perhaps content ourselves by remarking that the civil governor and his deputy, whom the Holy Community had identified as 'agents' of the Patriarchate and who had persistently interfered in their decision-making processes, were replaced; that an attempt was made, in January 1996, to bolster the cenobitic life of the Lavra by introducing the seventeen-member brotherhood of the cell of Bourazeri in Karyes (sadly this well-intentioned experiment failed and the Bourazeri brotherhood withdrew from the monastery); and that the Patriarchate has desisted from its aggressive policy of the early 1990s and no further incidents of patriarchal interference in the internal affairs of the Mountain have been reported. The unofficial schism between 'the six' and the other monasteries has ceased to have any real significance and is more or less forgotten, and at the same time relations with the Patriarchate have greatly improved. Groups of senior monks have been invited to visit the Phanar on a number of occasions in recent years and Patriarch Bartholomew, as part of his celebration of the millennium, planned to spend several days on Athos in July 2000, though this visit unfortunately did not take place.

EXHIBITING THE TREASURES OF MOUNT ATHOS

In 1997 the city of Thessaloniki, once joint capital of the Byzantine empire, was proclaimed that year's Cultural Capital of Europe. The centrepiece and single most successful event of the celebration was an exhibition entitled 'Treasures of Mount Athos', which filled the six halls of the recently built Museum of Byzantine Culture. Comprising some 650 items, most of them never seen before outside the Holy Mountain, it was the largest exhibition ever to have been mounted in Greece.

That the exhibition took place at all was a triumph of diplomacy. Several years of inconclusive discussion had preceded the agreement of the Holy Community in 1995 to loan the treasures of the monastic communities for this purpose. Even so, not all the monasteries participated: four of them (Megiste Lavra, Philotheou, Esphigmenou, and Konstamonitou) refused to contribute on the grounds that their 'treasures' were liturgical and devotional objects and that it was inappropriate to take them out of their religious context and treat them as secular exhibits in a museum. This did not prevent some overexcited visitors from trying to venerate certain exhibits, and it was no doubt a wise decision not to include in the exhibition any of the miracle-working icons and relics. Nevertheless the sheer assembly of items—manuscripts, paintings, sculpture and minor arts—was astonishing. No visitor, however privileged, to any monastery, however wealthy, ever saw such an array of Byzantine and post-Byzantine art. Everything was well displayed, beautifully lit, and accurately captioned; the catalogue, an invaluable 695-page work of reference, constituted a treasure in itself. Furthermore, the exhibits could at least be seen and lingered over, which is by no means always the case when they are in their usual location.

The agreement of the monks to loan their treasures was motivated by two principal concerns—the first was that they should be seen by that half of the world's population that is normally denied access to them (and they were keen that a majority of the tour guides and museum attendants should be women), the second the promotion of Orthodoxy in general. That the exhibition attracted half a million visitors in its first six months and was extended to Easter 1998, that it was greeted with great warmth by the world's press, and that most of its reviewers were women is some measure of its success. There was also a direct benefit for the monks: all the items exhibited were given the most thorough treatment by an expert team of conservators and a substantial sum of money was also received for the general benefit of the Holy Mountain.

But undoubtedly the greatest benefit to accrue to the fathers from the risk they took in exhibiting their treasures was the raising of the profile of the Holy Mountain. Athos was brought to the attention of millions of people throughout the world, many of whom were previously unaware of its existence, let alone its importance. Following major exhibitions of Byzantine art in Geneva, New York and Moscow, the Thessaloniki event attracted wide coverage in the media, both in Greece and abroad; and even if some of the reportage was ill informed or misguided, it served to bring the message home that Athos is a uniquely valued treasure-house and a dynamic and vigorous witness to the traditions of pan-Orthodox monasticism. The representatives and principals of the twenty monasteries wrote in the Foreword to the Exhibition Catalogue:

> Mount Athos, it has been said before, is not merely a transient episode in the life of the Orthodox Church. Created by the Byzantine Hellenic spirit at a time of spiritual maturity, artistic vigour, and worldwide influence, it is an age-old institution, the most important centre of monastic life, pan-Orthodox in character and global in its influence. Down the ages, many currents of religious art have intersected here and the cultures of the neighbouring Orthodox peoples meet here peacefully and fruitfully.
>
> As it moves through the second millennium of its uninterrupted life, vital and flourishing, despite the earth-shattering upheavals taking place in the world around it, Athos remains true, sheltered by its guardian Our Lady the Mother of God, to its *raison d'être*, as a place of silence proper to monastic renunciation and ascesis, but also as a centre of culture, learning, and artistic achievement.[36]

ATHOS REGAINS ITS *RAISON D'ÊTRE*

After the long centuries of Ottoman rule the Athonites had been faced with a twofold dilemma—how to reassert their independence and how to rediscover their reason for being. Their autonomy was established once and for all by the charter of 1924. Since then, despite occasional disputes, the monks have had the security of knowing exactly what their rights were and how far their independence stretched. But defining their *raison d'être* was another matter. During the Tourkokratia they had assumed a vital and unchallenged role as the guardians of Hellenism. Of course they continued to pursue their spiritual obedience in the time-honoured way, but their most tangible contribution was the preservation of Greek cultural identity by means of care for the language, literature (both secular and liturgical) and religion of their forebears. They did this supremely well; not for nothing was Athos known as the 'ark' of Hellenism.

Once they were liberated from the Turkish yoke, once Athos became part of the young and vigorous Greek state, the monks were stripped of this role. Suddenly they lost a large part of their *raison d'être*. Ironically it seemed that the Turks, like Cavafy's barbarians, were 'a kind of solution'. Even though the Great Idea (of a Greek state that would embrace all the Greeks of the Ottoman empire, including most importantly the city of Constantinople) was in ruins and Greece was overrun by impoverished, starving, unemployed refugees, the Greeks were a free people with their own land, their own language, their own culture, and their own religion. Finally released from its political/cultural responsibility, the Mountain needed to find a new role. It faltered—for half a century—and by the 1960s, when Athos was celebrating a past of thousand years, it seemed to many observers to have no future at all.

But the spiritual traditions of Athos are extremely resilient. They had not died at all and, as we have seen, they swiftly began to revive. The monks succeeded in fending off the attacks of ill-informed politicians who saw the Mountain as a cheap way of boosting the country's tourist industry. They resisted suggestions that they needed reform—that they should become more ecumenically minded, that they should adopt European time, that they should do something about their economy, sell off their treasures, invest more heavily in their timber industry, build proper roads, even admit women. Athos needed none of these things. And, more to the point, Athos was once again responding to a need that clearly existed, a need for a radical alternative to the fast-growing, fast-moving secularization of modern society in the outside world. Moreover the monks succeeded in parrying the demands of an insecure Patriarchate, obedient to the whims of a nationalist government in Athens, that they should abandon their ancient rights of autonomy and traditions of pan-Orthodoxy and allow the whole peninsula to be Hellenized. In so doing, the monks found that they were being listened to, that they still had access to powerful friends when they needed them, and that they commanded an authoritative voice in the world. In short, they had regained their original role as the spiritual heart of Orthodoxy.

ATHOS TODAY: FOR THE MONK

U ntil very recently anyone wishing to write positively about Athos had to talk about the past. Thirty or forty years ago, looking at the sad state of affairs into which most of the monasteries had fallen, who could pretend that the Mountain's future was likely to be as glorious as its Byzantine or even its post-Byzantine past? Who indeed could confidently predict that it had a future at all?

The Greek statesman Eleftherios Venizelos (1864–1936) was aware of the problem as early as the 1930s when he said, 'The Greek state and the Greek people as a whole look to the Holy Mountain as to the ark of our religious and national traditions . . . The changed mentality of the world does not regard monastic life as it was regarded in earlier centuries; but the Holy Mountain has exceptional reasons [for continued existence], and we are internationally bound, and it is to our national interest, to preserve monastic life there.'[1] As the crisis deepened, others echoed his words. In 1944 the celebrated iconographer Photis Kontoglou (1895–1965) wrote of Athos as 'a priceless treasure, something unique in the world, . . . where everything is calm and sanctified, where men find spiritual consolation, become holy and pray day and night for mankind'.[2] In 1963, on the occasion of the Athonite millennium, Basil Laourdas (1912–1971), Director of the Institute for Balkan Affairs in Thessaloniki, said: 'We must preserve intact the presence of the Holy Mountain as a spiritual power, as the Greek people have preserved it intact for one thousand years. And we must hand it over intact to the generations that will come.'[3]

Writing a few years earlier, Philip Sherrard reflected on the capacity of the Mountain to survive 'a gigantic and turbulent past', but the picture that he drew of the few survivors, however evocative it may be, is scarcely encouraging:

> Yet through all this history the life of the monastic community has persisted. On the sheer naked rocks at the base of the great peak still cluster the hermits, like watchful eagles in their eyries; the wooden gong still summons from their cells to the central church—the *katholikon*—monks of each of the twenty surviving monasteries. 'Forsake the world and join us', some of the monks told a traveller of the last century; 'with us you will find your happiness. Do but look at the Retreat there with its fair walls, at the hermitage on the mountain, how the westering sun flashes on its window panes! How charmingly the chapel peeps out from the bright green of the leafy chestnut forest, in the midst of vine branches, laurel hedges, valerian, and myrtle! How the water bubbles forth, bright as silver,

from beneath the stones, how it murmurs along the oleander bushes! Here you will find soft breezes, and the greatest of all blessings—freedom and inward peace. For he alone is free, who has overcome the world, and has his dwelling in the laboratory of all virtues on Mount Athos.'[4]

How charming! How romantic! How utterly antipathetic to the siren voices of secularism and materialism that beckoned the vast majority of young men born into a society that prided itself in being modern, postmodern, and even post-christian. How could Athos ever be the same again?

OUTWARD AND VISIBLE SIGNS OF RENEWAL

We have already seen that, despite appearances, the spiritual tradition of the Mountain was alive and well, though its centre of operations had moved temporarily from the monasteries to the cells. The influx of new recruits never dried up completely, though the few that did come shunned the crumbling towers and faltering spirituality of the ruling monasteries, choosing instead the harsher conditions of a life in the desert, joining the circle of some charismatic elder. Statistics of new monks arriving on the Mountain give an indication of how long it took before the downward trend was truly reversed. In the five years from 1972 to 1976 143 new monks arrived, an average of just 29 a year. In the decade from 1977 to 1986 284 new monks came, at the same average rate of 29 a year. But the decade from 1987 to 1996 saw the arrival of no fewer than 609 new monks, an average of 61 a year.[5] From these figures it is clear that the influx has been more than sustained and that it more than doubled in the 1990s. By this time the monasteries were functioning again; but they had had to change their ways: they were very different places from what they had been in the 1960s and 1970s.

At one level, a rather superficial level, monasteries may be said not to be in the forefront of change; some would no doubt describe them as bastions of tradition. But even monasteries have had to admit that life in the world changed rapidly in the course of the twentieth century; they were eventually persuaded to accept some of the changes and they must acknowledge that some of the changes have been beneficial. There was, for example, no particular virtue in serving food that was positively unappetizing, or in refusing the services of a qualified doctor when someone fell ill, or in turning a blind eye to the obvious advantages of modern technology as a means of communication. The fact that these changes were accepted undoubtedly contributed to the ease with which the monasteries were able to regain their vitality.

Novices arrived with a whole new range of skills, many of them portable.

The Mountain was attracting young men with inquiring minds who in many cases already had a university degree. Qualified doctors and dentists were warmly welcomed, as were theologians, philosophers, linguists and men of letters. Even a doctorate in bioethics offered valuable applications in the context of an intellectual brotherhood while a degree in business administration helped to ensure that the restoration of the fabric was in safe hands.

Such men came from all over the world. Many of course were Greeks; others came from the traditional Orthodox heartlands of Russia, Serbia, Bulgaria, and Romania, and there are currently four Georgian monks on the Mountain, though none of them at Iviron. But many came from other parts of the world—from Western Europe, North America, Australia, the Middle East and South Africa. This is partly a reflection of the worldwide Orthodox diaspora, but it also reflects the increasing popularity that the Orthodox Church is enjoying in the west as a whole.[6]

Nor were they all necessarily intellectuals. Men with artistic talents facilitated the revival of many of the Mountain's traditional arts. Music, for example, had followed an interesting progression during the twentieth century. During the first two decades, when Russians dominated so much of Athonite life, Athos yielded to the current vogue for Italianate harmony that was being propagated by musicians trained in the west. In the 1920s and 1930s, as the Russian population declined and there was at the same time an influx of refugees from Asia Minor, Anatolian sounds were introduced into the repertoire and some of these may be detected even to this day. In the post-war decades there was a new fashion for virtuoso solo performance, most famously represented by the voice of Deacon Dimitrios Firfiris (d. 1991), who was in constant demand for his improvisations not only on the Mountain but also in the outside world. Since the mid-1970s there has been a shift back from solo to choral singing and a revival of traditional Byzantine chant. New settings have been composed to complement the renewed emphasis on the Book of Psalms and at several monasteries full double choirs are now a feature of every service.[7]

One aspect of the current intellectual renaissance is the ability of the monks to examine the ancient manuscripts and treasures that they possess in order to rediscover the traditional practices of their predecessors. This applies to painting as much as to music. As a result, there has been a revival of traditional icon painting, not only in the sketes (where the art had always flourished in the past) but also in the monasteries, where some very fine work is now being done according to strict Byzantine principles. Perhaps even more important is the attention that many monasteries are now giving to restoring, studying, and publishing full and scholarly catalogues of the icons and other works of art in their possession.

Libraries too have benefited from the current revival. The facilities in

90 A revival in the arts. Icons are once again being painted in the monasteries according to strict Byzantine principles.

91 A revival in learning. Manuscript libraries are being put in good order and made accessible to scholars.

many monasteries have been modernized or even rebuilt. Funds have been made available for the acquisition of new printed books. And after many decades of neglect manuscripts are being properly cared for, often in controlled environments. Librarians tend to know more about the collections of which they have charge and are more willing than they used to be to admit visitors and show off some of their more prized possessions. Scholars are given much easier access to documents they need to study; many new catalogues are in preparation, and the ongoing programme of editing and publishing the archives of the monasteries has received a new impetus.

The recent publication of a large number of important books bears witness to the revival of theological scholarship on the Holy Mountain. We have already mentioned *Hymn of Entry*, a translation of *Eisodikon*, first published in 1974 by Archimandrite Vasileios of Iviron (formerly of Stavronikita). In his Foreword to the English edition Bishop Kallistos places it firmly in the tradition of the early fathers:

The quality that characterizes this remarkable book is above all a sense of organic wholeness, such as may be found in St Maximus the Confessor. The unity of the divine and the human in the incarnate Christ, the unity of heaven and earth in the Divine Liturgy, the unity between theology and spirituality, between theology and life—such are the author's master-themes.[8]

An earlier work, *Between Heaven and Earth* by Fr Theoklitos of Dionysiou, first published in 1956, was a trail-blazer. Emmanuel Amand de Mendieta, writing in 1972, described the author as 'perhaps the best theologian now living on Mount Athos'.[9] Written in the form of a Platonic dialogue, the book presents an imaginary but highly plausible conversation between a visiting monk (the narrator), two lay pilgrims (a lawyer and a theologian), two Athonite monks, and a hermit. The lawyer is initially very sceptical about the religious life, but as the discussion proceeds he slowly begins to understand its value. Though a member of a cenobitic monastery, the author believes that the only way for a monk to achieve perfection is by living a life of complete isolation and ceaseless prayer. In a striking passage the hermit explains that in order to experience divination (*theosis*), the ultimate goal of every spiritual person, the monk must devote himself to a self-crucifying programme of asceticism:

'To reach this stage, to become passionless in the patristic and not in the Stoic meaning of the word, requires struggle, time, hardship, fasting, vigils, prayer, sweat "like drops of blood", acceptance of contumely, humiliation, crucifixion, the body nailed to the Cross, wounds in the side, the vinegar, the desertion by all, the mockery of some silly brother crucified at one's side, the blasphemy of those that pass by . . . Then follow Resurrection in the Lord, and Easter in the incorruptibility of the holiness . . . Or else . . .'

The hermit's voice dropped; he fixed his eyes on a large painting of Christ on the Cross, of the Cretan school, which was hanging on the east wall of the room. Christ's head was pale, intensified by the twilight, death-like; all the beauty of his features was gone . . .[10]

More recently, Fr Makarios of Simonopetra has produced a magnificent collection of saints' lives of the Orthodox Church in six volumes entitled *The Synaxarion*. First published in French (1987–96), it is now being translated into English (1998–). In his Preface to the English edition Archimandrite Aimilianos explains that its appearance is due to the demands of pilgrims,

[who] with a sense of something missing or lacking, have spoken from the depths of their souls of the need, as of their daily bread, for an Orthodox Synaxarion in their own language . . . On account of these earnest entreaties, we have laid upon the priest-monk Makarios, a brother of our Monastery, the task of editing a Synaxarion of the Orthodox Church for the Orthodox friends of the Holy Mountain in the Diaspora who have asked it of us and, at the same time, to respond to the needs of the Orthodox Mission, as we have also been urged to do.[11]

92 Improving the cuisine. A new kitchen rises beside the refectory at Iviron.

Other books worthy of note include the writings of Fr Aimilianos himself, of which three volumes have appeared in Greek and one (so far) in English. These discourses provide valuable information on the early days of the monastic revival and its origin, in this instance, at Meteora. In his enthronement address to the assembled elders, for example, the abbot addressed the practical issue of the integration of the newcomers with the survivors of the old brotherhood:

> When we arrived and settled in this sacred, soaring and holy monastery, we were accorded such a reception on the part of the older fathers living here that we were amazed. We were left speechless and filled with emotion. How often have we seen tears in the eyes of the elders of our monastery, how often have we seen them expressing their love in a thousand ways, their confidence, their respect and their esteem! We came as humble servants and we found more than we had anticipated. We came humbly to venerate them, but instead, they wanted to venerate us.[12]

We have already mentioned the biography of Elder Joseph the Hesychast by his disciple, Elder Joseph of Vatopedi, which vividly describes the evolution of one of the most dynamic cells in the revival at New Skete.[13] A selection of the elder's letters has also been published and includes a fifty-four-page 'Epistle to a Hesychast Hermit'. Most of the letters are addressed to monks, but they have a universal application to any reader with a spiritually inquiring mind. More than one ends with these comforting words: 'Don't despair! We will go to paradise together. And if I don't place you inside, then I do not want to sit in there either.'[14] Another of the elder's disciples is Elder Ephraim, who in 1973 became abbot of Philotheou. He attracted so many recruits to that monastery that he was able to send them out to revive as many as three other monasteries on Athos (Xeropotamou, Konstamonitou and Karakalou). Since then he has extended his activities to North America and in the 1990s he founded no fewer than sixteen monasteries in the USA and Canada. A selection of his writing has recently appeared focusing on the theme of repentance.[15]

No survey of literature resulting from the monastic revival on Mount Athos should omit the ongoing translation of the *Philokalia*, the great anthology of hesychastic texts by spiritual masters of the Orthodox Christian tradition compiled in the eighteenth century by St Nikodimos of the Holy Mountain and St Makarios of Corinth, edited by Gerald Palmer (d. 1984), Philip Sherrard (d. 1995) and Kallistos Ware and currently being translated into English. Four volumes have appeared to date; the fifth and final volume is eagerly awaited. Its completion will mark a milestone in making the spiritual resources of Orthodoxy available to western readers. The work is dedicated 'to the memory of Father Nikon (1875–1963), Hermit of St George's, Karoulia, on the Holy Mountain of Athos, without whose inspiration this work would not have been undertaken'. Karoulia may not have yielded a harvest of men comparable to that of some of the other sketes, but its harvest of souls will be equal to none as a result of this monumental achievement.

Perhaps the most visible sign of the revival is the restoration of the monastic buildings themselves. Many of them were in a serious state of disrepair due to decreasing numbers of occupants and diminishing sources of income. Idiorrhythmic monks paid scant attention to the fabric of the house as a whole and rarely went further than applying a coat of paint to their own apartment every ten years or so. When new cenobitic brotherhoods arrived, they found themselves faced with an enormous problem of decay. Every monastery soon instituted a programme of restoration, on the basis of which it could apply for grants to fund the work. Some brotherhoods preferred to undertake the bulk of the work themselves, not always with very happy results. Some have been more careful than others to preserve the best of what they inherited. But on the whole the work has been carried out to a high standard; experienced architects and craftsmen have been employed wherever practicable; and as much care as possible has been taken to ensure that any new construction conforms to traditional models and styles and employs the same materials and methods as in the past.

The experience of one monastery will serve as an example of the scale of operations being undertaken to a greater or lesser extent by all the ruling monasteries. In 1996 Vatopedi published an illustrated volume which included details of its programme of restoration, how much had so far been achieved and how much remained to be done. Given that the new brotherhood had been in place for a mere six years, the record is impressive:

> Restoration has already finished in the old refectory, the kitchen, the gatehouse, the old workers' quarters, the stable and part of the underground passage (to be used for fire safety, power lines and water pipes, and for cables of all kinds). Work is also nearing completion on the lodgings for the Ministry of Culture's restorers, and also on the arsenal buildings to accommodate the necessary services. Restoration is progressing in half of the west wing to provide guest quarters, and in the icon repository where the study envisages an exhibition centre for the monastery's movable, spiritual and cultural heritage...Restoration work is also continuing on the treasury, as well as on the roofs and facades of the Katholikon.[16]

The monastery's 'architectural heritage programme' listed under 'operations of top priority' the following building works 'to answer the principal immediate needs of the brotherhood':

1. *Katholikon*: The maintenance and restoration of the roofs and facades of the Katholikon is a priority because of its special spiritual, historical, and artistic value . . .
2. *Clocktower*: A solution to certain structural problems, support of the top floor, restoration of the walls, maintenance of the roof.
3. *Refectory*: Restoration, and where necessary replacement, of embrasures, repair of the roof, and conservation of the ancient decoration.
4. *Kitchen*: The installation of a new kitchen in the north wing is necessary because the existing one is inadequate . . .
5. *Operations on half of the east wing*: The aim is the preservation of this important building and the modernization of its facilities so that the fathers of the Holy Monastery can live in it . . .
6. *Tower of the Virgin Mary*: The Tower of the Virgin Mary accommodates the old library which contains manuscripts, early printed materials, the archive, and other treasures. The tower presents problems due to penetration of damp and various structural faults . . .
7. *The 'Hatoularion' workers' house*: The aim is to preserve this nineteenth-century building and to modernize and improve the living conditions of the workers . . .
8. *Olive-press*: The survey has been completed and work is beginning.
9. *South-west and west wings*: Operations of limited extent are required so that decay may be arrested and the fathers housed while restoration is carried out on the east wing . . .
10. *North-west wing*: Operations of limited extent are required to improve the living conditions of the numerous pilgrims and visitors . . .[17]

Costs of Renewal

Renewal on such a scale inevitably incurs costs. Apart from the sheer financial burden, much of which has been borne by the European Union, the Greek government, and other sympathetic organizations, there have been other costs which have to be weighed against the numerous manifest benefits.

To help fund the programme of restoration, many monasteries were tempted to exploit their forests for timber, one of the few natural resources of the Mountain. There had been a small-scale timber industry in operation since the early years of the twentieth century. The Aleppo pine, particularly widespread in the northern parts of the peninsula, grows tall and straight and has apparently provided the raw material for the great majority of Greece's telegraph poles. Among the less well-advised business ventures of recent years one monastery leased some 500 hectares of Aleppo pine to the papermakers Softex. The company promptly bulldozed the whole area and tried to reforest it with faster-growing sorts of pine. These did not flourish and the entire scheme was a failure, prompting monks to comment wryly on the relative merits of telegraph poles and lavatory paper in the Garden of the Mother of God. Many of the other monasteries protested loudly at this commercial exploitation of Athonite territory, but the contract remains in place.

Until recently the only means of transporting timber overland on Athos was by mule. Every monastery had its own jetty, where the mule trains would deposit their burdens for export by sea. But once the first road had been built in 1963, the monks began to see the advantages of using motorized vehicles in place of mules, and in a very short space of time a large number of dirt roads had been cut into the forests, initially for the sole purpose of extracting timber. It was a short step from allowing roads for timber lorries to allowing roads for other forms of communication, and there is now a network of such roads across the whole peninsula connecting monasteries with each other and with the capital, Karyes. The surfaces are still rough and unsuitable for ordinary motorcars; but every monastery now has at least one or two four-wheel-drive vehicles, and even some hermits are motorized, though happily there are still no roads (nor any planned) crossing the frontier into the world or desecrating the desert at the southern tip of the peninsula.

The building of roads has resulted in a number of associated phenomena that are commonly deplored by visitors to the Mountain. The atmosphere is polluted by diesel fumes; the roadside is littered with empty cans, used tyres, and other detritus; the paths and tracks, originally built for mule traffic but also greatly enjoyed by pilgrims, have in many cases been destroyed in order to make way for the roads; there is even at times a parking problem at Karyes; and, worst of all, the silence of Athos is disturbed.[18]

Since 1963 there has been a regular bus service, however rudimentary and uncomfortable, connecting Daphne with Karyes, and sometimes Iviron.

It is a hair-raising journey and the bus is invariably packed to capacity, but the service is at least regulated by the state which charges a modest sum for tickets. The existence of other roads has bred a new spirit of commercial enterprise among the monks, and there is now a monastic taxi service, offering rides (to those who can afford the fares) to all points on the peninsula.

Other forms of commercialization have crept into the Athonite way of life. The number of shops selling books and religious paraphernalia at Daphne and Karyes is greater than that which was prescribed by any ancient *typikon*. Lay pedlars find their way on to the Mountain and are often to be seen displaying their wares in the streets of the capital. Similarly, most monasteries have seized the opportunity to market their products in the form of CDs or tape cassettes, mass-produced icons, prayer ropes, postcards, books, wine, and different flavours of incense. There is nothing wrong with this and most pilgrims welcome the chance to buy souvenirs of their visit to take home as well as the ability to contribute in however modest a way to the monks' economy, but it is symptomatic of a general trend towards greater commercialization of the Mountain.

The downside of the intellectual and artistic strengthening of Athos is the loss of certain skills that were once *de rigueur* for monks. Just as Greece was until recently a largely rural society, so monks were drawn largely from a peasant background. Several monasteries had close associations with a particular region or particular island, and as a result monks shared an interest in fishing or farming or whatever occupation was carried on by the folk of that place. Nowadays most monks come from an urban background and few come equipped with these traditional skills, though there is a remarkable range of talents in most monasteries. Faced with the need for self-sufficiency, many now have to learn trades that were second nature to their predecessors.

Some specialized lore, such as knowledge of certain medicinal plants, has probably been lost completely and a number of crafts that were once commonly practised on the Mountain seem to have died out. There were, for example, until recently many metalworkers—blacksmiths, locksmiths, tinsmiths, coppersmiths, silversmiths, brass founders, bell founders, etc. Eighteenth-century Athos was an important centre for the production not only of clocks but also of guns. Records show that there were as many as ten gunsmiths' workshops in Karyes, one of which was still active as late as 1920.[19] Their disappearance may not be any cause of regret to a more politically correct generation, though the fact that hunting is outlawed so vociferously is a sure indication of its continued practice. But the replacement of the Athonite artisan by the quartz chip is as much to be regretted as the loss of the mule and what followed from that.

INWARD AND SPIRITUAL SIGNS OF RENEWAL

The majority of monks welcome the fact that renewal is taking place, though such approval is far from being universal, and many deplore certain facets of the new order. But for the monk *qua* monk none of these changes is of any real consequence. Nor are the monks particularly concerned about numbers or statistics. Their confidence in the Mother of God's ability to ensure an adequate supply of novices is exemplified in the words of Fr Theoklitos of Dionysiou, writing at the time of the millennium celebrations in 1963: 'The Holy Mountain will always remain as it is, a place of repentance, of purification and of incessant praising of the Lord, and a monastic centre that continues the ancient monastic tradition of the Orthodox Church.'[20]

The reasons why men become monks have not changed. There may be added incentive perhaps in the desire to escape from what appears to be the ever-increasing secularism and materialism of the modern world; but this is merely a negative reason for leaving it. Monks come to Athos for positive reasons, as they have always done. Constantine Cavarnos reports the following conversation with a hermit at Karoulia:

> 'Why did I come here? you will ask me', said the hermit, whose name was John. '*For the sake of eternity*. Our life here on earth, whether we are plain folks, scientists or professors, princes or kings, will inevitably come to an end. When we die, these titles and capacities will mean nothing, absolutely nothing. The only thing that will matter then will be the quality of our soul, whether it is good or bad, whether we have saved it or lost it. Heaven and hell are everlasting, whereas our earthly life is insignificantly brief.'[21]

The only aspect of the revival that has made any serious impact on the monks' way of life has been the final abandonment of the idiorrhythmic system. Within the space of a quarter of a century (1968–92) all nine remaining idiorrhythmic monasteries reverted to the cenobitic rule. And whereas in 1956 the monasteries housed only a minority of the monks on the Mountain (43.7%), now the position is reversed and in 2000 the monasteries contained a majority (56.4%). The Mountain continues, as always, to offer the full range of monastic life-styles; and life in the cells and most of the sketes could never be anything other than idiorrhythmic. But the majority of newcomers made it clear that their overriding preference was for the cenobitic life, at least as regards the monasteries, and that change cannot be reversed.

Certain changes flow automatically from the return to a common life. Daily services in the katholikon are now regularly attended by the vast majority of the monks: there was no such requirement in idiorrhythmic monasteries. Refectories too are once again in regular use, and on most days

93 Inside the refectory at Vatopedi. The ancient marble tables are once again in daily use after centuries of neglect in idiorrhythmic times.

monks eat together twice: idiorrhythmic monasteries opened the doors of their refectories only on feast days. In many monasteries, simple tasks like preparing vegetables are often performed by most of the brotherhood working together—in silence, but with one monk reciting the Jesus Prayer. 'Work and pray!', cries the abbot, encouraging the pilgrims, willing but hesitant, to join in too. The overall impression is of a brotherhood living, working and praying together in harmony and love.

The Jesus Prayer is central to the spiritual revival. The injunction of St Paul, echoed by Elder Joseph the Hesychast and other Athonite teachers, to 'pray without ceasing' is eagerly followed by monks today. Inner prayer, or prayer of the heart as it is often called, was preached on the Mountain in the fourteenth century by St Gregory of Sinai, in the eighteenth century by the leaders of the Kollyvades movement, and in the twentieth century by all the luminaries of the current revival. As Archimandrite Aimilianos has written,

Inner prayer is the attribute of the angels. It is the unceasing activity of the angelic hosts. It is the bread, the life, the language of these immaterial beings and their way of expressing their love of God. And the monks, who precisely live the angelic life in the flesh, affirm their love of God through the same unceasing prayer as that of the angels . . . The prayer of the monks is the warming up of their heart. It places them in touch with the Father and Creator of the world. It is their elevation to Heaven. Prayer is the encounter and sweet embrace of the monk with the Bridegroom and Savior of our souls.[22]

There is no vow of silence in Orthodox monasteries (except sometimes for novices), but the urge to gossip is countered by recourse to the prayer, in almost any situation. Prayer ropes are just as often to be seen in use when monks are out walking or travelling as they are during pauses in church services. In fact most monks never go anywhere without one; and they are the gift most frequently given to and most gratefully received by visitors to a monastery.

Frequency of communion has long been a matter for debate in Orthodoxy and until recently many monks would receive the sacrament on only a few occasions in the year. Today abbots and spiritual fathers proclaim the importance of more frequent communion and in most monasteries the practice is for the monks to receive at least three times a week. The doctrine of 'continual communion', propounded with such vigour by St Nikodimos of the Holy Mountain and the leaders of the Kollyvades movement in the eighteenth century, is once again in favour. Although confession is not a prerequisite on every occasion, it is clear that monks are making their confession to their spiritual fathers on a more regular basis than was previously the practice.

Perhaps the most significant development of all is the importance now attached to the role of the spiritual father (*pnevmatikos*) or elder (*geron*) in guiding the new generation of novices and younger monks. There is nothing new about the ministry of the spiritual father, and indeed this has always been a valued feature of Athonite monasticism. We have already remarked on the high regard in which numerous elders, such as St Paisy Velichkovsky, St Silouan and Fr Gabriel of Dionysiou, were held by their spiritual children both on and off the Mountain. Athos has produced a continuous stream of such men who continue to operate in the tradition of the saints and who preserve and transmit to their successors the wisdom that they have themselves inherited and accumulated in the course of a life that they have shared with God.[23] It is the presence of so many charismatic elders in the sketes and monasteries, drawing so many devout young men to the Mountain, that is remarkable. As Bishop Kallistos has written, 'What draws them is the *abba* rather than the abbey.'[24] The first task of any would-be monk is always to find the right spiritual father who will offer him the benefit of his wisdom and accept him as a disciple. The advice given to Elder Joseph the Hesychast and his companion Fr Arsenios by Elder Daniel of Katounakia, when they decided to undertake their struggle together, is as valid now as ever it was:

'Do you have an elder? [Fr Daniel asked them.] Without the blessing of your elder, nothing can prosper. Without this seal of a paternal blessing, no spiritual work in our own monastic life bears fruit. This is why I insist that you pass through this requirement, that the grace of God may be with you throughout your lives. Go to an old man, however simple he may seem, and submit yourselves in obedience to him; and when he dies and you have laid him in his grave, you will receive as your inheritance the blessing of God, accompanying you and leading you to advancement of every kind.'[25]

Archimandrite Aimilianos of Simonopetra has himself set a shining example as one of the leading architects of the monastic revival. Let him describe the role of the spiritual father in his own words:

> The monastery is a mystery, a sacrament, and the spiritual father is the visible element of this mystery, behind whom hides the invisible: God, and everything that escapes the senses, which can only be sensed by the spirit . . . The spiritual father is therefore, in fact, the same who takes his disciple, the monk, by the hand in order to introduce him to the Lord. He is the same who brings Christ down, who reunites that which was separated—the realities of heaven and of earth—in order to transform them into the one, unique, and genuine dance. Such is the role of the spiritual father and such is the manner in which the monks perceive him. This is why this discipline exists, this obedience, this charity, this gift of self and this confidence that addresses itself not so much to the superior—who is only a man—but to Christ Whom he represents.[26]

INITIATION PROCEDURES

The stages by which a candidate is initiated into the monastic life vary in some respects from one monastery to the next according to the *typikon* it follows and the preferences of the abbot. The description that follows is therefore not universally applicable, but it is more or less accurate for most houses, although most monasteries no longer tonsure to the little habit.

The candidate must fulfil certain preconditions. He must first of all be a baptized member of the Orthodox Church. This means that he must have been baptized in the Orthodox manner, namely by total immersion and emersion three times in the font which symbolizes a mystical burial and resurrection with Christ. For 'cradle' Orthodox this takes place usually in infancy as a matter of course. For converts from other Christian denominations, however, who are normally received into Orthodoxy by chrismation, it does present a problem. Ever since the mid-eighteenth century, when the Orthodox patriarchs of Constantinople, Alexandria, and Jerusalem declared Latin baptism to be invalid, there has been a debate within Orthodoxy about the rebaptism of converts. The patriarchs decreed that 'the baptisms of heretics are to be rejected and abhorred . . . [They are] waters which cannot profit . . . nor give any sanctification to such as receive them, nor avail at all to the washing away of sins.'[27] In the Greek Church this ruling remained in force until the end of the nineteenth century. On Athos it is still in force today. The fathers cannot accept that sprinkling with holy water has the same validity as baptism by total immersion. Those who have been received into Orthodoxy by chrismation have to be rebaptized if they wish to become Athonite monks.[28]

In addition to being properly baptized, the candidate must be at least eighteen years of age and either be unmarried or, if he has been married, divorced or widowed. He must have come to the monastery of his own free will and he must have settled any questions of inheritance beforehand, since a monk's property is automatically inherited by the monastery on his death.

He will first have to decide which monastery he wishes to enter. This decision is most often governed by the search for a sympathetic spiritual father. It is not uncommon for a prospective novice to travel from one monastery to another until he finds a spiritual father with whom he can establish a satisfactory rapport. Having done so, he will apply to the abbot for admission to the monastery as a novice (*dokimos*). Once accepted, he must serve a probationary period during which time he is assigned to one of the senior monks for instruction. For practical purposes he will live the life of a monk, but he will not yet wear the habit. The length of this period varies: for men under fifty it is not often less than three years (but readiness is more important than age); and the abbot alone will decide when it should end.

Having served his probationary period, the novice is now eligible to be tonsured a monk of the lowest rank, or rasophore (i.e. a wearer of the *rason* or tunic which forms part of his habit). During this simple ceremony the priest prays as follows over the candidate:

> We thank you, O Lord, for by your great mercy you have rescued your servant N from the vain life of the world, and have called him to this modest calling. Grant therefore that he may live worthily in this angelic community; guard him from the snares of the devil; retain his body and soul pure until death; and grant him that he may become your holy temple . . . Clothe him with the garment of sanctification; gird his loins with chastity; make him an advocate of all continence; and grant that to him and to us remain the perfect gift of your fatherly blessings.

The priest will then cut a lock of hair from the candidate's head while invoking the Holy Trinity; he will give him a new name by which he is to be known from now on; and he will cloak him with the *rason* and the head-dress of cap and veil.

The rasophore is not yet a fully professed monk and is not eligible for ordination, though he is expected to obey the rules of the brotherhood and to practise the monastic life. He is not obliged to progress to a higher rank, though assuming he remains in the monastery he is most likely to do so after a certain lapse of time. In idiorrhythmic monasteries (and some others) it was common practice after two or three years to confer the so-called little habit (or small *schema*). The monk would then take formal vows in the context of a much more elaborate ceremony, performed in the katholikon by the

94 A new monk is born. Elder Joseph pronounces his monastic name as Abbot Ephraim effects the tonsure.

abbot in the course of the Divine Liturgy. The service itself is symbolic of three central ideas: the first is that of marriage of the soul with Christ, the divine bridegroom; the second is the idea of a second baptism—like a candidate for baptism the monk was undressed in a side chapel and his head was shorn; and third is the idea of the prodigal son returning to his father's house. The assembled monks led the candidate back into the church singing on his behalf a troparion (hymn) of confession. The candidate prostrated himself before the royal doors where the abbot stood as the father ready to welcome his errant son. The abbot then questioned the candidate as follows:

Q. Why have you come here, brother, falling down before the holy altar and before this holy assembly?

A. I desire the ascetic life, venerable father.

Q. Do you desire to become worthy of the angelic habit and to be ranked in the company of those who are living as monks?

A. Yes, with God's help, venerable father.

Q. Do you come to the Lord of your own free will?

A. Yes, with God's help, venerable father.

Q. Not by any necessity or constraints?

A. No, venerable father.

Q. Will you remain in the monastery and in the ascetic life until your last breath?

A. Yes, with God's help, venerable father.
Q. Will you remain chaste, sober, and pious?
A. Yes, with God's help, venerable father.
Q. Will you until death be obedient to the superior and to all the brotherhood in Christ?
A. Yes, with God's help, venerable father.
Q. Will you endure all the strain and poverty proper to the monastic life, for the kingdom of heaven's sake?
A. Yes, with God's help, venerable father.

Having received acceptable replies to his questions, the abbot proceeded to instruct the candidate as follows:

Understand, my son, what terms you offer to the Lord Jesus Christ; for invisible angels are present recording your vow with which you shall be confronted at the second coming of Christ our Lord. I shall now introduce you to the most perfect life, which reflects the community of the Lord, pointing out to you the things that you must follow and those you must avoid . . . If you wish to become a monk, first of all cleanse yourself of all bodily and spiritual contamination; acquire modesty, through which you shall inherit eternal happiness, put away the impudence of the habits of the worldly life; be obedient to all; do all the work required of you without murmur; in your prayer be firm; in your vigils do not be indolent; beware of temptation; do not break your fasting; for know that through prayer and fasting you may propitiate God . . . The Lord himself said, 'If any man will come after me, let him deny himself, take up his cross, and follow me.' Which means that you must always be prepared, fulfilling his commands until death. You shall be hungry, and thirsty, and naked; insulted, ridiculed, and persecuted; and shall suffer many other misfortunes that life according to God entails. But when you suffer all those things, rejoice, for your reward in heaven shall be high . . .

There then followed first the tonsure, in which the abbot cut a lock of hair from the candidate's head; then the monk's habit was put on, followed by the girdle and the head-dress; and finally the candidate was given a candle, the gospel book, and a cross. After readings from St Paul's Epistle to the Ephesians and chapter 6 of St Matthew's Gospel the candle was lit and the abbot said: 'And the Lord said: Let your light so shine before men that they may see your good works and glorify your Father which is in heaven.' The abbot then embraced the new monk who, as the ceremony came to an end, joined the company of his brothers.

Nowadays most monasteries in accordance with Stoudite tradition leave out the small *schema* stage and proceed straight to the great *schema* or great habit, a higher rank to which the rasophore may be promoted after a slighter longer span of time. Only great *schema* monks may wear the full habit, which includes an elaborately embroidered apron or stole with numerous crosses and Greek acronyms picked out in red—beginning with

M[ichael] and G[abriel] and ending with the skull and cross-bones of Adam at the foot of the cross over the words 'T[opos] K[raniou] [the place of the skull, i.e. Golgotha] P[aradeisos] G[egonen] [has become Paradise]'. This garment symbolizes the cross that the monk takes up when he vows to follow Christ. Great *schema* monks undertake to accept for themselves the cross and death of Christ and take stricter vows than other monks with regard to prayer and fasting. Initiates go through a ceremony similar to that for the small *schema* but of longer duration and more solemn tone. The Divine Liturgy is interrupted at the same point and the choir sings three antiphons which begin:

> By my tears, O Lord, I would blot out the record of my sins, and for the rest of my life I would endeavour to please thee by the practice of penitence. But the enemy never ceases from tempting me and from waging war against my soul. Save me before I am lost! . . .
>
> Having received, in the mystical fountain of regeneration, adoption and redemption, and yet having wasted my life in negligence and in sins, I now cry to thee, good Lord: grant me a fountain of tears of penitence and wash away the stain of my sins, almighty and merciful Saviour . . .
>
> Where is the vain endeavour of the world? Where is the fleeting show of transitory things? Lo, do we not see that they are dust and ashes? Why then labour we in vain? And why do we not renounce the world, and follow him who crieth, He that will come after me, let him take up my cross, and he shall inherit eternal life? . . .

The abbot then asks the same series of questions as in the service for the small *schema*, but the fifth question involves a more serious commitment to total renunciation of the world:

> *Q.* Do you renounce the world and the things of the world, in accordance with the teaching of our Lord Christ?
> *A.* Yes, with God's help, venerable father.

Then the abbot instructs the monk on the subject of penitence, and continues with a description of what renunciation involves:

> According to the plain meaning of the words of Christ, the monastic renunciation is an absolute promise to accept for yourself his cross and his death. Be certain, therefore, that, from today, through this most perfect renunciation by which you are now bound, you are crucified and dead to the world. You renounce your parents, your brothers and sisters; you renounce wife and children; you renounce your fellow citizens, your kindred, your clubs and societies, your friends and your habitual associates; you renounce the tumult and the shouting of the world and its cares; you renounce goods, property and riches; you renounce empty and vain pleasures, and human glory. And, in addition to all the things which I have just enumerated, you renounce yourself . . .

95 'From today . . . you are crucified and dead to the world.' A wall painting in the katholikon of Esphigmenou.

Now the abbot proceeds with a wonderfully lyrical description of the mystical ideal of monasticism, reminding the candidate that through a second baptism he is about to enter the angelic service of God:

> Leap then with joy and thrill with gladness! For today Christ the Lord has chosen you for himself, and has separated you from the life of the world; for he has set you before his face, in the ranks of the army of his monks, among his troops who live a life like that of the angels, in the heights of this existence which resembles that of heaven. God has set you there to serve him as do the angels, to be altogether in his service, to ponder on the things which are above, and to seek the things which are above, for, as the apostle says: 'Our conversation is in heaven.'
>
> O new vocation! O gift of God's own mystery! Today, my brother, you are baptised a second time, through the superabounding graces poured out by our God who loves mankind. Today you are freed of your sins and become one of the sons of light. Christ our Lord himself and his holy angels rejoice at your penitence, and he kills for you the fatted calf . . .

At last the moment of commitment is reached. The abbot places his hand on the gospel and says:

> Christ is here invisible. Understand, no one forces you to come to the *schema* involuntarily; understand that you by your own free will desire the bond of the great angelic *schema*.
> *A.* Yes, venerable father, by my own free will.

A pair of scissors is then placed on the gospel. The monk picks them up and gives them to the abbot, who lays them down again. This action is repeated three times. Only on the third occasion does the abbot keep hold of the scissors and say, 'Look, you have received this from the hands of Christ. See to whom you are coming; whose ranks you are joining; and whom you are renouncing.' Then he cuts a little of the monk's hair in the shape of a cross, saying: 'Our brother *N* has his hair shorn in the name of the Father, and of the Son, and of the Holy Ghost.'

Once monks assume the great habit, they are supposed never to take it off, even in death. In many monasteries the apron is worn only on feast days and days on which communion is received, but monks are otherwise expected to wear the habit night and day. Great *schema* monks are eligible to be ordained to the diaconate or the priesthood, though in practice only a small minority proceed to take orders. They are selected by the abbot, who invites a visiting bishop to perform the ordination. Every monastery needs a sprinkling of priests to serve the Liturgy and hear confessions; the abbot is always a priest and is given the title of archimandrite. Otherwise most monks are content to remain laymen.

Once professed, how does an Athonite monk occupy himself? It is a common misconception that monks spend long periods of time thinking beautiful thoughts in idyllic locations in between consuming large meals and attending interminable church services. In practice, the life of a monk on the Holy Mountain is very different from this. It is traditionally divided into prayer, work and sleep, with eight hours theoretically being available daily for each of these activities. We shall examine below how this schedule works in practice; but first we shall attempt to dispel the myth of monastic idleness.

Monks at Work

An Athonite monastery is a complex living organism that depends on the co-operation of all its members to ensure that it runs smoothly and provides the best possible environment for its inmates and visitors. According to the cenobitic rule every monk must play a part and perform it to the best of his ability. Only those who are pronounced medically unfit or infirm by virtue of their years are excused from working.

The abbot (*hegoumenos*) is theoretically responsible for everything that happens in the house. No one comes or goes, no decision is taken, no rule is made or unmade without his blessing. Within the territory of the monastery he is lord, though in practice he takes the advice of a governing body or council of elders (*synaxis*). When important visitors come to the monastery, he is there to receive them. He will personally represent his monastery when called to attend gatherings elsewhere on the Mountain or in the outside world. His routine is demanding and he is often away on business. He therefore needs a reliable deputy who can stand in for him as necessary and share the burden of office. If the abbot is renowned for his spirituality, it is often the case that his deputy will have administrative skills to complement the spiritual gifts of the abbot.

The abbot is not usually the sole or even the principal father-confessor of the monastery. If the brotherhood is numerous, it is more than one man can do to hear the confessions of all the fathers, in which case the more senior priest-monks will share the responsibility. Answering to the priests are one or two sextons (*ekklesiarches*) who ensure the smooth running of the services in the katholikon; their duties include the maintenance of icons, vestments, and lamps, the supply of candles and incense, the striking of the *simantron* (an iron bar) or *talanto* (a wooden plank used instead of a bell to summon the fathers to prayer), and bell-ringing. Other officers (*epistimonarches*) are charged with ensuring proper behaviour (among both monks and pilgrims) in church and refectory.

Other senior posts requiring administrative skills include that of the treasurer (*tamias*) who is responsible for the financial affairs of the monastery; depending on the size of its endowment or the extent of its

96 Abbot Ephraim of Vatopedi with some of the members of his brotherhood. Standing at the monastery gate they await the arrival of a visiting bishop.

estates, this can be an extremely onerous and responsible job; income from a variety of sources needs to be invested appropriately and expenditure handled in a wise and judicious fashion. The secretary (*grammatefs*) of the monastery handles much of the day-to-day correspondence on behalf of the abbot. The librarian (*bibliothikarios*) is in charge of the manuscript and printed-book collections of the monastery: he may operate a lending service for the brotherhood; he may superintend visiting scholars consulting the archives or manuscripts; and he may be responsible for a programme of conservation or instruction. The monastery's representative (*antiprosopos*) attends the meetings of the Holy Community in Karyes and normally occupies the residence (*konaki*) belonging to the monastery in Karyes during the working week, reporting back to the abbot and attending the Divine Liturgy at weekends.

A sizeable number of monks are involved with provisioning the monastery, headed by the steward (*oikonomos*) who is assisted by the storekeeper (*dochiaris*). The cook (*magiros*) runs the kitchen and ensures that the food he and his staff prepare is wholesome and that it accords with the calendar of fasts and feasts. The baker bakes bread for use not only in the refectory but also in the katholikon: liturgical loaves are kneaded with holy water and blessed by a priest before they are put into service. The cellarer (*kellaritis*) looks after the wine, which has a similar double function. By tradition he needs to be of sober character and not susceptible to temptation. The Russian houses had particular problems with alcohol, as Fennell relates of the Prophet Elijah skete:

We read in the 1904 minutes of the same month that Monk Vladimir swore at the prior, was violent and threw stones at people; this was hardly surprising, as he was at the time the cellarer and had unlimited access to alcohol. Monk Ioasaf was caught being drunk and disorderly, and was banned from drinking raki. These incidents were in March alone; two months later there was a major drink scandal. Three monks were caught, two were severely punished and the worst offender, Monk Parfeny, was forbidden raki after his expulsion from the skete had been revoked.

As a result of this incident the following measures were taken:

* no more written permission to be issued for raki;
* no raki was to be given to brethren washing laundry at the spring;
* only one glass of raki would be permitted in the cellar at certain times;
* singers were to be forbidden raki during rehearsals; instead one glass of wine per singer would be permitted on certain days, excluding fasts;
* no raki was to be issued to brethren celebrating namedays.[29]

The guest house also has to be adequately staffed to cope with the demands of the large numbers of visitors that enjoy the monastery's hospitality every night of the year. Rooms have to be swept, sheets laundered, fires lit in winter, washrooms kept clean; guests have to be received, provided with sustenance if they are late for refectory, informed about the monastery, disciplined if they are inclined to be rowdy, woken in time for services, and sent away happy. Providing hospitality without charge is one of the principal *raisons d'être* of the monastery. Not every monk has the appropriate combination of talents to be able to dispense it.

The monastery's gate has to be manned during daylight hours. The monk in charge will supervise all comings and goings and will check that pilgrims have the necessary documentation and direct them to where they should go. He may also operate the telephone switchboard and have radio contact with vehicles or boats that have business with the monastery. The post requires vigilance, but not much escapes the gatekeeper's eye. During the hours of darkness, when the gate is closed, the monastery is patrolled by a night watchman.

The monastery is likely to have workshops manned by members of the brotherhood. The tailor ensures that all monks have an adequate supply of clothing. Mechanics take care of the motor vehicles. Computer-literate monks handle communications with the outside world and prepare documents for circulation within the monastery or for publication in printed form. Craftsmen are needed on a regular basis to carry out repairs and

97 Below: Monks do much of the gardening for themselves nowadays.

98 Right: At Simonopetra land is at a premium but the narrow terraces are highly productive.

maintenance of the buildings. Such tasks may be performed by lay workers, but they still have to be supervised by monks. Similarly the fields and gardens require a great deal of labour: this is often 'farmed out' to foreign workers, but just as often the work is done by monks themselves. In idiorrhythmic monasteries such work was always performed by hired labourers—as recently as 1934 the Great Lavra employed as many as eighty lay servants—but cenobitic communities often make a point of sharing at least some of the physical tasks with the lay workers.

The philosophy of work in a cenobitic monastery is that every monk, regardless of his position in the hierarchy, performs a vital role. No matter how skilled or unskilled, his contribution is equally essential to the smooth running of the house as a whole. Work has a spiritual quality, which means that every able-bodied monk must participate in it in order to fulfil his ascetic obligations. Every task, however lowly, must be carried out as if for Christ himself. It is no less important than prayer. As Fr Aimilianos has written:

> Those who are allotted the tasks of the Monastery receive, at the beginning of each year, from the hand of Christ and of the holy Founder, through the Abbot, their keys and tools as sacred liturgical vessels. Each monk, in serving the needs of his brethren, is performing the liturgy of the one body and giving an account of himself as a faithful steward. He who serves practises his obedience in the midst of the brotherhood, hastening with zeal to anticipate the speediness of humility. But he who is self-willed, self-ruling and independent remains alone; and he who performs what appear to be the most 'humiliating' tasks is the most blessed.[30]

Monks at Prayer

Wherever possible, as we have already seen with the common task, work and prayer are combined. Many monks will recite the Jesus Prayer as they go about their daily routine. If their work keeps them from attending services in church (e.g. because they are preparing a meal or laying the tables in the refectory), they either recite the office themselves while working or they can sometimes listen to it broadcast on the monastery's radio system.

Most Athonite monasteries follow Byzantine time, which means setting clocks at 12 at sunset. The hours of darkness are regarded as a time of silence, for prayer and sleep. For practical purposes prayer times govern the monastic timetable.

At sunset the gates of the monastery are shut and by then everyone, pilgrims and monks alike, must be safely inside. Depending on the time of year, there may be a little time available for monks to enjoy some leisure or to converse with pilgrims before retiring early to their cells for private prayer and rest. Most monks spend at least two or three hours in prayer

99 'To talanto, to talanto, to ta to ta to talanto.' The rhythmical striking of the wooden *talanto* summons the monks to prayer.

every night. It is customary to begin by recalling the sins of the past day. This is followed by the performance of prostrations: their number, prescribed by the spiritual father, increases as the monk matures and it is not uncommon for a senior monk to make 300 or 400 prostrations every night. (The term 'spiritual athlete' takes on real meaning on Athos.) After prostrations the monk makes his confessional prayer (of thanksgiving, confession of sins, and petitions for others). He then ends with a prescribed number of recitations of the Jesus Prayer. All of this is subject to variation from one house to another, but the general pattern is universally applied.

At about 3 am the first call to prayer is struck on the *talanto* and monks congregate in the katholikon for the midnight office followed by matins and the daily offices known as the first, third, and sixth hours. This lasts for about three hours, or a little longer on Sundays and feast days. Upon completion of the office, the Divine Liturgy is celebrated every day (except during Great Lent), on Sundays and feast days in the katholikon; on other days probably in one of the smaller chapels; and in larger monasteries several liturgies are celebrated simultaneously in different chapels. At the end of the Liturgy there is usually a meal in the refectory (frugal on fast days). The refectory is normally located opposite the entrance to the katholikon so that monks can process directly from one to the other. Meals are thus demonstrably incorporated into the liturgical pattern and acquire a sacred quality that renders them an extension of the church services.

Fasting is as much a part of this liturgical pattern as prayer, and the two are often joined together (as in the New Testament) to define the essentials of Orthodox practice, for laymen as well as for monks and clergy. There are four extended fasts in the church year: Great Lent and Holy Week, the Dormition (1–14 August), Advent (15 November–24 December), and the Apostles' fast (from eight days after Pentecost to 29 June). Outside these periods, every Wednesday and Friday is a fast; and in monasteries every Monday also. There are different levels of fasting and not all are observed on every fast day; but monasteries generally follow a strict pattern and abstain from any consumption of meat (which monks never eat anyway), dairy products, fish, wine, and oil. The notion is that through fasting the body shares in the work of prayer; and fasting gives the faithful a sense of freedom and lightness. 'Fasting and self-control are the first virtue', wrote Kallistos and Ignatios Xanthopoulos, 'the mother, root, source, and foundation of all good.'[31] Great Lent is the strictest fast of the year and involves a complete change of the daily schedule: then there is no daily celebration of the Divine Liturgy, though there may be a liturgy of the presanctified gifts on Wednesdays and Fridays; vespers happens at 12.30 pm and is followed (at about 2 pm) by the only meal of the day.

The monastic diet is much the same as the traditional Greek peasant diet and consists largely of vegetables, bread, olives, salads, cheese, soya and fruit. On non-fast days there is usually plenty of food on the monks' table and an ample supply of wine; and on feast days there is often fish. But meals are eaten at great speed, and whatever is not eaten by the time the abbot rises for the final thanksgiving is left behind. There is a general rule of silence except that one monk will read aloud from patristic or religious literature. Sometimes the abbot will interrupt the reading to give his own commentary; and at the end of the meal he may read any notices about forthcoming events of the day. As soon as the meal is over, the abbot will lead the brotherhood, following in order of seniority, out into the courtyard and he will stand at the door to give a final blessing to his flock and their guests. Beside him stand the cook and his assistants, all of them bowing very low to indicate their contrition for any shortcomings in the meal. Any food that remains uneaten is carefully preserved for use on another occasion; or if is not reusable, it is fed to the cats, of which every monastery has a large flock, principally to act as mousers.

By now it is perhaps 8.30 am and every monk disappears to go about his work for the morning. Suddenly the courtyard empties of men in black and all that remains is a straggle of pilgrims planning their next move. Monks probably work for about four or five hours from this time until the early afternoon when they may take a few hours' rest, especially in the heat of summer. At about 4.30 pm (earlier in winter) the *talanto* is struck again, calling the brotherhood to the katholikon for vespers (preceded by the ninth hour). This service, technically the first of the daily offices, coincides with the close of the day and in most monasteries is celebrated with full double choir and great dignity amid the gathering gloom of early evening. It leads straight into another meal in the refectory, which does not differ much in style or content from the first meal of the day (except that on fast days it generally offers a little more). This is followed by compline, the last service of the day, which lasts for about three-quarters of an hour.

After compline monks are free either to finish off any work that was not completed earlier in the day or to enjoy a period of leisure until sunset when the routine for the following day begins.

CELEBRATIONS FOR A FEAST

Orthodox church services are long, dignified affairs; but they are not static or uneventful. Every few minutes something different happens: a new chant begins; the deacon comes round again with the censer; more candles are lit or extinguished; a coloured lamp is hoisted high into the dome; the priest emerges from the sanctuary for a reading; one by one monks disappear into a side chapel where the abbot is hearing confessions. So it is with the church calendar: the routine is never tedious because it is so often punctuated by red-letter days. Even periods of fasting make way for the celebration of a major feast. There are twelve such feasts in the course of the year, and many minor ones besides. On Athos special attention is paid to those relating to the life of the Theotokos.

In addition to the feasts of the calendar, every Athonite monastery puts on a special annual celebration (*panegyri*) for the feast of its dedication (just as every Orthodox Christian celebrates his or her name day). In anticipation of the day, many of the monks are released from their usual duties in order to make the necessary preparations. The church has to be cleaned from top to bottom; special treats have to be prepared for the large numbers of pilgrims (sometimes as many as 300) who are expected to attend; reception rooms must be made ready for visiting dignitaries. The invitation to attend a *panegyri* in a neighbouring monastery is the one occasion (other than sickness) that will persuade monks (and especially, but not exclusively, abbots) to leave home and visit each other.

There is no entirely regular pattern for the celebration of a feast. In fact the order of service is fixed and only its length varies, from four to sixteen hours, according to the significance placed on the occasion. Each time it seems to be different in certain respects; but the central feature is invariably a vigil, or all-night service (*agrypnia*), in the katholikon; this is always followed by a celebratory meal in the refectory. I shall describe in the next chapter my own experience as a pilgrim attending such a feast. In the present context it is appropriate to cite an Athonite's response:

> The most festal of all the liturgical offices is the all-night vigil. The mind is kept alert by the all-night service, while the heart leaps with might and main, sharing in the awesome vigour of the Powers on high and the delight of the saint whose day it is, or of the feast day. Laxity is lightly cast aside, vigilant eyes follow the round of the oil-lamps being lit and of the chandeliers and the great candelabra being swung in symbolic motion. Those present derive joy from heaven, absorb the dew of contrition and sport with men and angels. Thus the mind climbs like a unicorn to the sanctuary on high and the spirit is carried aloft in holiness and fear in order to discover, mystically, the mercy-seat of the sacred ark and to share in those things which 'no eye has seen, nor ear heard, nor the heart of man conceived'.[32]

LIFE IN THE SKETES AND CELLS

It is even harder to generalize about the sketes and cells than about the monasteries because they all do things differently according to their own rhythm. No doubt it is largely because of the great gulf that exists between the sketes and the monasteries that some of the old antagonisms that have characterized the Mountain since the days of St Athanasios survive to this day. Of course a cenobitic skete such as Prodromos or St Andrew's or the Prophet Elijah operates in much the same way as a monastery. To look at, they are more or less indistinguishable from monasteries and apart from certain differences in nomenclature (e.g. the abbot is called a prior or *dikaios*, and the katholikon is called the *kyriakon*, that is, the place to go on Sunday), the only difference of substance is that they do not send a representative to the Holy Community in Karyes. Nor are they so well endowed, and for their prosperity they are largely dependent on the good will of their parent monasteries. But the brotherhood (in each case numbering about 20) lives a common life, work is shared as in the monasteries, and both the church and the refectory are in daily use.

Idiorrhythmic sketes operate rather differently. Each forms a cluster of cells, and life centres round the cell or house in which a group of monks live together. Each cell has a chapel for weekday services, and a dining room where residents of the cell eat together. They usually come together for worship on Sunday in the kyriakon, but otherwise they may not see much of the monks in other cells. All the monks follow a rule of obedience to the prior, but there is a good deal of flexibility about how it is interpreted. Work may incorporate a wider range of activities than in the monasteries and there is often a greater emphasis on certain arts or crafts. New Skete, for example, once renowned as the place where woollen socks were knitted for use by monks all over the Mountain, is now more famous for its icon painters. One of the skete fathers has an international reputation for producing icons according to traditional Byzantine principles; students flock from all over the world to learn the technique from him and stay as guests in his well-equipped and hospitable cell.

Other sketes, particularly those in the region known as the desert down near the southern tip of the peninsula, are better known as centres of extreme asceticism. Karoulia is such a settlement and is located at a point where the terrain is vertiginously steep. The name means the place of the pulleys and recalls the system of communication by which hermits could only reach their cells by hauling themselves up by ropes or chains that passed over makeshift pulleys. Now there is a mule track; but still the cells cling to the cliffs in a most alarming fashion and overhang the sea many metres below. It remains no more than a collection of hermitages and has never achieved the status of a proper skete. Sydney Loch knew it fifty years ago and wrote about it during the lifetime of Fr Nikon (to whose memory the translation of the *Philokalia* is dedicated):

> Karoulia is still spectacular from a boat. A precipice of hermit eyries joined by chain-and-rope banisters, with its roots everlastingly chid by waves. It is still spectacular, but not as it was a few years before someone moved with the times sufficiently to scratch a track from top to bottom to allow a loaded mule to slither down, and his driver to follow, after crossing himself. This path has done away with the lower chains by which the caller hauled himself out of the boat up to those heights, and by so much has the power to astonish been lost to the world.
>
> Father Nikon, charming, educated, a Russian, and once a man of the world, survives there in his chapel cell, lying down to sleep with a stone for a pillow and the skulls of seventeen of his predecessors staring at him from a shelf. There he shed his association with courts and kings, and gained an ease of soul that shines from him. He is possibly the last of the educated solitaries left on the Mountain, and to spend an hour or two in his company is something out of this world. Only the stout-hearted can face the chains leading down to his eyrie.[33]

Kafsokalyvia, four or five kilometres east of Karoulia, is an idiorrhythmic skete that is a dependency of Megiste Lavra. Here a string of whitewashed cottages and chapels with domes and slate roofs winds up the side of a steep but fertile gulley between bay trees. There are forty cells but not all of them are occupied. Today the brotherhood numbers about thirty-five. Its official name is the Skete of the Holy Trinity and it celebrates its annual festival (*panegyri*) at Pentecost.

Isolated cells and hermitages are scattered all over the Mountain, though

certain areas (such as the desert, and Kapsala to the north of Karyes) contain a preponderance. Some are still inhabited, many are not, though it is not always easy to tell. They vary in form from a cave or simple stone shelter to a substantial farmhouse, and the activities within encompass a similar range. In most cases the monks who resort to them are in search of that complete isolation and rigorous asceticism that St Antony first found in the Egyptian desert. Instead of the sand, these men have chosen a world of dense forest or vertical cliffs. They spend their lives in prayer and are rarely seen. Some withdraw completely and never leave their cave, living in total silence and complete solitude. At regular intervals a monk from the parent monastery lowers a basket of simple provisions. Only if the basket remains unemptied may he then lower himself to visit the hermit. If he has died, his body is removed and buried; after exhumation his skull remains at the hermitage to take its place beside his predecessors and the cave is made available to a new occupant. Such men continue to come forward, often still in their twenties. It is not uncommon for them to endure sixty or seventy years of such solitude. Such is the desert of Athos.

Many stories are told of the great desert fathers of Athos. As an example let us look at Elder Kallinikos the Hesychast (1853–1930), who as a young man left Athens where he had received a good education. He came to the Holy Mountain towards the end of the nineteenth century. Finding the idiorrhythmic life at Iviron not to his taste, he was advised that if he was seeking the hesychastic life he should move to the desert, where many ascetics had their abode. He found his way to the cell of the renowned hesychast and spiritual father, Elder Daniel of Katounakia. The elder doubted that this refined young man from the city could endure the rigours of life in the desert, but finally he agreed to test him. Archimandrite Cherubim records the scene:

'Costas, my child [Kallinikos's baptismal name], here we have only one meal a day, and that without oil. We have oil only on weekends and feast days. We pray most of the night. We sleep little, and must do our handiwork in the daytime so that we may earn our bread.'

'May it be blessed, Elder. This is the life I have longed for. If I had wanted a different way of life, I would have chosen a cenobitic monastery or skete.'

'We have no spring here, Costas. The water collected in our cisterns must be used with great care. Among these rocks it is impossible to have a garden and so we taste neither fruits nor vegetables. We feed ourselves with a few wild greens, olives, sometimes with beans, or with a fig, or whatever else can be bought from the store in Daphne. And in place of fresh bread, we eat rusks.' (Bread which is left over from trapeza in the monasteries of the Holy Mountain is dried and distributed to the hermits. Father Daniel was supplied with this dried bread, or

100 Left: Karoulia from the sea. Hermits' cells cling perilously to the cliffs and overhang the waves below.

101 Fr Nikon of Karoulia, the celebrated Russian hermit who died in 1963.

102 The *kellion* of St Demetrios near Bogoroditsa. With its wooden gallery on the first floor it is typical of isolated cells in agricultural areas.

rusks, by Xeropotamou Monastery.)

'Costas, we have here neither milk, cheese, nor eggs. At Pascha, we have no red eggs to eat. One that is preserved from year to year is brought out that we may see it and remember the Feast.'

Costas listened with great interest and attention . . .[34]

In due course Fr Daniel tonsured Costas as the monk Kallinikos, and when Fr Daniel died, Fr Kallinikos took his place as the elder of the cell. He acquired disciples of his own together with a reputation for humility and loving-kindness. But still he longed for the solitary life. 'Four years after the death of his Elder', writes Archimandrite Cherubim,

he made the brave decision to shut himself up completely, to confine himself as if in a prison to his cell and to a small space around it. For however many years God would grant him, he would remain enclosed in these limits.

In fact, he lived thus for his remaining forty-five years. On no account did he break this principle. When he needed to notify somebody he used to raise a big pole with a sail on the end like a flag. The neighbors would see it and come to see what was the matter.

His sacrifice was great. For forty-five years he lived as a recluse in a cell in that desert ravine of Katounakia, depriving himself of ventures out-of-doors, walks, trips, and all human contact. Only with his death did he leave his enclosure, and even then, only his soul departed. His body remained faithful to the physical bounds of his ascetic labors.

This heroic step was richly blessed by God. 'Observe how when a cask of wine is kept still in one place, it becomes magnificent, reaching the peak of its bouquet' as the *Philokalia* says (Evagrios).[35]

Despite this self-imposed rule of isolation, Elder Kallinikos found the time to devote two hours a day to his spiritual sons. Monks and ascetics, priests and laymen, Greeks and Russians flocked to his cell from all over Athos and beyond to sit at his feet and hear his teaching. After his death, when his bones were exhumed, it was noticed that they were tinged with the same sweet yellowish shading that graces the relics of the saints.

Life in the desert of Athos is unchanged, untouched by the revival taking place elsewhere. The harsh environment ensures that only the most dedicated can survive there. It continues to elicit a lyrical response even from contemporary Athonites:

Here the hum of the unceasing prayer and the constant secret sigh of fallen man is detected. Here the world's fate is determined. Here God strains His ear, and here He decides. For this is the place of His rest. In this desert you can hear the echo of the angelic hymns, the doxological silence of the saints, and the melody of the everlasting godly word.

In the desert of the Holy Mountain you can meet more easily an angel than a man. The place is so savage that human beings cannot endure it; it is so immaterial that angels envy it. Here angels are in excess. The environment is more hospitable for them. It resembles heaven more than earth. Angels are recognized more easily than men. For hermits have eyes that can see angels, while angels are unable even to imagine the existence of such human beings. The people who can endure life here can see, but cannot be seen. They are more angelic than human; they are more heavenly than earthen, more eternal than temporal. This is why, along with God's rest, they cause the amazement of angels who take pleasure and find rest in this desolate place.

The clarity of the desert is so great that it transforms you. Your soul becomes transparent. Without any efforts your inner world emerges. You confess spontaneously and, if you have the blessing to meet a hermit, he reads your soul without difficulty. Here people possess souls and eyes that can be seen.[36]

THE MYSTERY OF ATHOS

Renewal has now spread to all of the seventeen Greek monasteries on the Mountain. It is more evident in some monasteries than others and each preserves its characteristic flavour or atmosphere: some emphasize intellectual activity, others are more pragmatically inclined; some are very strict in their observances, others adopt a more outward-looking approach. In practice every monastery takes on the personality of its abbot, and no two abbots share exactly the same attitude to the monastic life. It is important that this variety should be retained, so that the Mountain will appeal to and cater for a wide cross-section of recruits.

It is not easy to account for this renewal. At first it was no more than a redistribution of the existing population as some of the hermits were persuaded to move into the monasteries with their groups of disciples. Then there was the intake from monasteries elsewhere in Greece such as the Meteora, from where monks came in search of the solitude that Athos alone can still provide. But since then, there can be no doubting the increase in the numbers of new monks, their relative youthfulness, their intellectual capacity, their spiritual integrity, their devotion to all that Athos stands for. Why should this be? The renewal is in no sense a reform, except in the abandonment of the idiorrhythmic way of life; it is in every sense a revival of traditional cenobitic Athonite monasticism. Some see it as the Mother of God ensuring that her garden remains well tended. Others see it as a reaction to the secularizing tendencies of the modern world leading to a renewal of man's search for his spiritual self. Cynics speak of escape; but who would choose escape to such austerity without the promise and the delivery of rewards not available in the world? No doubt all these factors have played a part; but perhaps the greatest single reason for the renewal is the presence on the Mountain today of so many outstanding spiritual fathers and abbots of international renown whose reputations and publications and personalities have attracted disciples in ever-increasing numbers.

There is a new icon of the Theotokos, similar to the nineteenth-century Russian icon referred to in Chapter 2 which represented her as the abbess of Athos, but the new one has her as the 'ephor', or overseer, of the Holy Mountain (see frontispiece). Dressed as a nun, she floats above the peak of the Mountain, casting a gentle and kindly eye over her flock below. Clustering around the coastline and foothills are accurate but stylized representations of all the monasteries and sketes. It is a modern interpretation of an entirely traditional picture. For many monks it symbolizes what the renewal is doing, and this is what Athos is all about for the monks. It is holy ground, a station in sacred space, closely connected with the events of the gospel story, a place where miracles have happened and continue to happen. Athos is not of this world, nor are the monks of this world; they live in a world set apart. When a monk is tonsured, he dies to this world and is born again.

Using language that consciously evokes the writings of St John Klimakos,[37] Fr George Kapsanis, abbot of the monastery of Grigoriou and one of the architects of the current revival, has written about the spiritual life of Mount Athos in these words:

Athonite life is fundamentally a Mystery, a Mystery which defies any description. Our eyes must be opened if we are to behold the Mystery. We must be initiated into the Mystery. Initiation does not spring from rational understanding alone; it is a question of spiritual ascent. As Man ascends and God descends, it is at the point where they meet that the Mystery is celebrated. It is this Mystery which makes Athos not merely a mountain, but a Holy Mountain.

The Mystery is open to anyone, whether Athonite or not, who wishes to approach it. The approach, however, means ascent; ascent requires abstraction; and abstraction demands courage. The way life is organised on Athos, the architecture, painting, nature, cobblestones, bells, the wooden sounding boards striking day and night, the hospitality, the prayers—all of these express something of this Mystery. It is in them all and at the same time beyond them all. Whatever expresses the Mystery may be described up to a certain point, yet at the same time its core remains undescribed. Being undescribed it is offered in communion of life.[38]

8

ATHOS TODAY: FOR THE PILGRIM

M en travel to Athos for a variety of reasons, reasons that have evolved over time. In past centuries travellers from the west were often in search of manuscripts, lured by the faint hope that in the monastic libraries might lurk some yet undiscovered text of a lost work of classical antiquity.[1] Occasionally they were lucky; more often they had to content themselves with rescuing a few scraps of parchment which would otherwise have been consigned to the incinerator or more likely left to moulder away for another century or so on neglected library shelves. Others simply enjoyed travel for its own sake, especially in more exotic parts where their experiences provided material for tales of adventure that might subsequently be published. At the same time the Mountain continued to attract travellers from the east, Orthodox Christians from various parts of the Ottoman empire and from Russia, who often had more pious motives for making their journey, and, if they published an account of it, concentrated rather on the holy places and sacred treasures of Athos.[2] The passion for collecting manuscripts may have waned; but *mutatis mutandis* similar motives are to be found in many of today's visitors to the Holy Mountain. Much of what follows here is based on my own experience, gained in the course of ten visits between 1988 and 2000.

Visitors are flocking to Athos in increasing numbers. In the early 1970s no more than about 3000 came each year. By the mid-1980s that number had multiplied by a factor of 10. Ten years later, as many as 40,000 entry permits were being issued each year. As the renewal took hold among the monasteries, so they began to attract not only monks but also pilgrims. If steps had not been taken to control the numbers of visitors, there was a real risk that the monasteries would have been overrun and they would have been forced to revise their cherished traditions of offering free hospitality to pilgrims. But just as there was nothing new about the Mountain attracting increased numbers of monks, so in the past there had often been large numbers of pilgrims too, especially at major feasts. When the Englishman John Covel visited the Mountain in 1677, he recorded in his *Athos Notes* that the Lavra received about 500 visitors at major festivals, and that the previous Easter there had been 2000 at Koutloumousiou.[3] Just as now, resources of the poorer foundations were sometimes stretched when they had to accommodate and feed such an influx, but the facilities for doing so existed and great efforts were always made to provide for visitors' needs.

Pilgrims or Tourists?

Naturally the majority of the Mountain's visitors are Greeks: Athos lies within Greece, its common language is Greek, and the Greeks like to think of it as *their* Holy Mountain. As the renewal spread to the Greek monasteries, it became fashionable for more and more Greeks to visit them: access was easy; hospitality was free; it made a pleasant break from the daily routine. At the same time foreign tourism was increasing in Greece as a whole. The invention of the package holiday suddenly made Greece more accessible to large numbers of visitors. The climate was tempting; the cost of living was low; the local people were rumoured to be friendly. Hippie colonies were established in certain parts of the country and word spread that free hospitality was available on Mount Athos. It was a combination of these factors—the fashion-conscious Greeks and the hippie influx—that persuaded the authorities that steps had to be taken to protect the monasteries.

A quota system was first introduced in the 1970s and remains in place today. Each day a finite number of entry permits is issued: 100 for Orthodox, 10 for non-Orthodox. Permits are issued usually for four nights, which means that there should never be more than about 450–500 visitors on the Mountain at any one time, and if the quota is filled throughout the year, the annual total should never exceed about 40,000. Furthermore permits are not simply handed out to anyone arriving at the border. The quota is administered from Thessaloniki (formerly by the Ministry of Northern Greece, now by the Athos Pilgrim's Bureau); a consular letter was required (no longer the case) and pilgrims are expected to have a serious reason for wishing to visit the Mountain. The bureaucracy is deliberately complicated in order to deter the idly curious visitor.

That is not to say that many do not visit the Mountain, at least for the first time, out of mere curiosity. For many it is a combination of factors. Men are drawn to Athos from a wide variety of backgrounds. Some are artists who draw their inspiration from its scenery. Some are students of history, anxious to experience this last surviving fragment of the Byzantine empire. Some are art historians, wanting to see for themselves this living treasure-house of eastern Christian art and architecture. Some are priests from other Christian confessions, eager to be allowed to participate in the liturgical life of an Orthodox monastery. Some are environmentalists, zealous for a greener world, bringing the gospel of organic farming, disciplined forestry and proper drains. Some just want to stand back from the world and be still.

All these are perfectly valid reasons for visiting Athos. Most people come with some such reason at the forefront of their minds. The question then arises: are they pilgrims or tourists? Every visitor to the Holy Mountain is by definition a pilgrim: his entry permit admits him specifically in order 'to visit the holy relics and venerate the holy places of our faith' and he will be received as a pilgrim wherever he goes. How many visitors to the Holy Mountain are conscious of this purpose? Philip Sherrard is in no doubt:

> at least ninety per cent and possibly an even higher percentage of the visitors to Athos today are not pilgrims. They are tourists, however much they may like to think they are not . . . They do not walk the long, steep, often relentless paths, so that inner change, for the production of which walking is an essential element, cannot take place in them.[4]

But then we have to ask: what is pilgrimage? Here is Sherrard's answer:

> [A] pilgrimage is not simply a matter of getting to a particular shrine or holy place. It is a deliberate sundering and surrender of one's habitual conditions of comfort, routine, safety, convenience. Unlike the tourist, whose aim is to see things and to travel around in conditions which are as comfortable, secure, familiar, convenient and unchallenging as possible, the pilgrim breaks with his material servitude, puts his trust in God and sets out on a quest which is inward as much as outward, and is, in varying degrees, into the unknown. In this sense, he becomes the image of the spiritual seeker. He removes himself as far as possible from the artificiality within which he is enclosed by his life in society. Of this spiritual exploration, inward and outward, walking is an essential part. His feet tread the earth—the earth from which he is made and from which he is usually so cut off, especially in the more or less totally urbanized conditions of modern life. Through his eyes, ears, nose, he renews his sense of natural beauty—of the beauty of God's creation. He watches the flight of bird or insect, the ripple of light on leaves, the tameless vistas of the sea; he listens to the song of water, the calls of God's creatures; he breathes in the scent of tree and flower and soil. His feet tire, his body aches, sweat drips from his head and trickles into his eyes and down his neck. He tastes rigour and hardship. But through all this—and only through all this, and through his prayer and dedication and confidence—slowly an inner change is wrought, a new rhythm grows, a deeper harmony. The pilgrimage is at work.
>
> The crucial point in all this is that a pilgrimage is also a process which must not be hurried. The bonds of routine, dependence on material comforts and conveniences, on the familiar and the settled, have a far stronger hold than one is aware of. The conditions of modern life have so blunted the senses that it may take days, weeks even, until they begin to respond truly to the beauty about them. . . . If the would-be pilgrim attempts to speed this process up, or refuses to face the conditions, including the rigours and hardships under which alone it can develop, then he simply aborts his pilgrimage. He degenerates into being a tourist.[5]

Sherrard knew and loved the Mountain as well as anyone who has written about it in the last century. He lived much of his life in Greece and he converted to Orthodoxy; but he was still a westerner. René Gothóni has written at length about the difference between the concept of pilgrimage in the west, where the word 'pilgrim' means a traveller to a holy place or shrine, and in the east, where the word *proskynitis* (normally translated into English as 'pilgrim') actually means one who worships and bows down, i.e. before the icons, relics, and holy places.[6] In other words, for a western pilgrim the journey and the hardships relating to the journey are an essential ingredient of the pilgrimage, whereas for the eastern pilgrim what matters is not how he gets to the shrine but what he does when he has got there. Sherrard stopped going to Athos in 1980, even though he lived another fifteen years after that. He preferred to remember it when every visitor perforce conformed to his definition of a pilgrim, because there were no roads and no vehicles and there was no alternative to walking. The 'tourist' invasion was more than he could endure.

It is true that of the large numbers of visitors to the Holy Mountain today the vast majority choose to travel by road, largely because it is more convenient: it saves effort, and it saves time. Those of us who still choose to walk are often branded as romantics and laughed at for preferring the old routes. But we are not entitled to claim that only we are the true pilgrims. In Greek terminology those who ride in motor vehicles are no less pilgrims than we. In fact, if we do not venerate the relics and the icons and the holy places when we reach our destination, we are completely failing in our duty as *proskynites*.

But what about the visitor who is motivated by curiosity, or by his desire to study the architecture, or the butterflies? Is he a pilgrim or a tourist? Gothóni has conducted fieldwork in Ouranopolis and interviewed many visitors both before and after their journey to Athos. His research leads him to conclude that, while many said beforehand that they were going out of curiosity, nearly all realized by the time of their return that they had made a pilgrimage. They were moved by what they had seen and experienced; some were even reborn by it and felt that they now saw the world in a new light. Moreover he suggests that laymen have now discovered pilgrimage to be a way of distancing themselves from their everyday lives and concerns:

> This type of pilgrimage, where the travellers only realise later that they have made a pilgrimage, is usually connected with the search for a direction in life, often with a religious search. During their journey many of the visitors deal with the tension between what their life is and what they would like it to be. The pilgrimage provides a cooling off period, a means by which the traveller can reorient himself into his life situation. It contributes to a self-renewal, and, if it is successful, the traveller gains a fresh insight into his worldly problems. In this sense a pilgrimage really sets the traveller free.[7]

Perhaps the last word on the subject should be said by the monks, for it is they who have to suffer this formidable daily invasion of visitors. When

Gothóni asked an elderly father how they coped with it, he received this reply: 'Everyone who comes to the Holy Mountain is a pilgrim, whether he knows it or not. Originally each of us was a visitor. Who is to say in what way the will of God acts? Who is to say why the visitors really come? For many visitors a pilgrimage to this Holy Mountain has become a yearly habit.'[8]

Departure from the World

When is the best time to go to Athos? Winter on the Holy Mountain is long, wet, and often cold. Snow is by no means a rare occurrence, even at lower levels; and stormy seas often confine boats to harbour. As a result there are fewer visitors at this time, so for those who are not bothered by climatic uncertainty and who want to have the Mountain to themselves, winter can be a good time to go. Several monasteries have now installed central heating, and others use wood-burning stoves. By contrast, high summer (mid–June to mid–September) can be very hot and it is also the time that attracts the greatest numbers of (mostly Greek) visitors. This means that long–distance walking can be uncomfortable and guest facilities at many monasteries are overstretched. Of those who are free to choose, many will prefer to plan their visit either in the spring (mid–April to mid–June), when the temperature is more congenial for walking and the wild flowers are at their best, or in autumn (mid–September to late October), when the selection of fruit and vegetables on offer may be more appealing.

How does one get there? The first step is to reserve a place in the quota for the day on which one wishes to enter Athos. The bureaucratic procedure for this is occasionally subject to change at short notice,[9] but it goes without saying that the more notice one can give, especially in summer and around the time of major feasts, the better one's chances of success. Once the necessary procedures have been completed, pilgrims travel to Ouranopolis, which is the usual point of departure for Athos and literally the end of the road.

Founded in 1922 as a village for refugees from Asia Minor, Ouranopolis is now a summer resort for tourists. The only building of note is a Byzantine tower beside the quay. Known as Prosphori (meaning 'the offering'), the tower was built in the thirteenth century by Emperor Andronikos II and 'offered' to the monastery of Vatopedi in perpetuity. It is said that the emperor's wife stayed there. In 1922 the land surrounding the tower was confiscated from the monastery by the Greek government. The village that sprang up there was initially known as Pyrgos ('tower'), but when the population grew to more than 500 it was renamed Ouranopolis, after an ancient town of that name that stood on the other side of the peninsula between Ierissos and Nea Rhoda. In 1928 the tower became home to a remarkable couple, Sydney and Joice Loch. Sydney Loch (1889–1954) was British, and a veteran of the Gallipoli campaign, Joice (1893–1982) was Australian; both were writers and together they played an important part in providing employment for the villagers. They founded a rug-weaving enterprise, using designs from paintings on Mount Athos—the phiale at Lavra, the tree of life at Esphigmenou, an animal fresco at Vatopedi—and for many years carpets of high quality were produced.[10] Sydney became a regular visitor to the Mountain and numbered abbots, monks and hermits among his close friends.[11] Many Athonites passed through the tower when making an excursion into the outside world, as did pilgrims travelling in the opposite direction. The Lochs' hospitality became famous and the tower remained an important meeting-point for monks and laymen until Joice's death in 1982. Sadly the tower today is an empty shell and pilgrims must find other accommodation in the town, but the Lochs are still remembered with great affection and respect by older residents.

From Ouranopolis there is a boat every morning (in high summer there is sometimes a second departure), which is the only reliable means of access to the Mountain. (On certain days of the week there is also a boat in the morning from Ierissos for monasteries on the east coast as far as Iviron, but this service is unreliable because of frequent stormy weather.) Before embarking, the pilgrim obtains his *diamonitirion*, the official permit entitling him to hospitality at the monasteries for (usually) four nights.

The voyage from Ouranopolis is the final stage in the process of departing from the world and entering Athos. Womenfolk are left behind on the quayside as the ferryboat heads out to sea. Soon the tower of Prosphori disappears behind a headland, and a glimpse of the wall that marks the boundary indicates that the ship has entered Athonite waters. Regrettably, mobile telephones do not have to be left behind and Greek businessmen make their last frantic calls to colleagues and clients in Athens as they struggle with the prospect of cutting links with their mundane concerns for the next four or five days. Anyone wearing shorts on the boat will be asked to change into long trousers out of respect for the monks; anyone spotted using a video camera will have it confiscated for the duration of his visit. There is an air of expectation as first-time pilgrims pore over their maps and try to identify passing settlements, while others toss morsels to Athonite seagulls and keep a watch for monastic dolphins.

The ships now in service between Ouranopolis and Daphne are very similar in style to the sort of car ferries that operate on short-distance routes between Greek islands. The lower deck is likely to be occupied by lorries serving the timber industry on the Mountain or carrying building materials for the numerous reconstruction projects now in progress and smaller commercial vehicles bringing in supplies to supplement what the monks produce for themselves. The middle deck is an enclosed saloon which provides shelter and refreshments. If the weather is fine, most passengers make for the top deck, which is open to the sky and offers a good view of the passing coastline.

After about 45 minutes the hillside skete of Thivais comes into view. A dependency of St Panteleimonos, it had long been a deserted ruin until a year or two ago when it was repopulated by a pair of Russian monks. Half an hour later the boat makes its first call, at Megali Jovantsa, a cell of Chilandar, which has recently been carefully restored and extended. Perhaps a couple of people disembark here, and the boat is quickly off again and heading for the attractive port buildings of the inland monastery of Zographou. For the handful of pilgrims who get off here, the path follows a beautiful valley up to the Bulgarian monastery, which can be reached in less than an hour's walk. The boat then calls briefly at the port of Konstamonitou, another inland monastery, before moving on to Dochiariou, the first of the monasteries that can actually be seen from the sea.

The monastery clings to a steep hillside and the architecture has to obey the terrain. Seen from outside, with its high walls dominated by an even taller defence tower, it looks much like a castle; inside, the courtyard is narrow and terraced and the tightly packed buildings present a charmingly ramshackle appearance. There is a small brotherhood of just 25 monks. They have done much of the restoration work themselves, with some rather unhappy results.[12] A few years ago half the monks rebelled against the abbot's rule and, refusing to work to his demanding regime, left the monastery; the guest house was forced to close for several months.

From Dochiariou it is a short journey to the next monastery, Xenophontos. In 1998 it celebrated its millennium; the founder, the blessed Xenophon, was officially canonized and the celebrations attracted a remarkable array of distinguished guests including the Ecumenical Patriarch, the President and Prime Minister of Greece, the Archbishop of Athens, numerous bishops and government ministers, and as many as 2000 pilgrims. There was even a postage stamp issued to mark the event, and a *catalogue raisonné* of the monastery's icons was published in Greek and English. There are 35 monks here.

The last monastery at which the boat calls before reaching Daphne is the Roussikon, St Panteleimonos. Robert Byron called it a 'barracks' when he visited the place in the 1920s. 'Block after block of huge tenements that would disfigure a Clydeside slum, balconies rusting, windows broken, stretch down to the sea, six or seven stories high . . . Over all, more squalid than romantic, broods an air of disuse.'[13] When he wrote that, there were still over 600 monks there; now there are about fifty. The 'tenements' remain, though they were further damaged by a serious fire in 1968 and

103 Pilgrims and monks preparing for departure from the port of Daphne. Bags are inspected by customs officers to ensure no treasures are being smuggled out.

much of the monastery is deserted; but it seems to have found a number of wealthy benefactors and the parts that are occupied have seen great improvements in recent years.

At about midday the boat arrives in the little port of Daphne, where it terminates and disgorges all remaining passengers and vehicles before taking on a fresh load for the return journey. For an hour or so either side of noon the jetty and seafront are crowded with arriving and departing pilgrims, for this is the point at which most visitors to Athos begin and end their pilgrimage. At other times it reverts to being a sleepy fishing village with one or two shops, a post office, a police station, and one (recently refurbished) café. But the newly arrived visitor is confronted by a bustling scene of monks and pilgrims jostling for a place on the (alarmingly distressed) bus that will shortly begin the arduous climb up to the monastery of Xeropotamou and on to Karyes. It is not a comfortable ride, and for many it is an unsettling introduction to life on the Holy Mountain. But there is some comfort in knowing that within about 45 minutes one will arrive in the capital.

KARYES

As capital cities go, Karyes is somewhat unprepossessing. It is little more than a village, with a population of about 300 or 400 and, though attractive from a distance, presents a run-down appearance to the visitor arriving from the outside world. But it is the administrative centre of the whole Mountain, the seat of its parliament, the Holy Community, and its executive body, the Holy Epistasia. The main street, aptly named Holy Ghost Street, is lined with shops selling basic provisions, ecclesiastical supplies, clothes, books and souvenirs. Some are manned by monks, others by laymen; all operate more as centres of gossip than of commerce. There is also a police station, a post office, a (recently opened) branch of the Agricultural Bank of Greece, and a couple of eating-houses, one of which also offers accommodation. The lunchtime scene described by Sydney Loch in the 1950s is no different today:

> The bare dining-room was full of munching labourers, and monks entertaining relations from the world. Talk drowned the clatter of cutlery. The Greek diner found enough in a little red wine, or a thumbnail glass of raki, to magnify a saucer of salted herrings and another of salted cucumbers into a repast, capable of being lengthened indefinitely by optimistic talk. A waiter moved between the

104 Capital of Athos, Karyes presents a ramshackle appearance to the visitor.

tables calling, 'Command me!' but nothing of account was ordered, except a bottle of beer for me to garnish the beans.[14]

In the centre of the town is the church of the Protaton, the oldest church and the nearest thing to a cathedral on Athos. Inside, the magnificent frescos, painted by Panselinos around 1300, await much-needed and long-delayed conservation. The Protaton also contains the famous miracle-working icon known as the *Axion Estin* which every year on the day after Pascha is borne through the streets of Karyes in an imposing procession down to the nearby monastery of Koutloumousiou. At other times it remains in the sanctuary of the church to be venerated by the faithful. Other treasures belonging to the Protaton are stored in the tower that is adjacent to the building occupied by the Holy Community and some of them are displayed in a museum there.

Unless he has business with the Holy Community (such as the need to extend a *diamonitirion*) or with the representative of one of the monasteries (whose crumbling residences are scattered around the town), there is little to detain the pilgrim in Karyes. One's time on the Mountain is more profitably spent visiting the monasteries and sketes and enjoying the natural beauty of the peninsula.

Travelling on the Holy Mountain

Walking on Athos can be one of the most memorable aspects of one's pilgrimage. Large groups are not normally encouraged because they can disturb the peace and may be difficult for monasteries to accommodate. Small groups, however, are well suited to the conditions and walking with a close friend can be a most rewarding way to enrich an existing relationship. Walking alone is a deeply edifying experience and for many provides the best means to internalize their pilgrimage. Loch records the following exchange with a monk as he was about to leave the monastery of Dochiariou:

> 'Why do you always go round alone?' asked Veniamin, following to see the last of me.
> 'I like it that way, I suppose.'
> 'The Virgin goes with you', he said.[15]

But solitary walkers are warned of the need to exercise vigilance. Most paths are not much frequented and a broken ankle or worse could expose one to

105 Right: A typical Athonite path in springtime. Such paths are not much frequented by pilgrims and soon become overgrown.

106 Pilgrims boarding a monastic vehicle at Karyes. Motorized transport is a recent phenomenon on the Mountain and its spread is regretted by many.

serious danger. Furthermore there are said to be bands of wandering marauders, and there are stories of people disappearing in mysterious circumstances.

The paths of Athos provide some of the most delightful walking in Europe. Many of them were originally intended as mule-tracks and have a good stone base with steps for steeper gradients. They pass through a gloriously varied landscape, ranging from open moorland to dense forest to mountain scrub, and they afford fantastic views over both land and sea with regular glimpses of the summit of Athos itself. There was once a complete network of such paths covering the whole Mountain but sadly this is no longer the case. In many places paths have been destroyed in order to make way for roads that follow the same route and others are so badly neglected that they are no longer passable. But a good many of them remain and by using them pilgrims help to keep them open.

There is for example a delightful path from Simonopetra to St Paul's via Grigoriou and Dionysiou. The distance can be covered comfortably in a day, with pauses at the monasteries on the way. There are no intrusive motor roads and the path is easy to follow. There is a good deal of going up and down and, though the distances are not great, the walk can be tiring, especially on a hot day. But it is a rewarding experience and can be recommended as an introduction to Athos.

Even more dramatic is the walk round the southern tip of the peninsula, the area known as the desert of Athos. The landscape is incredibly desolate here and between settlements there are few signs of life. Because there is no alternative to them, the paths are quite well maintained, but they are often very hard going and the gradients can be exhausting. But this is in many ways the finest walk on Athos; the views, both down to the sea and up to the peak, are spectacular; and anyone who travels this way is in no doubt that he has made a pilgrimage.

Some other parts of the peninsula are less attractive to the walker. The coastal path from Lavra to Iviron, for example, has now largely been superseded by a dirt road; the route from Daphne to Simonopetra has suffered the same fate. On the west coast at least there is usually the option of taking the boat. There is a daily service from Daphne to Kafsokalyvia which calls at all the intervening monasteries and sketes. A similar service on the east coast starts from Ierissos but does not often go beyond Iviron. When it runs, it provides a relatively comfortable and inexpensive means of travelling from place to place and is used by monks and pilgrims alike. But when it was first introduced it aroused the same reaction of horror that now greets the arrival of motorized transport on land. 'Was the Mountain suffering from the motor-boat age, and all it represented?' wondered Sydney Loch in the 1950s:

> It was no longer secure in the old sense of the word from the outside world. Society no longer had sympathy with the monastic way of life. The modern man demanded speed, noise, change.
>
> The tourist was ousting the pilgrim of the past, who arrived after difficulty, in the mood to venerate. The sightseer now caught a bus across the mountains, or came in his own car to Erissos, and ran up and down either coast of the Mountain in a motor-boat. With him came the post, newspapers, and his own sceptical mind prepared to smile at what he found there, rather than regard a little enviously a single-mindedness beyond his own duplication.[16]

HOSPITALITY IN THE MONASTERIES

Be he tourist or pilgrim, today's visitor will sooner or later find himself at the gates of a monastery. It may be helpful to have some idea of what to expect within: the pattern does not vary much from one house to the next.

On arrival at a monastery, pilgrims should go straight to the guest house (*archontariki*) where they will be warmly welcomed by the guest master (*archontaris*) and offered refreshment (usually a tot of raki, a glass of water,

107 Inside the guest house at Stavronikita. A simple saloon is provided for the use of pilgrims.

a cup of Greek coffee, and a piece of loukoumi). Those who intend to stay the night will be given a bed, usually in a dormitory with a number of other guests. The guest master will also announce the times of services and meals; he may mention the rules of the house and he may offer a tour of the monastery (always worth taking). Otherwise visitors are left very much to their own devices. Some guest houses are now equipped with showers, though hot water remains a rarity. Visitors should always take care to be properly clothed when appearing in public. Those who wish to bathe in the sea should do so out of sight of monasteries: officially both bathing and fishing are forbidden.

Hospitality at the monasteries is free and to attempt to pay for it may cause offence. On the other hand it is usually expected that guests will stay only one night. Those wishing to stay longer should ask if this is possible, and usually permission is given. Then it may be appropriate to make a small offering 'for the church'. Even this may be refused but usually donations are gratefully accepted.

Meals on Athos are generally simple but wholesome. In most monasteries monks and pilgrims eat together in the refectory (*trapeza*), but usually at separate tables. The pilgrims' diet is the same as the monks'. Gone are the

108 More lavish quarters are available at Vatopedi for distinguished visitors. The wood-burning stove was made in Russia in the nineteenth century.

days when Covel would dine with a retired patriarch at the Lavra on 'fish, oil, salt, beans, artichokes, beets, cheese, onions, garlic, olives, caviar, rhubarb . . . oranges and wine . . . twenty or thirty good glasses at a sitting'.[17] Regardless of whether they are Orthodox, pilgrims will be expected to follow the calendar of fasts and feasts. Those who arrive too late for *trapeza* will always be given something to eat in the guest house.

The liturgical routine is the foundation of the religious life and visitors are generally encouraged to participate in it. Orthodox pilgrims are expected to attend services and are usually invited to make their confession and to receive communion. Non-Orthodox may not receive communion, and different monasteries have different customs about the attendance of non-Orthodox at services (this is true also of formal meals in the refectory). Restrictions are often imposed for the purely practical reason that there is not enough room for all in the body of the church; they are certainly never meant to cause offence. When non-Orthodox are asked to remain in the narthex or eat after the others have finished, it is the monks' way of showing how special Orthodoxy is to them. Athos has never been at the forefront of ecumenical dialogue. On the other hand many monks enjoy the opportunity to discuss questions of belief and practice with members of other churches. Pilgrims should take advice from the *archontaris* about what is possible.

At sunset the gates are shut, no further visitors are admitted, and monks soon retire to their cells. The hours of darkness are regarded as a time for silence and prayer, and visitors are asked to behave accordingly. Some monasteries turn off the electricity at night in an attempt to discourage idle chatter. Services resume in the early hours and it is assumed that most people will want to take some rest before then. Most monasteries run according to 'Byzantine time' which starts the clock for each new day at sunset. Depending on the season, therefore, clocks will be between three and six hours ahead of local Greek time. Guest masters however realize that this may be confusing and will generally translate the timetable into 'cosmic time' for the benefit of visitors. No such concession is likely to be made, however, with regard to the date. As mentioned above, the whole Mountain still follows the Julian calendar and is therefore thirteen days behind the outside world.

All the monasteries are veritable treasure-houses filled with priceless relics of their Byzantine past, many of which were displayed for the first time in the exhibition at Thessaloniki in 1997–8. Treasures of particular religious significance, such as relics of the saints and miracle-working icons, are often kept in the church and may be displayed at certain times for veneration by Orthodox pilgrims. Other items are likely to be kept in a strongroom to which supervised access can sometimes be arranged. Most monasteries also house important collections of manuscripts. The vast majority of these are liturgical, many date from the Byzantine period, and some are beautifully illuminated. A small proportion (five per cent) are classical texts.[18] Permission to read manuscripts can usually be obtained if the request is supported by a letter of recommendation. Printed books are often kept in another library to which access is less restricted. Books in various languages may also be available in the guest house.

Photographers find Athos irresistibly photogenic. Most monasteries permit photography within their walls, but not inside the church, especially during services. Monks do not normally allow themselves to be photographed; a request to do so may have to go to the abbot. The same procedure may be necessary for photography of icons, frescos and other treasures. The best advice is always to ask. Failure to do so may cause serious offence. Video cameras and camcorders are prohibited everywhere on the Mountain.

The common language in the Greek monasteries is Greek, in St Panteleimonos Russian, in Chilandar Serbian, in Zographou Bulgarian, and in the sketes of Prodromos and Lakkou Romanian. Some communities are more cosmopolitan than others, but many now include monks from overseas. As a result English is now quite widely spoken on the Mountain. To have no Greek remains a disadvantage, but not nearly so much as it was a few years ago.

THE SPIRITUAL HARVEST

The ever-increasing number of visitors makes it not uncommon, particularly at the major feasts, for the pilgrims to outnumber the monks. One cannot help wondering if such numbers do not present a distraction and a burden to the monks. A monk of Iviron responded to the question in this way:

> Besides praying for the world, hospitality is the Orthodox monk's traditional means of fulfilling the second commandment. How tiring this can be for the monks depends not so much on the numbers of visitors but on their reasons for coming. But even then, as Fr J once said to me, people have *their* reasons for visiting Athos, but God has *His*. An Austrian might come purely to climb Athos, but God meets him and changes him; the poor man finds that he has encountered a Holy Mountain more vast than the heavens!

Does this sort of encounter actually happen; or is this wishful thinking on the part of a monk? What is the pilgrim's experience? Here we may cite the response of a Greek medical student when questioned by René Gothóni about his recent visit to Athos:

> Walking was incredible—first of all tiring, physically very tiring. We walked from Megisti Lavra to Karakallou for about twelve hours. The eye could see a long way—the sky, the virgin nature, the mountain, the valleys. The spirit soars in these parts. You get a splendid feeling. We had many rests. Drank only water. We climbed about 1,000 meters, Athos was right over our heads and then from 1,000 meters down to the sea and then from the sea up to about 200 meters to Karakallou. I felt there, at 1,000 meters on Athos, between the trees—it is impossible for me to translate my thoughts into words, it was the kind of experience you can live, not explain—I found myself there, I returned to my roots as a human being. My mind became peaceful. I found myself as a human being.[19]

Archimandrite Aimilianos has written perceptively about the role of a monk's spiritual father, comparing it with the efforts made by a father in the world for his own children:

> The worker, the farmer, the professional man, all strive to make their living, to gather together their families, to enjoy their material goods and provide for their children. This is true of every father, but much more so of the spiritual father and the spiritual harvest. The seed which is sown and the garnered treasures are his children. And the children are the life of the father.[20]

In a vivid demonstration of the central role played by hospitality in the life of the monastery Fr Aimilianos then extends this image of fatherhood beyond the monk to the pilgrim:

And there is another harvest: not this time in the cell, but in the guesthouse. Each day men gather there—our brothers. They come from all parts. The hospitable monks offer themselves in sacrifice. Joy, faith, warmth and jubilation erupt in the hearts of the guests. Their life changes. They find meaning. They weep for joy, each finding what was necessary for him. They become one with the monks. A living change wrought by the right hand of the Lord. Here, then, is the other harvest in the hearts and the homes of those who have left the Monastery to return as soon as possible.[21]

A pilgrim's enjoyment of monastic hospitality is not only a privilege; it carries responsibilities too. The next few pages recount a few of my own experiences, beginning with some of the major feasts I have attended in the course of several pilgrimages.

PASCHA AT XEROPOTAMOU

In 1994 I was invited to celebrate Pascha at the monastery of Xeropotamou. In February of that year Archimandrite Joseph, the abbot of that monastery, had been deposed, together with the representatives of Dionysiou, Philotheou and Simonopetra, by a delegation of bishops sent by the Ecumenical Patriarchate,[22] and when I arrived on the Mountain, on Great Thursday of Holy Week, the depositions were still in place. This was my fourth visit to Athos and I travelled alone.

I went first to Simonopetra, striding south from Daphne in the pleasant April sunshine. Arriving at the monastery around 2.30 pm, I was warmly received in the traditional fashion and given a room to myself, a rare privilege in this already crowded monastery. The fathers were very frank in discussing with me the recent tension with Constantinople and explaining the background to it. The Friends of Mount Athos, of which I was Honorary Secretary, had published protests in the British press, the only group in the outside world to have responded to the monks' appeal for help, and for this they were truly grateful.

That night the depositions were retracted by fax from Constantinople. Whether our fumbling interventions had assisted the process we shall never know; but it was an exciting moment to be there. The monks insisted, however, that, even though the immediate crisis was over, the underlying problem had not gone away and they would continue to need our support. I left the monastery with many expressions of good will but with little material sustenance. My breakfast was a piece of loukoumi and a glass of water. But it was Great Friday and I was expected at Xeropotamou.

Pinning my hopes on the restaurant in Daphne, I retraced my steps along the dusty road that I had taken the day before and reached the port

109 Great Friday at Simonopetra. A coffee break during the preparation of fish to be eaten at the coming feast.

around 10 am. To my dismay the restaurant was closed, not because it was Great Friday but for refurbishment. Equally dismayed was a Lebanese doctor whom I had met at Simonopetra. He was travelling with two Serbs, and all three were going to Chilandar for Pascha. One of the Serbs, a journalist whom I had met the night before, spoke movingly to me about his country's guilt in the recent war in Bosnia.

Taking my leave, I followed the steep path up to Xeropotamou and reached the monastery at about 11.30. Fr B, an English monk whom I had met in Oxford some months before, emerged from the katholikon to welcome me. With his long, divided, white beard he seemed older than I remembered him. He quickly whisked me into church for the hours (third, sixth, and ninth) and went off to telephone the good news of the retracted depositions to the British press and the BBC. He later told me with some satisfaction that a journalist from the *Independent* newspaper would visit the Mountain the following week.

After the hours I went to the guest house where I met another Englishman, formerly Nicholas, now Evangelos, who had been baptized at the monastery of Philotheou. We became good friends and I was given a room to myself (containing five beds) next to his—sparsely furnished but pleasant enough and with electricity. After a short rest I went down to the katholikon for vespers at 5 pm. Xeropotamou is one of the monasteries that does not normally admit the non-Orthodox to the body of the church during services, and I was then not yet Orthodox. But since I had been invited to be there, I had earlier taken the liberty of making my acceptance dependent on my being allowed in. Fr B now gave me a bilingual service book which made it easier to follow what was going on. Great Friday vespers is a beautiful service lasting two hours during which the figure of Christ is taken down from the cross and placed on the Epitaphion (sepulchre). The tomb had already been decorated with flowers and bay and was now placed in the middle of the church. After compline the pilgrims were given a light meal of fruit, halva, olives, and water in the refectory while the monks fasted. I retired to my room at about 7.30 pm.

The next morning, Great Saturday, I was up in time for matins which began at 2.30 am. Everyone in church was given a candle to hold. At about 5.00 we processed once round the outside of the church, then came back in, stooping to pass under the Epitaphion as we did so. The service was over by about 6.00 and everyone retired to sleep for a few hours. By mid-morning I had wandered outside the monastery to take some photographs, but I was brought back by the sound of the *talanto*. Vespers began at 10.30 and was followed by the Liturgy of St Basil. Immediately after this, at 2 pm, there was *trapeza*—a fasting meal consisting of bean soup, a whole cucumber, a raw onion, bread, olives, halva, and water. The food was welcome, and for once there was time enough to eat it.

The weather was cool and cloudy, in tune with the Great Friday lamentations ('Today the sky is black, today is a black day'). I was pleased therefore to be invited to help Fr B with his work in the kitchen, chopping onion leaves and breaking eggs. Fr B was the monastery's chief cook and he had what seemed to me a very modern kitchen by Athonite standards—two large gas rings, several electric stoves, and a vast dishwasher. The community numbered 25 monks and one novice and there were as many as forty pilgrims to be fed too. Later, when he had an hour to spare, we strolled outside together and he told me something about his past life. He had been a pupil of Dimitri Obolensky at Oxford and then became a schoolmaster, first in England and later in Athens. He had first come to Athos as a pilgrim in 1961. Now he had been at Xeropotamou for seven years, having been baptized at Simonopetra by Fr Aimilianos. Archimandrite Joseph, he told me, had been abbot of Xeropotamou for ten years and was the youngest abbot ever when he was first elected. His predecessor had been killed in a road accident (a surprising fate for an Athonite) and Joseph was the only priest there at the time. But he was a good choice and had made a very successful abbot. He was busy hearing confessions that day but would

110 'Christ is risen! He is risen indeed!' Pilgrims and monks listen to the Resurrection story outside the katholikon at Vatopedi.

like to see me the next day after the services.

The next day was Pascha, culmination of the great fast and of all the long services of the preceding days. I was woken at 1.00 am and remained in the narthex of the katholikon until the end of the hours. At 1.30 all lights were extinguished, and the sudden darkness produced a silence that was pregnant with anticipation. Then at last Christ rose, and light was dispensed to all from the royal doors. Shielding our candles from the wind, we all processed outside to the *phiale* (the monastery's sacred fountain where every month water is blessed for use in the church). There the Resurrection story (Mark 16:1–8) was read and the great Easter hymn ('Christ is risen from the dead; trampling down death by death; and upon those in the tombs bestowing life') was sung endlessly. Returning to the church, we (the pilgrims) greeted each of the fathers individually with the words 'Christos anesti' ('Christ is risen'), starting with the abbot and moving all the way round the church, venerating the icons, the cross, and the gospel in passing. The great candelabra were now set swinging, creating a ballet of golden light, which was all very glorious and uplifting. The Easter hymn was sung in English by Fr B, in French by another father, and in Romanian by a priest from a nearby cell traditionally reserved for Romanians. Then followed the Liturgy of St John Chrysostom at which most of those present received holy communion. (At the end I took *antidoron*, which is blessed bread, sometimes available to the non-Orthodox.)

By 6.00 the Liturgy was over and monks and pilgrims processed without a pause into the refectory, the abbot in full regalia leading the procession. The icon of the Resurrection was carried aloft, hymns continued to be sung, censers to be swung, candelabra to be rotated, all combining to demonstrate that the festal meal about to be eaten in the refectory was in every sense a continuation of the liturgical meal that had just been celebrated in the katholikon. Fr B had taken immense trouble with the food. There was the traditional egg and lemon soup, steaming hot and good; a large piece of meaty fish, cold and (to my taste) less good; salad, cheese, a painted egg; and plenty of strong white wine. The meal was not hurried, but by 6.30 it was over and I was pleased to retire to my bed where I slept until 9.00. For the rest of the day there was peace and quiet in the monastery as most people relaxed and enjoyed the holiday.

At 4.30 pm there was a short service of vespers in the katholikon with readings in English, Romanian, and Greek, another ballet of candles, and another round of greeting all the fathers. Then there was a gathering in the *synodikon* (the monks' reception room, or senior common room as I referred to it in my diary) at which the abbot held court, talking about the recent retractions (which had particularly affected him) and answering questions from monks and pilgrims. Everyone there was given a cake, a glass of liqueur and an Easter egg. This was followed by dinner: a warm risotto with mushrooms and peas, artichoke hearts in an egg sauce, yogurt, wine, and another Easter egg (I now had three, all of which I kept as sustenance for my walking tour that was to come). After dinner I was summoned by the abbot and we discussed some of the problems that were of concern to the monks at the time and our hope that he would some day come to England.

The next morning, Bright Monday, I left Xeropotamou after *trapeza* on a journey that took me round the northern part of the peninsula, staying one night at Dochiariou and two at Chilandar, before arriving at Vatopedi on the Thursday. My feelings were similar to those of Donald Nicol, who wrote of his experience of Pascha at Chilandar in 1949, 'Somehow I feel that my Easter this year has been a real one and not just a matter of a special day in my diary.'[23]

CHRISTMAS AT VATOPEDI

I returned to the Mountain on Thursday 4 January 1996 (NS), this time travelling with a friend who was an Anglican ordinand. On Athos of course it was only 22 December 1995. We had already celebrated a snowy new year in Oxfordshire; but we were here for the festival of the Nativity of Christ.

Even though it was winter, there was standing room only on the bus from Daphne to Karyes, but it was not quite as crowded as it is in the summertime. In Karyes we were met by Fr A, a hermit monk, who had invited us to visit his hermitage at Kapsala, high up in the hills above Karyes.[24] There we were warmly received and given a feast of a meal, far more than we could possibly eat: spinach pie, ladies' fingers, yogurt, oranges, lemonade and coffee. In exchange we brought him a Christmas cake which my wife had made for him. His house, more like an Alpine chalet than an Athonite cell, is on two floors. Downstairs is a large living room with a wood-burning stove, a reception area, a bed, and enormous numbers of icons, photographs and treasures of all sorts. Fr A is very house-proud and everything is beautifully arranged. He played cassettes of a book by Fr Sophrony and Russian Orthodox chant. When we had eaten, I went outside to take photographs. The view from his garden was magnificent, taking in the Serai just below in Karyes and the whole of the east coast as far as the eye could see. Only the peak of Athos itself was, as usual, hidden by cloud. The garden was decorated in similar manner to the house, with numerous icons, painted ornaments and (in winter) plastic flowers. Fr A then showed us upstairs, where the space is divided into six very small rooms, including a library and a chapel. There were also two guest rooms but he was having trouble with the stove, he said, and the house was damp, so it would be more convenient if we were to continue our journey to Vatopedi, where he would join us in two days' time for the feast. We departed, leaving this eccentric but cultivated hermit to his favourite occupations of talking to the birds and feeding his pet lizards, and reached the monastery before the gates shut at sunset.

The next day, 23 December, was 'rather a churchy day', according to my diary. We attended the hours from 4.00 to 6.30. There was then a break for sleep until 9.00, and we were back in church until 1.30 pm when there was *trapeza*: soup with pasta, bread, olives, an apple and water. In wintertime the shortness of the days means that the liturgical routine is concentrated into a very few hours. At 3.30 we were back in the katholikon for vespers, followed again by *trapeza* (this time halva, bread, olives, an orange and water) and then compline. Since evenings are longer, more time is available after dinner for discussion with the fathers. Wood-burning stoves are lit in every room and a very warm and cosy atmosphere is created.

Vatopedi maintains a policy of openness which some have mistaken for worldliness. No monastery is more welcoming to its visitors, regardless of whether they are Orthodox; no brotherhood is more devoted to the cenobitic way of life or more serious in the way that they practise it. Thanks to the presence of inspiring spiritual fathers, it has attracted a steady flow of recruits from all over the world. No restrictions are put in the way of non-Orthodox pilgrims in either church or refectory. They are positively encouraged to do everything that the Orthodox do except receive holy communion.

The following day was Christmas Eve, a Saturday. We rose at 5.30 and attended church until 8.30 when there was *trapeza*—rice, olives, salad, potatoes, bread, an orange and (rather surprisingly) wine. At 1.00 we returned to the katholikon for Great Vespers, a beautifully sung service during which the great candelabra were swung for the first time. This was followed at 2.30 by a fasting meal of bean soup, olives, bread, a raw onion, an orange, and water. The monks processed in and out of the refectory singing hymns. We greeted Fr A who had just arrived for the coming feast. At 4 pm we retired to our rooms to rest and a period of silence began.

At 8 pm both monks and pilgrims gathered in the *synodikon* to listen to a homily by Elder Joseph, the disciple of Elder Joseph the Hesychast and principal spiritual father of the monastery. Then at 9 pm the vigil began. The church was alternately made light and dark with use of all the candles and candelabra at different times. The effect was highly theatrical and quite beautiful. At one point the brows of all were anointed ('for healing of body and soul') by a priest standing in the middle of the nave. The icons were venerated several times. And then a very exciting event took place: two novices were brought forward to be tonsured as monks. As the abbot cut a lock of hair from the head of each of them, so the Elder Joseph pronounced their new monastic names for the first time—Fr J, originally from France, and Fr A, from Arta in Epirus. To my even greater surprise I was instructed to photograph this rite of passage. As I stepped forward to do so, a shade whispered in audible tones, 'Your turn next!' In conclusion, the Liturgy of St Basil was celebrated by Abbot Ephraim, finishing at 6.30. The feast that followed included a generous portion of fish (*rophos*), with salad, cheese, and bread, full decanters of wine, and a portion of *kataiphi* to end with. It was now Christmas morning and we exchanged greetings with each other before retiring to our rooms where we slept contentedly until 11.30.

After the rigours of the vigil Christmas Day itself was a joyful and relaxed holiday. No work was done by most monks and a good part of the day was devoted to rest and leisure activities. Vespers was celebrated at 3 pm, and after that the abbot held a reception for the brotherhood and their guests. Drinks and sweets were served, Christmas greetings were exchanged, and the atmosphere was suitably festive. Roaring fires were lit in every room, ensuring that no one was cold, and as the darkness settled early, monks entertained pilgrims with stories of miraculous happenings and holy men of long ago.

After Christmas I stayed on at the monastery for a further week, reading the proofs of the Elder Joseph's biography of *Elder Joseph the Hesychast* as my *diakonima* (monastic obedience). This gave me an opportunity to get to know more of the fathers, and to see for myself how well the restoration of the monastery was progressing. Decaying buildings have been expertly and lovingly restored; gardens and vineyards have been brought back into full production; a completely new guest house has been constructed in a disused wing (though the constant flow of pilgrims means that the old one is still needed); icons and other treasures have been conserved and exhibited in a beautifully designed museum; manuscripts have been catalogued; an ambitious programme of publications is now bearing fruit. I also spent some time with Fr A, the deputy abbot, planning the forthcoming visit of Abbot Ephraim to England. The days passed all too quickly and very soon my fifth visit to the Mountain was ended.

PENTECOST IN THE DESERT

In June 1998 I returned to Athos, travelling with a friend who is a rug dealer. It was my seventh visit and the second that we had made together. We went first to Karyes to inspect the progress of work on the Protaton Tower. We were met by the architects, Petros Koufopoulos and Stavros Mamaloukos, and the architectural historian Ploutos Theocharides, who showed us over the building. Restoration of the fabric was almost complete and they were well advanced with plans for the interior refurbishment. Our interest focused on this part of the project because it was to be funded by the Friends of Mount Athos with the proceeds of the Onassis Prize won in 1997 by the President of the society, Sir Steven Runciman.[25] Having seen the tower, we were received formally by the Protos, who presented with us with silver plaques to commemorate our visit and kindly arranged transport for us to Simonopetra in his private vehicle (registration number AO 1). At Simonopetra, where we stayed a night, we were shown the monastery's new library, which had been designed by the same partnership that was now at work on the Protaton Tower. The work had been done beautifully using traditional materials and maintaining the highest standards of craftsmanship. It augured very well indeed for our project in Karyes and we were greatly encouraged. Next morning we took the coastal path via Grigoriou and Dionysiou to St Paul's. From there it was our intention to proceed into the desert and walk round the southern tip of the peninsula to the Lavra.

Setting out from St Paul's on the Saturday morning, we walked along the coast as far as New Skete where we sought out Fr N, the celebrated iconographer. He invited us to visit his cell and, having been assured that there would indeed be a boat to Kafsokalyvia in the afternoon, we were delighted to accept his hospitality. His balcony affords a delightful view of the surrounding cells of the skete (where about forty-five monks live today) and the sea below. Even at New Skete there was construction work in progress, the workers being Pontic Greeks from Russia; there were some terrible examples of new building in the worst modern concrete style. Happily Fr N's cell is older and built on traditional lines with a beautiful garden. Inside, he showed us his studio, where he was working on several icons, and the comfortable accommodation that he offers to his guests (mostly students of iconography). It was tempting to stay but we were anxious to reach Kafsokalyvia that night because there would be a vigil for Pentecost, together with a *panegyri*, since Pentecost is the feast to which that skete is dedicated. Having enjoyed a substantial meal of spaghetti and red wine, we ran down to the port in time to catch the boat at 1 pm.

It was a scenic voyage. The boat called first at St Anne's skete, a dependency of the Lavra and the biggest and oldest skete on the Mountain. There is currently a brotherhood of 105 monks, scattered among the fifty-odd cells. The next stop was Karoulia, where a collection of hermitages cling precariously to the sheer face of the cliffs, overhanging the sea itself 100 metres or more below. Some of the cells are still inhabited but only two or three passengers disembarked here. Everyone else stayed on board, eager to reach the boat's final destination, the skete of the Holy Trinity at Kafsokalyvia.

Arriving at about 2 pm, we began the stiff climb up to the church, together with about two dozen other pilgrims. There were rumours that the skete would not be able to provide accommodation for all the pilgrims who were expected, so there was some incentive not to be last. But in the event, as usual on Athos, there were beds and food for all and we need not have worried. On arrival we were received with traditional hospitality and shown to a room that contained eight beds. After a short rest we explored the skete, which is home to thirty-five monks, and conversed with some of the fathers and other pilgrims. A sense of expectation hung in the air as we all waited for things to happen.

At 8.30 pm there was a service of short vespers in the kyriakon, a large and beautiful building which occupies the only piece of level ground in the whole skete. This was followed by a great feast with vast plates of fish, cheese and salad, bowls of cherries, plenty of wine, and even macaroons. There was no nonsense about segregating the Orthodox from the non-Orthodox or the fathers from the pilgrims. There were roughly equal numbers of each and everyone sat at the same tables and tucked in to the same food with enthusiasm and a real sense of fellowship. There was a truly festive atmosphere that was much less formal than one would find in any of the ruling monasteries today, more reminiscent in fact of the stories told by Sydney Loch and others who had visited the Mountain in the first half of the twentieth century.

After the meal, monks and pilgrims returned to church for the vigil which would continue through the night. But since we planned an early start the next morning, we (rather reluctantly) retired to our beds in the early hours. When we rose at 6.00, the vigil was still in progress, so we stole quietly away in the direction of Agios Neilos, and from there across the desert to the Romanian skete of Prodromos which we reached by about

10.00. Refreshed by a suitably festive meal generously provided by the kind fathers of this cenobitic skete, we continued on our way to the Lavra where we established ourselves in the guest house for the night.

Lavra seemed to have changed very little since my last visit ten years before, except that the buildings were in a much worse state of collapse and the monks were ten years older. Many of the fathers still appeared to be living according to the idiorrhythmic system, despite the fact that it was formally abandoned in 1980. They did not come to services in the church or meals in the refectory, nor did they attempt to fraternize much with pilgrims, though those on duty in the guest house were friendly enough. There had been some reconstruction work carried out on the buildings, though it did not look particularly well done to me; and in places there was a good deal of rusting old scaffolding that looked as if it had become permanent. Staying here was not an uplifting experience. But one other Pentecost-related incident must be recounted.

The service of vespers at Pentecost includes a sequence of so-called kneeling prayers that require prostrations. We attended this service at the Lavra and took our places in the body of the katholikon. My prostrations obviously did not pass muster and drew the inevitable challenge from a fierce-looking monk:

‘Are you Orthodox?’
‘No.’
‘Would you please take a seat in the narthex.’

I obeyed, with some reluctance. My bitterness towards the brotherhood was not sweetened by the fact that my rug-dealing companion, no more Orthodox than I, had prostrated himself with sufficient conviction to be permitted to remain in the church. I was of course happy for him; but such incidents, all too common in certain monasteries, do nothing to promote the virtues of Orthodoxy. The next morning we left for the Romanian skete of Lakkou, where happily such discriminatory thoughts would never cross the minds of the fathers—fathers who have themselves suffered more than their fair share of persecution at the hands of the Greek civil authorities.

Visiting an Elder

In August 2000 I made my tenth visit to the Mountain, this time at the behest of the abbot of Vatopedi who summoned me to act as godfather to a young American catechumen (candidate for baptism). I felt greatly honoured to be asked to play this responsible role and I had no hesitation in accepting.

A few days before the baptism, my prospective godson and I decided to visit Elder Dionysios, the renowned Romanian elder who lived at Kolitsou, about an hour's walk from Vatopedi in the direction of Pantokrator. Then aged ninety-two, he had been on the Mountain for seventy-four years, but he continued to receive visitors for a few hours each morning. He was highly regarded by the fathers of Vatopedi and we were encouraged to seek the benefit of his wisdom.

I have always felt a sense of anxiety and awe when approaching any of the great holy men of Athos who have become legendary figures in their time. Nor am I alone in this. Fr Nikolaos writes movingly of his 'encounter with a living saint' when he visited the famous Greek Elder Païssios (1924–1994) for the first time in 1971:

> His humble hut was situated at the lowest point of a ravine, but maybe it was the highest place on earth! While we descended the pathway on foot, we ascended it with our soul. We did not talk to each other. It seemed we were anticipating something sacred. Here, absolute quietude prevailed, even if we could hear the birds, cicadas or the rustle of the leaves. This quietude was not only peculiar or unusual, but it radiated a deep sense of mystery. It did not invite you to enjoy it, but rather it created a deep feeling of contrition. It was not relaxing, but stimulating. You were silent and everything in you functioned as intensely as ever. You worried, but you felt unusually serene. You anticipated something great.[26]

We felt something of this as we approached the remote settlement of Kolitsou. Here, as at Lakkou, the true ascetic life continues, unaffected by what is happening in the monasteries. We felt privileged to find it.

We were received by a youngish monk who brought us the traditional tray of hospitality. When we explained that we had come to see the elder we were asked to wait for a few minutes. We sat on a bench in the reception room where we were soon joined by a frail and diminutive figure who greeted us warmly. On learning that the young American sitting next to him was about to be baptized, the elder beamed and began to talk freely about the life that lay ahead of him in the world and the temptations that it would bring.

> 'And what would be your advice to a young man who is about to be baptized?' asked my godson.
>
> 'You must either marry or become a monk', was the elder's immediate and slightly puzzling response. To emphasize that no other option was possible, he repeated it. 'You must either marry or become a monk.'

The explanation of this apparently stark choice is provided for us by Fr Alexander Golitzin who quotes the advice given to him by an Athonite abbot:

> 'We Christians are not meant to live alone. We are called to be part of a family. We thus have a choice: we can either make a new family [i.e., marry], or join an existing one [become monks].' To choose the first, although certainly worthy and

blessed by Church and Tradition, is still to remain within the circles of blood and kinship, nor will it elicit cries of outrage from near and dear (unless, of course, it is marriage to the 'wrong' person. . .). To choose the second, on the other hand, is really and truly a break with the 'world', a kind of death, and it is accompanied by the same sort of mourning as would be expected at a funeral. One's kin will respond to it as to a desertion, an abandonment, a kind of familial apostasy. The Athonite, in particular the Greek Athonite, genuinely does depart here from the secular norm. He has, in embracing the family of monks, left the 'world' and set out on the road to a different society.[27]

STAYING ON

The Mountain exercises strong powers over those who visit it. We have already remarked on the fact that even those whose journey was originally motivated by mere curiosity return to the world conscious of having made a pilgrimage. Some are so moved by their experience that they do not return at all, or only after an extended stay. Just as one or two undergraduates each year are likely eventually to become senior members of the institution at which they studied, so one or two pilgrims each year will turn into novices.

111 'Master, give the blessing.' A baptismal feast at Vatopedi.

Nor is it uncommon for non-Orthodox pilgrims to choose to be received into Orthodoxy on the Mountain. The monks do not recognize the validity of sacraments conferred by other Christian churches. This means that a non-Orthodox who wishes to become Orthodox on Athos has no choice but to be baptized or, in the case of those who have been baptized already, rebaptized. As was noted in the last chapter, this issue has long been debated and the idea of rebaptism is anathema to those who feel committed to 'one baptism for the remission of sins'. But for those who have fallen under the spell of the Holy Mountain there is no alternative.

Like a novice, a candidate for baptism will first be assigned to a senior monk for a course of instruction lasting several weeks. This normally involves a study of the gospels and also a study of Orthodox doctrine, on which he is examined. In other respects he lives like a monk, attends services in the katholikon, eats in the refectory, but has little contact with pilgrims or anyone else in the monastery, and prepares himself for the coming event. As the time approaches, the abbot will ask the monk in charge of the candidate if he is ready; he may also require the candidate to make a confession of his past life; and he will need to assure himself that the candidate is indeed ready. Meanwhile the candidate, like a novice, is likely to experience a whole range of emotions from serious doubt to wild euphoria as this course proceeds. By the end of it he will probably yearn so much for baptism that he can think of nothing else. The day will be chosen by the abbot, as will the form of the service and the place where it is to be performed. In summer it is sometimes done quietly in the sea; otherwise, like a tonsure, it takes place in the katholikon in the middle of the Divine Liturgy on Sunday, thus ensuring maximum exposure before the whole body of monks and pilgrims.

On the appointed day the candidate must present himself early in the narthex where the priests of the monastery will read exorcisms over him in order to achieve a spiritual catharsis of the soul and body. Later, when the Liturgy has reached a suitable point (usually after the reading of the epistle), the abbot will lead the monks and pilgrims to the narthex where the candidate is waiting with his sponsor or godfather. Taking the candidate out of the church, the abbot then questions him. He asks him to renounce the devil, to breathe and spit on him, and to turn to Christ. The candidate is then asked to recite the creed three times and, as he re-enters the church, to prostrate himself and invoke the Holy Trinity. The candidate, like a novice, then retires to a side chapel where he removes his clothes. Naked except for a pair of shorts, he returns and is anointed with oil, tonsured, and then totally immersed three times in the font 'in the name of the Father, the Son, and the Holy Spirit'. He is then dried and receives chrismation when the abbot anoints certain parts of his body (forehead, eyes, nose, lips, ears, chest, hands, and feet) with myrrh. Each time the abbot

112 The mystery of Athos: a wayside cross near Simonopetra.

says 'the seal of the gift of the holy Spirit', summoning the Spirit to endue the newly baptized with divine grace. The candidate then retires once more to the side chapel to change into a brand new set of clothes, symbolizing his rebirth as a new man. Returning to the narthex, he is clothed in a white baptismal robe and processes with the abbot back into the body of the church where he is given a seat of honour next to his godfather. The Liturgy then resumes. The neophyte and his godfather are called to the royal doors twice, for special prayers and for the sponsor to place a baptismal cross round his godson's neck; and they receive communion ahead of everybody else. At the end of the service they process out of the church with the abbot, whereupon they receive congratulations and are embraced by the whole company of monks and pilgrims. After weeks of preparation the endurance test is finally over and everyone can relax. The newly baptized is warmly welcomed as an honorary member of the monastic brotherhood; and to symbolize this reception he and his godfather are honoured with seats at the abbot's table in the refectory where the meal that follows is truly a joyful feast.

After baptism the neophyte is required to stay on at the monastery, usually for another week, to receive communion daily and to begin to practise his Orthodoxy with the full support of a loving brotherhood. The difference between the neophyte and the novice is that the latter stays on for ever, while the former returns to the world. The world can seem a harsh, evil and frightening environment after a long period of time spent on the Holy Mountain. The neophyte is warned that he can expect to be assailed by temptations, demons will lie in wait for him at every turn. At the same time he has the comfort of knowing that he is for the rest of his life an honorary member of the most exclusive Orthodox brotherhood in the world.

EPILOGUE

The exclusiveness of Athos is essential to its survival. If it were to be compromised, there is no doubt that within a very short space of time the sole surviving holy mountain would suffer the same fate as the others, like Meteora and countless other monasteries in Greece and the Middle East that are now either museums of Byzantine art or deserted ruins. Thirty years ago it seemed that this was the inevitable fate of Mount Athos. But the Mother of God was not willing to surrender her garden. Its soil has been refertilized and has given birth to a new spring. The garden is blooming again as freshly as ever, welcoming newcomers to its groves, and exporting its fruits to the world.

Despite appearances to the contrary, the Mountain is not a place of total isolation and introspection. It is a world apart; but it does not shun the rest of the world; nor can it afford to do so. It relies on the world for supplying it with new blood and for supporting its economy. But the relationship with the world is a true symbiosis. Just as the Mountain needs the world, so the world needs the Mountain. The monks see their principal duty as being to pray for the world, a world of which they no longer form a part, a world to which they have died, but a world which they continue to cherish almost as if it were their creation. The world needs those prayers as never before. What could be more reassuring for us as we lie in our beds at night than to know that there are 1600 or so monks on Mount Athos praying now, *for us*?

The monks' care for the world takes concrete as well as spiritual form. We cannot close this book without mention of the Holy Convent of the Annunciation at Ormylia, a daughter house of the monastery of Simonopetra, where a thriving community of some 125 nuns live an ascetic life that is consciously modelled on that of their parent monastery. Under the inspiring leadership of the Abbess Nikodeme the sisters provide countless benefits to their neighbours and visitors. Their organic farming methods are an example to local agriculturalists; their community centre cares for both the physical and the spiritual needs of the local population and specializes in the early diagnosis of cancer in women; they also have a centre for the treatment of distressed icons and other works of art. They too provide hospitality for numerous pilgrims, and are a living witness that Athos cares for women as well as men.

The monks also demonstrate their mission to the world in practical ways. In 1992 four Athonites went to Albania to help to reinvigorate the Church there after many years of communist oppression and persecution. The following year the abbot of Xeropotamou twice visited Georgia to co-ordinate efforts being made by the Church to alleviate suffering in that country. In 1996 the Holy Community expressed its support for refugees from Bosnia by sending a sum of money to the patriarchate of Serbia. The monastery of Koutloumousiou is closely involved with a number of initiatives to improve the lot of young people in Greece. Athonite monks have recently been seconded to Calabria in order to repopulate an eleventh-century Byzantine monastery there. Relics of the saints and miracle-working icons are regularly sent out into the world for the faithful to venerate. In 1999 the *Axion Estin* icon of the Mother of God was taken from Karyes to Athens where it succeeded in raising 470 million drachmas for the victims of the recent earthquake disaster. These are just a few examples of the Athonite mission to the world during the 1990s.

But what does the future hold for Athos? How will the monks cope with the advent of the third millennium? How will they respond to the demands brought to bear by membership of the European Union, the relentless growth of tourism, the invasive tendencies of new technology? Will they withdraw into their shell and revert to being a collection of reactionary divines in the decline of life? Or will they be forced to yield to the raucous and ill-informed clamour of politicians who insist that they must 'mend their ways', abandon their Byzantine bureaucracy, Hellenize their remaining non-Greek monasteries, sell off their treasures, even admit women?

The monks know that in order to survive they must tread cautiously; they know that they must look for a middle way, and that to find it they need to summon up all their skills of tact and diplomacy. They may give the impression of inhabiting an otherworldly paradise where they are so close to God that they no longer have a care in the world; and at one level that image is not so far from the truth. But that is only part of the picture. There are some extremely astute men among them who are quite well aware of what is going on in the outside world and have a fairly shrewd idea of how to deal with it.

They know that, in order to survive, they must first of all protect their seclusion, and that without it any hope of preserving the true monastic way of life is lost. The vast majority of monks are also determined to maintain the pan-Orthodox traditions of the Mountain. Athos has survived threats to its autonomy in the past, and it owes its survival on numerous occasions to the unstinting support of the other Orthodox nations, notably Serbia, Romania and Russia. To turn its back on these former benefactors at a time when *they* most need the support and example of this supranational monastic model would be an act of unforgivable betrayal. Athos, like the Ecumenical Patriarchate, draws strength from its very supranational status; and nothing should stand in the way of its continuation.

There are signs that relations with the Patriarchate in Constantinople and with the government in Athens have at last begun to improve and that the tensions of recent years are becoming more relaxed. The Patriarchate itself is in a highly precarious position and knows that it must look for friends beyond Athens. More than once the Greek government has announced an undertaking to guarantee the ancient rights and privileges of the monks and the visits made by European commissioners to the Mountain and the remarks they have made at the time have gone some way towards allaying the monks' fears for their future security. It is important for all concerned that human rights should be respected and that a more constructive dialogue should take the place of the scenes of ugly confrontation that have characterized some recent episodes.

The fact is that once again Athos is operating in just the same way that it has done for centuries. It is providing a viable alternative to the rapidly spreading materialism and secularism of modern society, an alternative that is clearly much needed and much appreciated by large numbers of men, be they monks or pilgrims; and let it not be forgotten that daughter houses such as Ormylia provide the same alternative for women. Athos is also once again performing its traditional role as the spiritual heart of Orthodoxy. Thanks to the presence of spiritual fathers like Fr Vasileios, Fr Aimilianos, Elder Joseph, Elder Païssios and Abbot George, Athos has rediscovered its voice; and with God's help that voice will continue to be heard for many centuries to come.

NOTES

INTRODUCTION

1   R. Byron, *The Station. Athos: Trea-sures and Men* (1931, repr. London, 1984), p.98.
2   See P. Meyer, *Die Haupturkunden für die Geschichte der Athosklöster* (Leipzig, 1894), pp.113, 121.
3   M. Choukas, *Black Angels of Athos* (London, 1935), p.296.
4   P. Sherrard, *Athos: The Mountain of Silence* (London, 1960), p.26.
5   J.J. Norwich and R. Sitwell, *Mount Athos* (London, 1966), p.14.
6   C. Cavarnos, *Anchored in God: An Inside Account of Life, Art, and Thought on the Holy Mountain of Athos* (1st edn. Athens, 1959; 2nd edn. Belmont, MA, 1975), p.214.
7   Ibid., pp.214–15.
8   C. Cavarnos, *The Holy Mountain* (Belmont, MA, 1973), pp.128–31.
9   Ibid., p.129.
10 Gabriel, Abbot of the Monastery of Dionysiou, *The Voice of One Crying in the Wilderness* (Volos, 1955), quoted by C. Cavarnos, *Anchored in God*, p.216.

CHAPTER 1

1   Aeschylus, *Agamemnon*, 281–316, translated by Louis MacNeice (London, 1936).
2   Apollonius Rhodius, *Argonautica*, 1.601–4. See also Sophocles fragment 776 Pearson and commentary *ad loc.*
3   Herodotus 6.44, translated by Aubrey

de Sélincourt (Harmondsworth, 1954).
4   Herodotus 7.22.
5   M.G.A.P. de Choiseul-Gouffier, *Voyage pittoresque en Grèce*, 2 vols (Paris, 1782–1809), vol.2, pp.146–50.
6   W.M. Leake, *Travels in Northern Greece*, 4 vols (London, 1835), vol.3, p.145.
7   T. Spratt, 'Remarks on the Isthmus of Mount Athos', *Journal of the Royal Geographical Society*, 17 (1847), 145–50.
8   A. Struck, 'Der Xerxeskanal am Athos', *Neue Jahrbücher für das klassische Altertum: Geschichte und Literatur*, 10 (1907), 115–30.
9   B.S.J. Isserlin *et al.*, 'The Canal of Xerxes on the Mount Athos Peninsula: Preliminary Investigations in 1991–1992', *Annual of the British School at Athens*, 89 (1994), 277–84 and plates 43–4; 'The Canal of Xerxes: Investigations in 1993–1994', *Annual of the British School at Athens*, 91 (1996), 329–40.
10 V.K. Karastathis and S.P. Papamarinopoulos, *Geophysical Prospecting*, 45 (1997), 389–401. Reported by Norman Hammond in *The Times*, 5 January 1998.
11 B.S.J. Isserlin, 'The Canal of Xerxes: Facts and Problems', *Annual of the British School of Athens*, 86 (1991), 83.
12 J.N. Loch, *A Fringe of Blue* (London, 1968), p.114. Joice's husband Sydney Loch was a Scotsman who was welcomed as an honoured guest everywhere on the Holy Mountain and who

knew it as few laymen do, as is evident from his delightful book *Athos: The Holy Mountain* (London, 1957). On the Lochs see further, p.238.

13 Vitruvius, *De Architectura*, 2 praef., translated by F. Granger (Cambridge, MA, and London, 1931).

14 P.M. Fraser, *Ptolemaic Alexandria* (Oxford, 1972), vol.1, p.4 and note 12; Plutarch, *Life of Alexander*, 72.7.

15 G. Smyrnakis, *To Agion Oros* (Athens, 1903; repr. Mount Athos, 1988), p.12.

16 Leone Battista Alberti, *Ten Books on Architecture*, 1.4, translated by James Leoni, edited by Joseph Rykwert (repr. London, 1955).

17 Ibid. 6.4.

18 The scheme of Dinocrates and the subsequent fashion for mountain carving are well documented and illustrated in Simon Schama, *Landscape and Memory* (London, 1995), ch.7, 'Dinocrates and the Shaman: Altitude, Beatitude, Magnitude'. See also H. Meyer, 'Der Berg des Athos als Alexander: zu den realen Grundlagen der Vision des Deinokrates', *Rivista di archeologia*, 10 (1986), 22–30.

19 See J.C. Lawson, *Modern Greek Folklore and Ancient Greek Religion: A Study in Survivals* (Cambridge, 1910), p.185.

20 See Pomponius Mela 2.2.32; Lucian, *Macrobii*, 5; Aelian, *Varia Historia*, 9.10.

21 However, all five cities and the route of the canal are located with bold precision on a map in my possession printed in London in 1725.

CHAPTER 2

1 The monastery of Konstamonitou also claims a Constantinian foundation, but the claim seems to be based on a false etymology.

2 *Life of St Peter the Athonite*, 11 *PG* 150, 1005.

3 In this section I am greatly indebted to the writings of Bishop Kallistos of Diokleia (formerly Timothy Ware), in particular *The Orthodox Church*, rev. edn. (Harmondsworth, 1993), pp.257–60, and *The Orthodox Way*, rev. edn. (New York, 1995), pp.76–8.

4 *On the Annunciation*, 4–5 in *Patrologia Orientalis*, vol.19 (Paris, 1926), p.488.

5 V. Lossky, '*Panagia*', in *The Mother of God*, ed. E.L. Mascall (London, 1949), p.35.

6 T. Ware, *The Orthodox Church*, p.260.

7 See, for example, Hieromonk Alexander (Golitzin) (trans.), *The Living Witness of the Holy Mountain* (South Canaan, PA, 1996), p.105, an excellent collection of modern Athonite spiritual writings.

8 P. Meyer, *Haupturkunden für die Geschichte der Athosklöster*, p.113. See also *Actes de Xénophon*, No.1. 175 [a. 1089].

9 *Actes du Prôtaton*, No.8, 45–53.

10 Ibid., No.13, 71–2.

11 Ibid. 72–4.

12 On this whole question see Alice-Mary Talbot, 'Women and Mt Athos', in A. Bryer and M. Cunningham (eds.), *Mount Athos and Byzantine Monasticism* (Aldershot, 1996), pp.67–79. Talbot describes a range of business transactions between Athonite monks and women in the Byzantine period, often acts of donation that 'explicitly reveal women's strong yearning for spiritual links with the Holy Mountain which they could never visit' (p.77).

13 F.W. Hasluck, *Athos and its Monasteries* (London, 1924), p.12.

14 Ploutarchos L. Theocharides, 'Recent Research into Athonite Monastic Architecture, Tenth–Sixteenth Centuries', in Bryer and Cunningham

(eds), op. cit., p.212. Further archaeological investigation, made in 2000–1, has revealed traces of what is described as a basilica-style church of the Palaeochristian period beneath the north choir of the present katholikon

15 *The Great and Holy Monastery of Vatopaidi* (Mount Athos, 1994), p.21.

16 This section owes much to P. Oswald, 'The Flora and Fauna of Mount Athos', *Annual Report of the Friends of Mount Athos* (1995), pp.35–9. See also the essays in S. Dafis *et al.*, *Nature and Natural Environment in Mount Athos* (Thessaloniki, 1997) and O. Rackham, 'The Holy Mountain', *Plant Talk*, 27 (Jan. 2002), 19–23.

17 See M. and R. Higgins, *A Geological Companion to Greece and the Aegean* (London, 1996), pp.112–13, 212.

18 K. Ganiatsas, 'I vlastesis kai i chloris tis chersonesou tou Agiou Orous', *Athonike Politeia* (Thessaloniki, 1963), pp.509–678.

19 S. Papadopoulos (ed.), *Simonopetra: Mount Athos* (Athens, 1991), p.57.

20 G.E.H. Palmer, Silence over Athos', first published in the periodical *Orthodox Life* (Holy Trinity Russian Orthodox Monastery, Jordanville, NY), Nov.– Dec. 1968, p.33.

CHAPTER 3

1 A helpful summary of the iconoclast controversy may be found in J.M. Hussey, *The Orthodox Church in the Byzantine Empire* (Oxford, 1986), pp.30–68.

2 See D. Papachryssanthou (ed.), *Actes du Prôtaton, Archives de l'Athos* VII (Paris, 1975), pp.6–19.

3 See R. Morris, 'The Origins of Athos', in A. Bryer and M. Cunningham (eds), *Mount Athos and Byzantine Monasticism*, p.38 n.9.

4 The lives of these early Athonites are described by Kirsopp Lake in his *Early Days of Monasticism on Mt Athos* (Oxford, 1909).

5 Papachryssanthou, op. cit., pp.22–31; id., 'La Vie de Saint Euthyme le Jeune et la métropole de Thessalonique', *Revue des Etudes Byzantines*, 32 (1974), 225–45.

6 Lake, op. cit., pp.26–7.

7 *Actes du Prôtaton*, No.7.

8 E. Amand de Mendieta, *Mount Athos: The Garden of the Panaghia* (Berlin, 1972), pp.67–9.

9 On St Athanasios see P. Lemerle, 'La Vie ancienne de saint Athanase l'Athonite composée au début du XIe siècle par Athanase de Lavra', in *Millénaire du Mont Athos* (Chevetogne, 1963), vol. 1, pp.59–100; J. Leroy, 'La Conversion de saint Athanase l'Athonite à l'idéal cénobitique et à l'influence studite', ibid., vol. 1, pp.101–20; K. Ware, 'St Athanasios the Athonite: Traditionalist or Innovator?', in A. Bryer and M. Cunningham (eds), *Mount Athos and Byzantine Monasticism*, pp.3–16.

10 See R. Morris, *Monks and Laymen in Byzantium, 843–1118* (Cambridge, 1995), pp.34–5.

11 J. Noret, *Vitae duae antiquae Sancti Athanasii Athonitae* (Louvain, 1982), *Vita* A, 164. 37.

12 P. Meyer, *Haupturkunden für die Geschichte der Athosklöster*, pp.102–22.

13 *Vita* A, 140.1-2, 155.8, 8.11.

14 P. Meyer, *Haupturkunden*, p.117.

15 Vatopedi's precedence over Iviron did not become formally established until 1362.

16 *Actes d'Iviron*, vol.1, No. 7.

17 *Actes du Prôtaton*, No. 8.

18 On the early development of Vatopedi see N. Oikonomides, 'Byzantine Vatopaidi: A Monastery of the High Aristocracy', in *The Holy and Great Monastery of Vatopaidi*, vol.1,

pp.44–53; and *Actes de Vatopédi,* vol.1, pp.3–37.

19 O. Lancaster, *Sailing to Byzantium* (London, 1969), p.75.

20 On the landholdings of Iviron see *Actes d'Iviron,* vol.1, pp.25–59 and 70–91.

21 See the article by Dom Leo Bonsall, 'The Benedictine Monastery of St Mary on Mount Athos', *Eastern Churches Review,* 2:3 (1969), 262–7. See also P. Lemerle, 'Les Archives du monastère des Amalfitans au Mont Athos', *Epeteris Hetaireias Byzantinon Spoudon,* 23 (1953), 548–66 and A. Pertusi, 'Nuovi documenti sui Benedettini Amalfitani dell'Athos', *Aevum,* 27 (1953), 410–29.

22 The number of monasteries was now thought to exceed 40, but the figure of 180 clearly includes other lavras, cells and hermitages.

23 *Actes du Prôtaton,* No. 8. Illustrated in *Treasures of Mount Athos* (Thessaloniki, 1997), p.510.

24 Op. cit., pp.77–8.

25 P. Meyer, *Haupturkunden,* p.163.

26 For the latest assessment see Morris, op. cit., pp.275–8.

27 Ibid., pp.294–5.

28 For a sketch of the early Russian presence on the Holy Mountain see N. Fennell, *The Russians on Athos* (Bern, 2001), pp.51–5.

29 *Actes d'Ivirôn,* vol. 1, No.21.

30 See the biography by Dimitri Obolensky, 'Sava of Serbia', in his *Six Byzantine Portraits* (Oxford, 1988), pp.115–72. It includes a description of the foundation of the monastery 'which became for many centuries the fountain-head from which the Serbs drank at the source of Byzantine spirituality and culture' (ibid., p.7).

31 See *Actes de Chilandar,* vol. 1, Nos. 3 and 4.

32 Ibid., vol. 2, No. 132. Illustrated in D. Bogdanovic, V.J. Djuric, D.

Medakovic, *Chilandar on the Holy Mountain* (Belgrade, 1978), p.37.

33 *Actes de Zographou,* Nos. 3 and 4.

34 D. Obolensky, *The Byzantine Commonwealth: Eastern Europe, 500–1453* (London, 1971), p.383.

35 S. Runciman, *A History of the Crusades,* vol. 3 (Cambridge, 1954), p.130.

36 S. Runciman, *Byzantine Civilisation* (London, 1933), p.55.

CHAPTER 4

1 R.M. Dawkins, *The Monks of Athos* (London, 1936), p.300.

2 Several versions of the story are related by Dawkins, op. cit., pp.301–3.

3 M. Gedeon, *O Athos. Anamniseis, Eggrapha, Simeioseis* (Constantinople, 1885), pp.137–45, quotes from a hagiographical document which reports the tradition, but the document is of uncertain date.

4 Op. cit., p.89.

5 D.M. Nicol, *The Last Centuries of Byzantium 1261–1453,* 2nd edn. (Cambridge, 1993), p.122.

6 Op. cit., p.90.

7 See the discussion by I. Tarnanidis in S. Papadopoulos (ed.), *Simonopetra. Mount Athos,* pp.18–20.

8 *Actes de Dionysiou,* No. 4; illustrated in *Treasures of Mount Athos,* p.518.

9 N. Oikonomides, 'Patronage in Palaiologan Mt Athos', in A. Bryer and M. Cunningham (eds), *Mount Athos and Byzantine Monasticism,* p.109.

10 See S. Binon, *Les Origines légendaires de Xéropotamou et de Saint Paul* (Louvain, 1942), pp.185–8.

11 *Actes de Kutlumus,* No. 26.

12 E.A. Zachariadou, 'A Safe and Holy Mountain', in A. Bryer and M. Cunningham (eds), *Mount Athos and Byzantine Monasticism,* p.131.

13 See R. Gothóni, *Tales and Truth:*

Pilgrimage on Mount Athos Past and Present (Helsinki, 1994), pp.26–9. Interestingly, monk Isaiah listed Simonopetra as Bulgarian, Zographou as Wallachian, Koutloumousiou as Moldavian, and Philotheou as Albanian.

14 D. Bogdanovic, V.J. Djuric, D. Medakovic, *Chilandar on the Holy Mountain*, pp.40–2.

15 *Actes de Chilandar*, p.292.

16 Op. cit., p.255.

17 P. Meyer, *Haupturkunden*, pp.197–203.

18 See p.112.

19 *Triads in Defence of the Hesychasts*, 1.3.38, quoted by J. Meyendorff, *A Study of Gregory Palamas*, 2nd edn. (Crestwood, NY, 1998), p.151.

20 T. Ware, *The Orthodox Church*, pp.69–70.

21 L. Bréhier, *Les Institutions de l'empire byzantin* (Paris, 1949), pp.578-9, as translated by E. Amand de Mendieta.

22 S. Runciman, *The Last Byzantine Renaissance* (Cambridge, 1970), p.47.

23 D. Obolensky, *The Byzantine Commonwealth: Eastern Europe, 500–1453*, p.390.

24 See his lecture '"Act out of Stillness": The Influence of Fourteenth-Century Hesychasm on Byzantine and Slav Civilization' (Toronto, 1995).

25 Edited by F. Halkin from transcriptions made by E. Kourilas: 'Deux vies de S. Maxime le Kausokalyve Ermite au Mont Athos (XIVe s.)', *Analecta Bollandiana*, 54 (1936), 38–112. See also the brief account of his life in R.M. Dawkins, *The Monks of Athos*, pp.131–5, and the much fuller account by Kallistos Ware, 'St Maximos of Kapsokalyvia and Fourteenth-Century Athonite Hesychasm', in *Kathigitria: Essays Presented to Joan Hussey on her 80th Birthday* (London, 1988), pp.409–30.

26 K. Ware, 'St Maximos of Kapsokalyvia and Fourteenth-Century Athonite Hesychasm', p.411.

27 See K. Ware, 'The Fool in Christ as Prophet and Apostle', in *The Inner Kingdom* (New York, 2000), pp.153–80.

28 *Triads in Defence of the Hesychasts*, 1.3.43.

29 Ibid. 1.2.12.

30 K. Ware, 'St Maximos of Kapsokalyvia and Fourteenth-Century Athonite Hesychasm', p.430.

31 *The 'Painter's Manual' of Dionysius of Fourna*, tr. P. Hetherington (London, 1974), p.2.

32 See V.J. Djuric, 'Fresques médiévales à Chilandar', *Actes du XIIe Congrès Internationale des Etudes Byzantines* (Ochrid, 1961), pp.83–6.

33 This situation is in the process of being rectified. Recent years have seen sumptuous publications of the icons of Vatopedi (1998), Pantokrator (1998), Xenophontos (1999), and St Paul's (1999).

34 E.N. Tsigaridas, 'Portable Icons' in *The Holy and Great Monastery of Vatopaidi*, vol.2, p.394.

35 G.T. Stathis, 'The Musical Manuscripts' in *The Holy and Great Monastery of Vatapaidi*, vol.2, p.598.

36 S. Runciman, *The Last Byzantine Renaissance*, p.79.

37 P. Meyer, *Haupturkunden*, pp.203–10.

38 Ps-Sphrantzes, *Chronicon Maius*, ed. Grecu, p.320, quoted in D.M. Nicol, op. cit., p.338.

CHAPTER 5

1 S. Runciman, *The Fall of Constantinople 1453* (Cambridge, 1969), p.155.

2 C.G. Papadopoulos, *Les Privilèges du patriarcat oecuménique dans l'empire ottoman* (Paris, 1924), pp.27–41.

3   S. Runciman, *The Great Church in Captivity* (Cambridge, 1968), p.182.

4   G. Smyrnakis, *To Agion Oros* (Athens, 1903; repr. Mount Athos, 1988), p.110.

5   F. Dölger (ed.), *Mönchsland Athos* (Munich, 1943), p.19

6   On the history of this monastery see C. Patrinelis, A. Karakatsanis, M. Theocharis, *Stavronikita Monastery: History—Icons—Embroideries* (Athens, 1974), pp.17–38.

7   P. Meyer, *Haupturkunden*, pp.212–14.

8   Ibid., pp.210–12.

9   Ibid., pp.215–18.

10 The exact date is uncertain; but the skete is mentioned in a Lavra document of 1575, so it was certainly in existence by then.

11 See above, pp.90–2.

12 On the lives of Akakios and his disciples see E. Kourilas, *Istoria tou Askitismou, Athonitai* I (Thessaloniki, 1929), pp.66–87. Barsky's *Travel Diary*, describing his journeys to the holy places of Europe, Asia, and Africa in the years 1723–47, was published posthumously in 1778.

13 For details of their foundations see P. Meyer, *Haupturkunden*, p.84.

14 See C. Patrinelis in S. Papadopoulos (ed.), *Simonopetra: Mount Athos*, p.23.

15 K. Sathas, *Biographikon Schediasma peri tou Patriarchou Ieremiou B* (Athens, 1870), p.185.

16 K. Chryssochoidis in S. Papadopoulos (ed.), *The Holy Xenophontos Monastery: The Icons* (Mount Athos, 1999), p.32.

17 See P.S. Nașturel, *Le Mont Athos et les roumains. Recherches sur leurs relations du milieu du XIVe siècle à 1654* (Rome, 1984).

18 K. Chryssochoidis, 'An Outline of the History of the Iveron Monastery', in E. Vlachopoulou-Karabina, *Holy Monastery of Iveron: Gold Embroideries* (Mount Athos, 1998).

19 D. Bogdanovic, V. Djuric, D. Medakovic, *Chilandar on the Holy Mountain*, p.134.

20 N. Fennell, *The Russians on Athos*, p.58.

21 V.G. Barsky, *Travel Diary* (St Petersburg, 1793), pp.296, 300.

22 Quoted by C. Patrinelis in S. Papadopoulos (ed.), *Simonopetra: Mount Athos*, p.24.

23 G. Smyrnakis, *To Agion Oros*, p.591.

24 See S. Runciman, *The Great Church in Captivity*, pp.232-3, and T. Ware, *Eustratios Argenti* (Oxford, 1964), p.22.

25 Quoted by R.M. Dawkins, *The Monks of Athos*, p.69.

26 On the Athonite academy see P.M. Kitromilides, 'Athos and the Enlightenment', in A. Bryer and M. Cunningham (eds), *Mount Athos and Byzantine Monasticism*, pp.257–72; and id., 'Vatopaidi and the Greek Cultural Tradition: The Contribution of the Athonite Academy', in *The Holy and Great Monastery of Vatopaidi*, vol.1, pp.72–80.

27 I. Moisiodax, *Apologia* (Vienna, 1780), p.128.

28 A. Coray, *Mémoire sur l'état actuel de la civilisation dans la Grèce* (Paris, 1803), pp.65–6.

29 On this movement, its aims, and its achievements see Bishop Kallistos of Diokleia, 'The Spirituality of the *Philokalia*', *Sobornost*, 13:1 (1991), 6–24.

30 *Philokalia*, 5 vols (Athens, 1957–63; repr. Athens, 1974–6), vol.1, pp.xxiii–xxiv.

31 T. Ware, *The Orthodox Church*, p.100.

32 M. Gedeon, *O Athos*, p.216.

33 N.M. Vaporis, *Father Kosmas, the Apostle of the Poor: The Life of St Kosmas Aitolos together with an English Translation of his Teaching and Letters* (Brookline, MA, 1977), p.146.

34 Quoted in C. Cavarnos, *St Cosmas Aitolos*, 3rd edn. (Belmont, MA, 1985), p.45

35 A. Riley, *Athos or the Mountain of the Monks* (London, 1887), p.372.

36 This work is now available in English as *The New Martyrs of the Turkish Yoke*, tr. L.J. Papadopoulos and G. Lizardos (Seattle, WA, 1985).

37 See P. Meyer, *Haupturkunden*, pp.243–8.

38 It is worth noting that St Nikodimos opposed Greek independence on the grounds that it would expose Orthodoxy to the malign influence of the west.

39 G. Smirnakis, *To Agion Oros*, pp.173–83.

40 N. Fennell, *The Russians on Athos*, p.74. Both this section and the next owe much to Fennell's work.

41 Ibid., p.56.

42 The Greek brotherhood at Iviron banished its Georgian minority to a skete. See N. Fennell, op. cit., pp.132–8. The last Georgian monk of Iviron, Fr Tikhon, died in 1956.

43 N. Fennell, op. cit., p.81.

44 G. Smyrnakis, *To Agion Oros*, p.208.

45 See for example Dorotheos, Monachos Vatopedinos, *To Agio Oros* (Katerini, 1985), vol.2, p.185.

46 N. Fennell, op. cit., p.147.

47 See A.-E. Tachiaos, 'The 20th Century', in S. Papadopoulos (ed.), *Simonopetra: Mount Athos*, pp.26–7.

48 *I Thraki*, 1877, quoted by N. Fennell, op. cit., pp.175–6.

49 A. Riley, *Athos or the Mountain of the Monks*, pp.248–9.

50 N. Fennell, op. cit., p.178.

51 Ibid., p.317.

52 G. Smyrnakis, *To Agion Oros*, pp.705–7.

53 In the 1880s the monastery of Stavronikita fell seriously into debt. By 1889 the representative of St Panteleimonos at Karyes, one Fr Nathanail, had accumulated sufficient funds to write off the entire debt and with the encouragement of the senior monks intended to buy the monastery and have himself installed as abbot. This would have given the Russians another voice in the Holy Community; but Fr Nathanail died in 1890 and the scheme came to nothing.

CHAPTER 6

1 I. Smolitsch, 'Le Mont Athos et la Russia', *Le Millénaire du Mont Athos*, vol.1, p.318.

2 See A Monk of the Eastern Church [Fr. Lev Gillet], *The Jesus Prayer*, 2nd edn. (New York, 1987), pp.83–6.

3 N. Fennell, *The Russians on Athos*, p.218.

4 Ibid., p.318.

5 Article 105 of the 1975 Constitution, quoted by Charalambos K. Papastathis, 'The Status of Mount Athos in Hellenic Public Law', in A.–E. N. Tachiaos (ed.), *Mount Athos and the European Community* (Thessaloniki, 1993), pp.55–75 (p.59 n.10).

6 Ibid., pp.72–3.

7 For a discussion of the unwritten prohibition of women on Athos see Alice-Mary Talbot, 'Women and Mt Athos' in Bryer and Cunningham (eds), *Mount Athos and Byzantine Monasticism*, pp.67–79.

8 See V. Makrides, 'Aspects of Greek Orthodox Fundamentalism', *Orthodox Forum*, 5 (1991), 49–72.

9 In fact not all Athonites supported the Allies. Some of the Russians were believed to have collaborated with the Germans in the hope that a German victory would result in a restoration of the old order.

10 W.B. Thomas, *Dare to be Free* (London, 1951), pp.171–3.

11 S. Loch, *Athos: The Holy Mountain*, p.226.

12 G. Smyrnakis, *To Agion Oros*, pp.705–7.

13 Taken from G. Galitis *et al.*, *Glauben aus dem Herzen* (Munich, 1994).

14 J.J. Norwich and R. Sitwell, *Mount Athos*, p.98.

15 E. Amand de Mendieta, *Mount Athos: The Garden of the Panaghia*, p.45.

16 P. Sherrard, *Athos, the Mountain of Silence*, p.26.

17 Archimandrite Sophrony, *Saint Silouan the Athonite*, tr. R. Edmonds (Tolleshunt Knights, 1991), p.26.

18 Ibid., p.42 (his italics).

19 Hieromonk Alexander (Golitzin), trans., *The Living Witness of the Holy Mountain: Contemporary Voices from Mount Athos*, p.147.

20 The millennium also occasioned the publication of a most valuable collection of essays covering all aspects of Athonite history from the tenth century to the twentieth: *Le Millénaire du Mont Athos, 963–1963. Etudes et mélanges*, 2 vols (Chevetogne, 1963–4).

21 See I. Doens, 'La Célébration du Millénaire de l'Athos sur la Sainte Montagne', *Irénikon*, 36 (1963), 390–402.

22 When Constantine Cavarnos visited Chilandar in 1958, however, he was informed by Fr Domitian, 'We now have a tractor, too. It was sent as a gift to our monastery by Premier Tito.' *Anchored in God*, p.140.

23 See especially the new biography by Elder Joseph of Vatopedi, *Elder Joseph the Hesychast: Struggles—Experiences—Teachings* (Mount Athos, 1999).

24 Archimandrite Vasileios, *Hymn of Entry* (New York, 1984), p.9.

25 See Hieromonk Alexander (Golitzin), op. cit., p.15.

26 The first notice of the revival in English, so far as I am aware, was an article by Bishop Kallistos entitled 'Mount Athos Today' in *Christian*, 3:4 (1976), 322–33, followed by an article by Garth Fowden entitled 'The Orthodox Monastic Revival on Mount Athos' published in *The Times* on 8 January 1977.

27 But perhaps not universally. Sir Steven Runciman, President of the Friends of Mount Athos until his death in 2000, once told me that if he were to retire to an Athonite monastery he would have preferred it to be an idiorrhythmic one.

28 Official Journal of the European Communities 291/19.11.1979, p.186; quoted by C.K. Papastathis, 'The Status of Mount Athos in Hellenic Public Law', p.55.

29 The relevant documents are published in Fr Maximos, *Human Rights on Mount Athos* (Welshpool, 1990), pp.33–5.

30 N. Fennell, op. cit., p.309.

31 See for example the evidence adduced in Fr Maximos, op. cit., pp.39–42.

32 Bishop Kallistos of Diokleia, 'Athos after Ten Years: The Good News and the Bad', *Sobornost*, 15:1 (1993), 35.

33 The Prophet Elijah skete was not the only Russian house to be Hellenized in the 1990s at the behest of Constantinople. The Serai in Karyes, which had been deserted since the death of the last Russian monks in the 1970s, suffered a similar, if less violent, fate. Fearful that 'new blood' would arrive from Russia to revive it, the Patriarchate encouraged its parent monastery (Vatopedi) to repopulate the skete with Greek monks and this was duly done.

34 Communiqué of the Holy Community, 17 June 1994.

35 S. Runciman, 'Trouble on Holy Mountain', *The Times*, 17 April 1995, p.12.

36 *Treasures of Mount Athos* (Thessaloniki, 1997), p.xii.

CHAPTER 7

1 *Ekklesia*, 1–15 August 1963, p.398.

2 *Histories kai Peristatika* (Athens, 1944), pp.18–19.

3 The journal *Gregorios Palamas*, March–April 1963, p.145.

4 *Athos the Mountain of Silence*, p.3.

5 Figures taken from G.I. Mantzaridis, 'Athonite Monasticism at the Dawn of its Second Millennium', in the exhibition catalogue *Treasures of Mount Athos*, p.16.

6 See T. Ware, *The Orthodox Church*, pp.178–87.

7 See D. Conomos, 'The Musical Tradition of Mount Athos', *Annual Report of the Friends of Mount Athos* (1996), pp.26–40.

8 Foreword to Archimandrite Vasileios, *Hymn of Entry: Liturgy and Life in the Orthodox Church*, p.9.

9 E. Amand de Mendieta, *Mount Athos: The Garden of the Panaghia*, p.321.

10 Theoklitos, *Metaxi Ouranou kai Gis. Agioritikos Monachismos*, 2nd edn. (Athens, 1967), pp.128–9; quoted in Amand de Mendieta, op. cit., p.323.

11 Preface to Hieromonk Makarios of Simonos Petra, *The Synaxarion: The Lives of the Saints of the Orthodox Church*, vol.1 (Ormylia, 1998), p.v.

12 Archimandrite Aimilianos, *Spiritual Instruction and Discourses*, vol.1: *The Authentic Seal* (Ormylia, 1999), p.95.

13 Available in English translation as *Elder Joseph the Hesychast: Struggles–Experiences–Teachings*, by Elder Joseph (Mount Athos, 1999).

14 Elder Joseph the Hesychast, *Monastic Wisdom: The Letters of Elder Joseph the Hesychast* (Florence, AZ, 1998).

15 Elder Ephraim, *Counsels from the Holy Mountain: Selected from the Letters and Homilies of Elder Ephraim* (Florence, AZ, 1999).

16 *The Great and Holy Monastery of Vatopaidi: The Continuation of a Tradition* (Mount Athos, 1996), p.8.

17 Ibid., pp.42–5.

18 Philip Sherrard deplored this growing trend as long ago as 1977: 'The Paths of Athos', *Eastern Churches Review*, 9 (1977), 100–7.

19 See P.M. Koufopoulos and S.B. Mamaloukos, *The Metalwork of Mount Athos from the Eighteenth to the Twentieth Century* (in Greek; Athens, 1997).

20 *Ekklesia*, 1–15 August 1963, p.386.

21 C. Cavarnos, *Anchored in God*, p.183 (his italics).

22 Archimandrite Aimilianos, 'Mount Athos: Sacred Vessel of the Prayer of Jesus', in Hieromonk Alexander (Golitzin) trans., *The Living Witness of the Holy Mountain*, pp.182–3.

23 See for example the portraits of twentieth-century elders in Archimandrite Cherubim (Karambelas), *Contemporary Ascetics of Mount Athos*, 2 vols (Platina, CA, 1991–2).

24 Bishop Kallistos of Diokleia, 'Wolves and Monks: Life on the Holy Mountain Today', *Sobornost*, 5:2 (1983), 64.

25 Elder Joseph, *Elder Joseph the Hesychast: Struggles–Experiences–Teachings*, p.47.

26 Archimandrite Aimilianos, 'The Role of the Spiritual Father', in Hieromonk Alexander (Golitzin) trans., *The Living Witness of the Holy Mountain*, pp.165–7.

27 See T. Ware, *The Orthodox Church*, p.98.

28 On his own reception into Orthodoxy by baptism see Père Placide, 'The Question of Baptism', in Hieromonk Alexander (Golitzin) trans., *The Living Witness of the Holy Mountain*, pp.87–90.

29 N. Fennell, *The Russians on Athos*, pp.282–3.

30 Archimandrite Aimilianos, 'The House of God and the Gate of

Heaven', in S. Papadopoulos (ed.), *Simonopetra. Mount Athos*, p.119.

31 *Philokalia*, vol.4 (Athens, 1961), p.232; quoted in T. Ware, *The Orthodox Church*, p.300.

32 Archimandrite Aimilianos, *The Authentic Seal*, pp.120–1.

33 S. Loch, *Athos: The Holy Mountain*, p.220.

34 Archimandrite Cherubim, *Contemporary Ascetics of Mount Athos*, vol.1, pp.179–80.

35 Ibid., pp.191–2.

36 Fr Nikolaos Hatzinikolaou, 'Mount Athos: The Highest Place on Earth', *Annual Report of the Friends of Mount Athos* (2000), pp.77–8.

37 St John was abbot of St Catherine's monastery, Sinai, in the mid-seventh century. His most important book, *The Ladder of Divine Ascent*, which is based on his own experiences of nearly forty years as a desert anchorite, offers guidance to monks about how to progress through the stages of the ascetic life, breaking free of the earthly passions and ascending to a level where they can enjoy union with God. The *Ladder* is still greatly prized as a manual of monastic practice: graphic illustrations of it are to be found in the exonarthex of many katholika; and the text remains to this day prescribed reading in the refectories of Athonite monasteries during Lent.

38 Abbot George Kapsanis, 'Mount Athos and the European Community', in A.-E.N. Tachiaos (ed.), *Mount Athos and the European Community*, p.113.

CHAPTER 8

1 See e.g. G. Speake, 'Janus Lascaris' Visit to Mount Athos in 1491', *Greek, Roman and Byzantine Studies*, 34:3 (1993), 325–30.

2 See the useful summary of 'Travellers' Tales' in R. Gothóni, *Tales and Truth: Pilgrimage on Mount Athos Past and Present* (Helsinki, 1994), pp.46–92.

3 See R. Gothóni, op. cit., p.56.

4 P. Sherrard, 'The Paths of Athos', *Eastern Churches Review*, 9: 1–2 (1977), 102.

5 Ibid., pp.101–2.

6 R. Gothóni, op. cit., pp.165–71.

7 R. Gothóni, *Paradise within Reach: Monasticism and Pilgrimage on Mt Athos* (Helsinki, 1993), pp.134–5.

8 Ibid., p.135.

9 For the latest information readers are referred to the booklet produced by the Friends of Mount Athos (*A Pilgrim's Guide to Mount Athos*, 2nd edn., 2000) or the society's website (www.athosfriends.org).

10 The story is told in a booklet by Joice Loch, *Prosporion – Uranopolous: Rugs and Dyes* (Istanbul, 1964). See also her autobiography, *A Fringe of Blue* (London, 1968).

11 See his excellent account of his many journeys, *Athos: The Holy Mountain* (London, 1957).

12 See Archimandrite Ephrem Lash, 'Athos: A Working Community', in A. Bryer and M. Cunningham (eds), *Mount Athos and Byzantine Monasticism*, pp.81–8.

13 R. Byron, *The Station: Athos: Treasures and Men*, p.149.

14 S. Loch, *Athos: The Holy Mountain*, p.123.

15 Ibid., p.96.

16 Ibid., p.243.

17 See R. Gothóni, *Tales and Truth*, p.49.

18 See S. Rudberg, 'Les Manuscrits à contenu profane du Mont-Athos', *Eranos*, 54 (1956), 174–85.

19 R. Gothóni, *Paradise within Reach*, p.129.

20 Archimandrite Aimilianos, *The Authentic Seal*, p.124.

21 Ibid., pp.125–6.

22 See above, pp.189–90.

23 D. Nicol, 'A Sojourn on the Holy Mountain in the Year 1949', *Annual Report of the Friends of Mount Athos* (2000), p.107.

24 Fr A was formerly a monk at Ein Fara in the West Bank where he claims to have been the last of the desert fathers. His story is told in W. Dalrymple, *From the Holy Mountain: A Journey in the Shadow of Byzantium* (London, 1997), pp.355–7.

25 The project was duly completed and the building rededicated in July 2000 in the presence of Sir Steven who had travelled to Athos at the age of ninety-seven to witness the event.

26 Fr Nikolaos Hatzinikolaou, 'Mount Athos: The Highest Place on Earth', *Annual Report of the Friends of Mount Athos* (2000), p.66

27 Hieromonk Alexander (Golitzin), trans., *The Living Witness of the Holy Mountain*, pp.33–4.

Select Bibliography

1. Primary Sources

Archives de l'Athos
Chilandar: Vol. XX: *Actes de Chilandar*, vol. 1: *Des origines à 1319*, ed. M. Zivojinovic, V. Kravari, C. Giros (Paris, 1998).
Dionysiou: Vol. IV: *Actes de Dionysiou*, ed. N. Oikonomidès (Paris, 1968).
Dochiariou: Vol. XIII: *Actes de Docheiariou*, ed. N. Oikonomidès (Paris, 1984).
Esphigmenou: Vol. VI: *Actes d'Esphigménou*, ed. J. Lefort (Paris, 1973).
Iviron: Vols XIV, XVI, XVIII, XIX: *Actes d'Ivirôn*, vols 1–4, ed. J. Lefort, N. Oikonomidès, D. Papachryssanthou with H. Métrévéli and V. Kravari (Paris, 1985–95).
Konstamonitou: Vol. IX: *Actes de Kastamonitou*, ed. N. Oikonomidès (Paris, 1978).
Koutloumousiou: Vol. II: *Actes de Kutlumus*, ed. P. Lemerle (Paris, 1945; new edn Paris, 1988).
Lavra: Vols V, VIII, X, XI: *Actes de Lavra*, vols 1–4, ed. P. Lemerle, N. Svoronos, A. Guillou, D. Papachryssanthou (Paris, 1970–82).
Pantokrator: Vol. XVII: *Actes du Pantocrator*, ed. V. Kravari (Paris, 1991).
Protaton: Vol. VII: *Actes du Prôtaton*, ed. D. Papachryssanthou (Paris, 1975).
St Panteleimonos: Vol. XII: *Actes de St-Pantéléêmôn*, ed. P. Lemerle, G. Dagron, S. Circkovic (Paris, 1982).
Vatopedi: Vol. XXI: *Actes de Vatopédi*, vol. 1: *Des origines à 1329*, texte et album, ed. J. Bompaire, J. Lefort, V. Kravari, C. Giros (Paris, 2001).
Xenophontos: Vol. XV: *Actes de Xénophon*, ed. D. Papachryssanthou (Paris, 1986).
Xeropotamou: Vol. III: *Actes de Xéropotamou*, ed. J. Bompaire (Paris, 1965).

I. Doens, *Bibliographie de la Sainte Montagne de l'Athos* (Chevetogne, 1964; repr. Mount Athos, 2001).
P. Meyer, *Die Haupturkunden für die Geschichte der Athosklöster* (Leipzig, 1894).
P. Mylonas, *Atlas of Athos*, 2 fascs (Berlin, 2000).
R. Petit and B. Korablev (eds), *Actes de Chilandar*, 2 vols, vol. 1: *Actes grecs*, vol. 2: *Actes slaves* (St Petersburg, 1911–12; repr. Amsterdam, 1975).
W. Regel, E. Kurtz, B. Korablev (eds), *Actes de Philothée* (St Petersburg, 1913; repr. Amsterdam, 1975).
—— (eds), *Actes de Zographou* (St Petersburg, 1907; repr. Amsterdam, 1969).

2. SECONDARY SOURCES

Archimandrite Aimilianos, *Spiritual Instruction and Discourses*, vol. 1: *The Authentic Seal* (Ormylia, 1999).

E. Amand de Mendieta, *La Presqu'île des caloyers: Le Mont-Athos* (Bruges, 1955).

——, *Mount Athos: The Garden of the Panaghia* (Berlin, 1972).

D. Bogdanovic, V.J. Djuric, D. Medakovic, *Chilandar on the Holy Mountain* (Belgrade, 1978).

Dom Leo Bonsall, 'The Benedictine Monastery of St Mary on Mount Athos', *Eastern Churches Review*, 2:3 (1969), 262–7.

R.H. Brewster, *The 6000 Beards of Athos* (London, 1935).

A. Bryer and M. Cunningham (eds), *Mount Athos and Byzantine Monasticism* (Aldershot, 1996).

R. Byron, *The Station: Athos: Treasures and Men* (London, 1931; repr. Lodon, 1984).

C. Cavarnos, *Anchored in God: An Inside Account of Life, Art, and Thought on the Holy Mountain of Athos* (Athens, 1959).

——, *The Holy Mountain* (Belmont, MA, 1973).

M. Choukas, *Black Angels of Athos* (London, 1935).

R. Coate, *Mont Athos: La sainte montagne* (Paris, 1949).

R. Curzon, *Visits to Monasteries in the Levant*. 3rd edn (London, 1850).

R.M. Dawkins, *The Monks of Athos* (London, 1936).

F. Dölger, *Mönchsland Athos* (Munich, 1943).

Dorotheos, Monachos Vatopedinos, *To Agio Oros*, 2 vols (Katerini, 1985).

N. Fennell, *The Russians on Athos* (Bern, 2001).

M. Gedeon, *O Athos. Anamniseis, Eggrapha, Simeioseis* (Constantinople, 1885).

Hieromonk Alexander (Golitzin), trans., *The Living Witness of the Holy Mountain: Contemporary Voices from Mount Athos* (South Canaan, PA, 1996).

R. Gothóni, *Paradise within Reach: Monasticism and Pilgrimage on Mount Athos* (Helsinki, 1993).

——, *Tales and Truth: Pilgrimage on Mount Athos Past and Present* (Helsinki, 1994).

F.W. Hasluck, 'The First English Traveller's Account of Athos', *Annual of the British School at Athens*, 17 (1910–11), 103–31.

——, *Athos and its Monasteries* (London, 1924).

C. Hellier and F. Venturi, *Monasteries of Greece* (London, 1996).

The Holy and Great Monastery of Vatopaidi: Tradition—History—Art, 2 vols (Mount Athos, 1998).

F. Huber, *Athos* (Zürich, 1969).

J.M. Hussey, *The Orthodox Church in the Byzantine Empire* (Oxford, 1986).

Elder Joseph, *Elder Joseph the Hesychast: Struggles—Experiences—Teachings (1898-1959)* (Mount Athos, 1999).

S. Kadas, *Mount Athos: An Illustrated Guide to the Monasteries and their History* (Athens, 1979).

E. Kaestner, *Mount Athos, the Call from Sleep* (London, 1961).

C. Karambelas, *Contemporary Ascetics of Mount Athos*, 2 vols (Platina, CA, 1992).

E.N. Kyriakoudis *et al.*, *The Holy Xenophontos Monastery: The Icons* (Mount Athos, 1999).

K. Lake, *The Early Days of Monasticism on Mt Athos* (Oxford, 1909).

W.M. Leake, *Travels in Northern Greece*, 4 vols (London, 1835).

S. Loch, *Athos. The Holy Mountain* (London, 1957).

Fr. Maximos, *Human Rights on Mount Athos* (Welshpool, 1990).

Le Millénaire du Mont Athos, 963–1963. Etudes et mélanges, 2 vols (Chevetogne, 1963–4).

R. Morris, *Monks and Laymen in Byzantium, 843–1118* (Cambridge, 1995).

D.M. Nicol, *The Last Centuries of Byzantium 1261–1453*, 2nd edn (Cambridge, 1993).

J.J. Norwich and R. Sitwell, *Mount Athos* (London, 1966).

D. Obolensky, *The Byzantine Commonwealth: Eastern Europe, 500–1453* (London, 1971).

——, *Six Byzantine Portraits* (Oxford, 1988).

S. Papadopoulos (ed.), *Simonopetra. Mount Athos* (Athens, 1991).

S. Papadopoulos and C. Kapioldassi-Soteropoulos (eds), *Icons of the Holy Monastery of Pantokrator* (Mount Athos, 1998).

C. Patrinelis, A. Karakatsanis, M. Theocharis, *Stavronikita Monastery: History—Icons—Embroideries* (Athens, 1974).

S. Pelekanides *et al.*, *The Treasures of Mount Athos. Illuminated Manuscripts*, 3 vols (Athens, 1973–9).

M. B. Pennington, *O Holy Mountain! Journal of a Retreat on Mount Athos* (London, 1979).

F. Reichert and G.J. Schenk (eds), *Athos. Reisen zum Heiligen Berg 1347–1841* (Stuttgart, 2001).

D.T. Rice, 'The Monasteries of Mount Athos', *Antiquity*, 2 (1928), 443–51.

A. Riley, *Athos or the Mountain of the Monks* (London, 1887).

N.F. Robinson, *Monasticism in the Orthodox Churches* (London and Milwaukee, 1916).

S. Runciman, *Byzantine Civilisation* (London, 1933).

——, *A History of the Crusades*, 3 vols (Cambridge, 1951–4).

——, *The Great Church in Captivity* (Cambridge, 1968).

——, *The Last Byzantine Renaissance* (Cambridge, 1970).

P. Sherrard, *Athos, the Mountain of Silence* (London, 1960).

——, 'The Paths of Athos', *Eastern Churches Review*, 9:1 (1977), 100–7.

——, *Athos: The Holy Mountain* (London, 1982).

G. Smyrnakis, *To Agion Oros* (Athens, 1903; repr. Mount Athos, 1988).

A.-E.N. Tachiaos (ed.), *Mount Athos and the European Community* (Thessaloniki, 1993).

P. Theocharides, P. Foundas, S. Stefanou, *Greek Traditional Architecture: Mount Athos* (Athens, 1992).

S.P. Todorovich, *The Chilandarians: Serbian Monks on the Green Mountain* (Boulder, CO, 1989).

Treasures of Mount Athos, Exhibition catalogue (Thessaloniki, 1997).

M. Vassilaki, I. Tavlakis, E. Tsigaridas, *The Holy Monastery of Aghiou Pavlou: The Icons* (Mount Athos, 1999).

E. Vlachopoulou-Karabina, *Holy Monastery of Iveron: Gold Embroideries* (Mount Athos, 1998).

K. Vlachos, *I Chersonisos tou Agiou Orous Atho* (Volos, 1903).

K.T. Ware, 'Wolves and Monks: Life on the Holy Mountain Today', *Sobornost*, 5:2 (1983), 56–68.

——, *The Orthodox Church*, 2nd edn (Harmondsworth, 1993).

——, *The Orthodox Way*, 2nd edn (Crestwood, NY, 1995).

GLOSSARY

abaton: the traditional principle, common to all monasteries, that enables monks and nuns to close their doors to members of the opposite sex.

archontariki: guest house.

archontaris: guest master.

Axion estin: ('It is meet') a hymn to the Virgin sung at the Divine Liturgy and other services; also the title of the holiest icon on Athos, preserved in the sanctuary of the church of the Protaton in Karyes.

cenobitic system: the system by which monks live a common life in spiritual obedience to an abbot, worshipping and eating together, and contributing any wealth they may have to the common purse; cf. idiorrhythmic system.

chrysobull: a document or charter bearing the emperor's gold seal.

coenobium: a house in which monks live according to the cenobitic system (q.v.).

Deesis: a visual representation of Christ flanked by the Virgin and St John the Baptist in which the Virgin and St John intercede with Christ on behalf of the world.

diakonima: the work or duty allotted to a monk.

diamonitirion: the official permit or visa that permits a pilgrim to enter Athos and to enjoy hospitality at the monasteries.

dikaios: the prior of a skete.

dokimos: a novice.

enkolpion: a pendant bearing a sacred image that is worn 'on the breast'.

exonarthex: the antechamber to the narthex (q.v.) in an Orthodox church.

hegoumenos: the abbot of a cenobitic monastery.

hesychasm: a spiritual tradition developed by St John Klimakos (seventh century) for whom *hesychia* ('stillness', 'tranquillity') was a state of inner silence and vigilance, closely associated with the name of Jesus and the repetition of short prayers.

idiorrhythmic system: the system by which monks were permitted to set their own pattern, were not bound by the vow of poverty or of obedience to an abbot, and lived in separate apartments, often with their own servants and their own worldly goods, neither eating together nor contributing to a common purse; cf. cenobitic system.

katholikon: the main church of a monastery.

kellion: a monk's cell; also a separate monastic house with a chapel and several rooms, perhaps inhabited by three or four monks.

konaki: a monastery's residence in Karyes, inhabited by that monastery's representative to the Holy Community.

ktitor: the founder of a monastery; also used to refer to a major benefactor.

kyriakon: the main church of a skete, used for worship on Sunday (*Kyriaki*).

lavra: a group of cells for hermits.

metochion: a dependency of a ruling monastery.

narthex: the antechapel or vestibule at the west end of an Orthodox church.

panegyri: the annual celebration of a monastery or skete for the feast of its dedication.

prohegoumenos: the principal of an idiorrhythmic monastery.

proskynitis: a pilgrim.

protos hesychastes: the 'first hesychast', subsequently shortened to Protos ('first'), as the primate of Athos is still known.

rason: a loose-cut gown with billowing sleeves, part of the monastic habit.

schema: the monastic habit: the small *schema* (now rarely conferred) is the first grade; the great *schema* (or great habit) denotes the highest rank to which a monk may be promoted.

simantron: an iron bar used instead of a bell to summon the fathers to prayer.

skete: a monastic village or group of houses gathered around a central church (or *kyriakon*, q.v.), dependent upon a ruling monastery.

starets: elder.

synaxis: a meeting of the brotherhood of a monastery or of the representatives to the Holy Community in Karyes.

synodikon: a part of the monastery set aside for meetings.

talanto: a wooden plank used instead of a bell to summon the fathers to prayer.

Theotokos: the Virgin Mary or Mother of God, as she is known to the Orthodox.

Tourkokratia: the period of Ottoman ('Turkish') rule.

Tragos: the earliest imperial document (dated 972) concerned with the organization of the Holy Mountain as a whole, called *Tragos* ('goat') because it is written on goatskin parchment.

trapeza: the refectory of a monastery.

typikon: the rule or charter by which a monastery or group of monasteries is governed.

waqf: a charitable foundation in Islamic law.

INDEX

196, 204, 225–30, 245, 257, 259
de Valenciennes, Pierre-Henri 14, 15
diamonitirion 163, 234, 235, 238, 242
diet 222, 227–9, 246–7, 254, 256
Dimitrios Firfiris, Deacon 197
Dinocrates 13, 14, 15
Dionysios III, Patriarch 124
Dionysios of Kolitsou, Elder *187*, 189, 260
Dionysios of Phourna 93–5
Dionysiou, monastery of *77*, 143, *145*, 171, 244
    Myrovlitissa 24; foundation 76; chrysobull of Alexios III Komnenos 76, 78; Serbian house 81; gospel cover *103*; cross of Empress Helena *104*; supported by ruler of Wallachia *129*; becomes cenobitic 144; and World War II 167; twentieth-century decline 170; revived by Abbot Charalambos 181; representative deposed 189, 250
Dochiariou, monastery of *82*, 239, 242
    Gorgoypekoös 24; supported by Stefan Dushan 74; Serbian house 81; revived in 1979 179
Dormition, feast of 25

Ecumenical Patriarch 3, 63, 85, 114–15, 176, 188, 266
    and the Charter of 1924 162; tensions with Athos 164, 189–92, 194, 250, 266–7
Eden, Garden of 19
enamel *83*, *103*, 107
enkolpia 107
Enlightenment 138, 140
entry permit *see diamonitirion*
Ephesus, Council of (AD 431) 19
Ephraim, Abbot of Philotheou 175, 181, 202, 251–2
    founder of monasteries in North America 202
Ephraim, Abbot of Vatopedi *211*, *216*, 256, 257, 259
Epirus, despotate of 71
Esphigmenou, monastery of 66, 142, *214*
    tradition of early foundation 28; supported by Stefan Dushan 74;

becomes cenobitic 144; a Zealot monastery 164, *165*, 166; refuses to exhibit treasures 192
Euboea 1, 179
Eugenius IV, Pope 112
eunuchs 25–6, 61, 62
European Union 182–4, 188, 191, 204, 266
Eustathios, Archbishop of Thessaloniki 68–9
Euthymios of Iviron 55
Euthymios, Abbot of Vatopedi 72
Euthymios the Younger, St 38
Evgenios, Abbot of Simonopetra 129

fasting 222
Fennell, Nicholas 151, 155, 161, 217
flora 8, 34
Florence, Council of 86, 111–12
Franks 69, 70
frescos 8, *94*, *95*, 98–106
    of Panselinos 95–6, *96*; of Theophanes the Cretan *118*
Friendly Society 145
Friends of Mount Athos 191, 250, 257
Fyodor Ivanovich, Tsar 130

Gabriel, Abbot of Dionysiou 6, 171–2, 208
Gabriel, hermit monk of Iviron 21
Gabriel IV, Patriarch 138, 143–4
Galla Placidia, Empress 25
Gallipoli 74, 113
Ganos, Mount 91
Genesios 38
Gennadios, Patriarch 109, 114
Genoese 74
geology 29
George I, King of the Hellenes 157
George, St *49*, *54*
George (Kapsanis), Abbot of Grigoriou 179, 231–2, 267
George Scholarios *see* Gennadios, Patriarch
Georgia 265
Georgians 55–8, 79, 150, 197
    support for Iviron 130
Gerasimos, Abbot of St Panteleimonos 146, 151

PHOTOGRAPHIC ACKNOWLEDGEMENTS

Jacket image, 1, 5, 7, 8, 9, 10, 11, 12, 13, 14, 15, 19, 24, 25, 26, 27, 28, 29, 31, 32, 33, 36, 37, 51, 52, 53, 57, 58, 59, 62, 64, 68, 69, 70, 74, 75, 77, 80, 81, 84, 86, 87, 88, 90, 91, 92, 93, 94, 96, 97, 98, 100, 102, 103, 104, 105, 106, 107, 108, 109, 111, 112 © Graham Speake; 2 Restricted gift of Mrs Harold T. Martin, 1983.36 The Art Institute of Chicago; frontispiece, 3, 23, 39, 65 Holy Community, Karyes; 4, 34, 35, 40, 41 © monastery of Chilandar; 6 © Romanian skete of Prodromos; 16, 17, 38, 42, 43, 44, 49, 50, 83, 85, 110 © monastery of Vatopedi; 18 © Anthony Hazledine; 20, 45, © monastery of Iviron; 21 © monastery of Xenophontos; 22 © Fr John Maitland Moir; 30, 47, 48, 61, 67 © monastery of Dionysiou; 46 © monastery of Xeropotamou; 54,55 © monastery of Stavronikita; 56 © monastery of Pantokrator; 60 © monastery of Grigoriou; 63 © monastery of Simonopetra; 66 © Ashmolean Museum, Oxford; 71 © Skete of St Andrew; 72, 73, 76, 79, 82 © Mount Athos Photographic Archive; 78, 101 © Gerald Palmer; 95 © monastery of Esphigmenou.